THE
AUSTRALIANS

The Russian Revolution

Eyewitness (*an anthology of Eyewitness Reporting*)

Eighteen Fifteen

The Elysian Fields (*France in Ferment 1789–1804*)

JOHN FISHER

THE
AUSTRALIANS
From 1788 to Modern Times

Illustrated

ROBERT HALE · LONDON

Printed in Great Britain
by Ebenezer Baylis and Son, Limited
The Trinity Press, Worcester, and London

CONTENTS

		page
1	The Way to Botany Bay	9
2	Starvation Corner	25
3	Mutineers Defeat Governor Bligh of the Bounty	44
4	Macquarie the Magnificent	57
5	Growing Pains	69
6	When Free Men Flowed Out-back	87
7	Days When the World was Wide	102
8	Golden Dawn	113
9	Linking-up Time	126
10	Anthony Trollope Ignores Ned Kelly	147
11	Australia Looks Out	182
12	The Gay and Not-So-Gay Nineties	192
13	From Hughes to Gallipoli	209
14	The Great Depression	224
15	MacArthur Was Here	233
	Notes on Books	243
	Index	247

ILLUSTRATIONS

facing page

1   The First Fleet in Botany Bay   48

2–5 Arthur Phillip; Lachlan Macquarie; William Bligh; John Macarthur   49

6   Arrival of Government gold conveyance at the Colonial Treasury, Sydney, 1851. From a sketch by Marshal Claxton   64

7   A Government jail gang in Sydney around 1830   64

8   The squatter's first home   65

9   Gold washing on Summerhill Creek near the site of Hargreaves' gold discovery of 1851, by G. F. Angas   65

10   Officers of the Sydney Volunteer Corps   160

11   Native police   160

12   "Bailed Up", oil-painting of a bushranger's hold-up in the 1860s, by Tom Roberts   161

13   Sheep-shearing in Australia in the 1860s   176

14   A miner's hut in New South Wales   176

15   William Morris Hughes "The Complete War Winner": cartoon by Low from the *Bulletin*, 13th December 1917   177

ACKNOWLEDGEMENTS

The illustrations in this book are reproduced by permission of the following: National Maritime Museum, 1; Public Library of New South Wales, 2, 4, 7, 8, 10, 11, 13, 14; Trustees of the Mitchell Library, Sydney, 3; Camden Park Estate, New South Wales, 5; *Illustrated London News*, 6; National Library of Australia, 9; Art Gallery of New South Wales, 12; Australian Consolidated Press, 15.

The quotations from poems by Henry Lawson are included by permission of Angus and Robertson Limited.

1

The Way to Botany Bay

At first sight it might seem a mystery that Australia, a land mass of nearly three million square miles, one and a half times the size of Europe, should have remained virtually untrodden by Europeans until two hundred years ago. But the mariners of Tudor and Stuart times found little difficulty in accounting for this neglect.

"We have not seen one fruit bearing tree, nor anything that man could make use of; there are not mountains, or even hills . . . this is the most arid and barren region that could be found anywhere on the earth; the inhabitants, too, are the most wretched and poorest creatures I have seen," said Jan Carstensz, the Dutch explorer who visited New Holland, as Australia was then called, in 1623.

William Dampier, the Somersetshire sea-captain who touched there later in the same century agreed with Carstensz: "If it were not for that sort of pleasure which results from the discovery even of the barrenest spot upon the globe," Dampier wrote, "this coast would not have charmed me much. . . . The inhabitants of this country are the miserablest People in the world. The Hodmadods of Monomatapa, though a nasty People, yet for wealth are Gentlemen to these."

But there were other reasons, too, why this half-legendary land-mass in the southern seas remained uncharted. The Spaniards, though well established in the Philippines two thousand miles *Spaniards* to the north of Australia, were far more interested in their treasures on the eastern side of the Pacific. The Dutch, from about 1613 onwards, often sailed along the west coast of Australia, but they did so only because this route gave them a faster passage from the Cape of Good Hope to the East Indies than they would have got by following the coast of Africa. They were interested solely in cargoes from the spice islands, which brought a high return for little shipping space and which were desperately needed for flavouring the otherwise tasteless European smoked or salted meat and fish.

One other obstacle served to isolate Australia from New Guinea, only 150 miles away, and therefore from other islands further to the west as well as from India, Malaya and China: this was the weather.

From November to early March, during the north-west monsoon, when the direction of the wind is favourable, conditions are undependable. There are calms in which a ship could drift for days . . . and storms. A hurricane can swirl down any time between December and May. From then till September a fine steady sailing wind sets in but it blows from the south-east, in other words dead on the nose of any ship approaching *poor* Australia from the open sea. Neither the Indonesian Trimarans, *sea* nor Arab craft, nor even Europe's square-riggers fancied such a *conditions* beat to windward. Only one thing had been heard in favour of this enigmatic territory. It was said to be "a region where the Portingales [Portuguese] see popingays [parrots] commonly of a wonderful greatness".

And so, in May 1787 when the first fleet of marines, seamen and convicts cleared the English Channel for Botany Bay, their ships were sailing toward an almost unknown world. The interior of their new domain, nearly ten times that of the United States of the day, had never been penetrated, and its coast was notoriously inhospitable.

Most of what was known had been provided by Joseph Banks, an amateur botanist, often described as the father of Australia, who had landed with Captain Cook nearly twenty years earlier at seven places only in the whole of the sub-continent and who knew almost nothing of the famous Australian bush.

Banks, born in 1744, had the unusual distinction of having been educated at both Harrow and Eton. As an undergraduate at Oxford he imported and paid for his own teacher of botany. On his twenty-first birthday he came into a fortune and, at twenty-two, departed aboard a naval vessel to look for plants in Newfoundland. In 1768 the Royal Society, of which Banks was already a Fellow, was organizing an expedition to Tahiti to observe the transit of the planet Venus across the sun on 3rd June 1769, an event which would help astronomers to calculate more exactly the distance of the earth from the sun. The Society asked the Admiralty to take Banks and his personal staff of seven aboard the ship *Endeavour*, commanded by the famous navigator Captain Cook. The new arrivals could have been a heavy liability to the expedition but, instead, Banks's charm, ability and hard work made him an asset and Cook even "lifted" parts of Banks's journal to make us his own log of the trip.

Endeavour sailed to Tahiti via Madeira, Rio de Janeiro and Cape Horn, and Cook, after observing the transit, began to explore the unknown South Pacific, to find perhaps Terra Australia, the continent that cartographers had filled in so hopefully on their maps. He made a landfall on New Zealand and, by sailing round the two islands, proved that they at least were not the missing continent.

In April 1770 *Endeavour* and her crew sailed westwards from New Zealand and across the Pacific for nearly three weeks with only a gannet (which flew with a steady uninterrupted flight as if it knew the road was going to lead to the shore) to encourage them.

But, at 6 a.m. on 20th April, land was sighted and, when they closed it the following day, they could see that it rose in "gentle sloping hills which had the appearance of the highest fertility; every hill seemed to be cloth'd with trees of no mean size; at noon a smoke was seen a little way inland and in the evening several more." This, they soon realized, was the unexplored east coast of New Holland.

It was of course difficult for small boats to beach on an open coast through the Pacific surf and equally difficult to find a safe anchorage without soundings having been taken first from a smaller vessel. It was nine days before they found a secure inlet which, because of the great quantity of new plants collected there, was afterwards named Botany Bay.

The voyage by Cook and Banks up the east coast of Australia lasted roughly four months and covered some two thousand miles as the crow flies—and a good deal more as the ship sailed. During that time the expedition never really left the coast. They sailed right past the entrance to Sydney Harbour without investigating it, and even New South Wales, the name of the territory which Cook took possession of before leaving, was supplied later, after Cook had sent off his first report to the Admiralty.

Years later, Banks was criticized for having been over-optimistic about the prospects for settlers in Australia, but the journal that he kept of his voyage showed that, from the start, he had had misgivings as well as hopes. For example, six days after his arrival he wrote: "The countrey tho in general well enough clothd, appeared in some places bare; it resembled in my imagination the back of a lean Cow, covered in general with long hair, but nevertheless where her scraggy hip bones have stuck out farther than they ought, accidental rubbs and knocks have intirely bard them of their share of covering."

Four months later, as *Endeavour* drew out of sight of land on her way to New Guinea, Banks summarized his impressions and again we see that he had no dreams of paradise:

For the whole length of coast which we saild along there was a sameness to be observd in the face of the countrey very uncommon; Barren it may justly be calld and in a very high degree, that at least that we saw. The soil in general is sandy and very light: on it grows grass tall enough but thin sett, and trees of a tolerable size, never however near together, in general 40, 50, or 60 feet asunder. This, and spots, sometimes very large, of loose sand constitutes the general face of the countrey as you sail along it, and indeed of the greatest part even after you have penetrated inland as far as our situation would allow us to do. . . . Inland you sometimes meet with a bog upon which the grass grows rank and thick so that no doubt the soil is sufficiently fertile. The Valleys also between the hills where runs of water come down are thick clothd with under-wood, but they are in general very steep and narrow, so that upon the Whole the fertile soil Bears no kind of Proportion to that which seems by nature doomd to everlasting Barrenness.

Water is here a scarce article or at least was so while we were there, which I believe to have been in the very hight of the Dry season; some places we were in where we saw not a drop, and at two places where we filld for the ships use it was done from pools not brooks. This drought is probably owing to the dryness of a soil almost intirely composd of sand in which high hills are scarce. That there is plenty however in the rainy season is sufficiently evincd by the channels we saw cut even in rocks down the sides of inconsiderable hills; these were in general dry, or if any of them containd water it was such a ran in the woody valleys, and these seldom carried water above half way down the hill. Some indeed we saw that formd brooks and ran quite down to the sea but these were scarce and in general brackish a good way up from the beach.

A soil so barren and at the same time intirely void of the helps derivd from cultivation could not be supposed to yield much towards the support of man.

For the article of timber, there is certainly no want of trees of more than the midling size and some in the valleys very large, but all of a very hard nature; our carpenters who cut them down for fire wood complained much that their tools were damaged by them. . . .

For quadrupedes, Birds, fish etc. I shall say no more than that we had some time ago learnd to eat every identical species which came in our way: a hawk or a crow was to us as delicate and perhaps a better relishd meal than a Partridge or Pheasant to those who have plenty of dainties: we wanted nothing to reccommend any food but its not being salt, that alone was sufficient to make it a delicacy.

The sea however made some amends for the Barreness of the Land. Fish tho not so plentyfull as they generaly are in higher latitudes were far from scarce; where we had an opportunity of hauling the Seine we generaly caught from 50 to 200 lb of fish in a tide. To the Northward again when we came to be entangled within the great Reef . . . was plenty of Turtle hardly to be credited, every shoal swarmed with them.

Then, in the very next paragraph of Banks' journal comes the decisive judgement, "Upon the whole New Holland, tho in every respect the most barren countrey I have seen, is not so bad that between the productions of sea and Land, a company of People, who should have the misfortune of being shipwrecked

Overall Banks thought it barren but bearable.

upon it might support themselves, even by the resources that we
have seen. Undoubtedly a longer stay and visiting different
parts would discover many more."

Banks was impressed by the fact that, "This immense tract of
Land, the largest known which does not bear the name of a
continent, as it is considerably larger than all Europe, is thinly
inhabited even to admiration," and concluded that although it
might be due to the barrenness of the soil and scarcity of fresh
water, it was more likely due to tribal wars.

However this somewhat grudging encouragement even from
a man as eminent as Banks would not have been enough to
launch the first fleet on its way to Botany Bay, almost a generation later, if there had not been other political reasons, too, for
such an undertaking. These reasons were largely connected with
the American War of Independence.

James Maria Matra, whose family had fought on the
"loyalist" side in the American War of Independence, had sailed
with Cook as lieutenant aboard *Endeavour*, and had been struck
by the possibilities of finding territory in New South Wales to
compensate the loyalists for what they had lost in America.
"I am going to offer an object to the consideration of our
Government which may in time atone for the loss of our
American colonies," he wrote in a proposal made in December
1784 to Lord Sydney, Secretary of State for the Home Department:

Matra

By the discoveries and enterprise of our officers, many new
countries have been found which know no sovereign, and that hold
out the most enticing allurements to European adventurers. None
are more inviting than New South Wales.

Captain Cook first coasted and surveyed the eastern side of that
fine country from the 38th degree of South latitude down to the
10th, where he found everything to induce him to give the most
favourable account of it. In this immense tract of more than two
thousand miles, there was every variety of soil, and great parts of it
were extremely fertile, peopled only by a few black inhabitants,
who in the rudest state of society, knew no other arts than such as
were necessary to mere animal existence, and which was almost
entirely sustained by catching fish.

The climate and soil are so happily adapted to produce every
various and valuable production of Europe and of both the Indies,

that with good management and a few settlers, in twenty or thirty years they might cause a revolution in the whole system of European commerce, and secure to England a monopoly of some part of it, and a very large share in the whole.

He suggested that the Admiralty should provide frigates for an expedition.

Lord Howe, First Lord of the Admiralty, did not, however, share Matra's enthusiasm. Writing to Lord Sydney he said:

I return, my dear lord, the papers you left with me today, which are copies only of the former sent to me on the same subject on Friday evening.

Should it be thought advisable to increase the number of our settlements on the plan Mr. Matra has suggested, I imagine it would be necessary to employ ships of a different construction. Frigates are ill adapted for such services. I conceive that ships of burthen to contain the various stores, provisions, implements, etc., wanted for the first colonists meant to be established there, and composing the chief part of the company of the ship, should be provided for the purpose; though an armed vessel of suitable dimensions might be previously appointed to inspect and fix on the preferable station for forming the intended establishment.

The length of the navigation, subject to all the retardments of an India voyage, do not, I must confess, encourage me to hope for a return of the many advantages, in commerce or war, which Mr. Matra has in contemplation.

Matra, however, remained undaunted by the unfavourable opinion of the First Lord and, early in 1785, he induced Sir George Young an admiral of the White Squadron to prepare a further proposal on the same subject. Like Matra's, it drew attention to the advantages of having a naval station in New South Wales in the event of war with Spain and suggested that enough New Zealand flax could be grown there to make the navy independent of Russia for its supply of cordage and canvas. Sir George also argued that a settlement offered immense opportunities for trade with China and Japan.

Both Matra and Young mentioned in their proposals that the loyalists would make admirable settlers in New South Wales since they were used to the rough life of a pioneer country. Both plans, however, pointed out that New South Wales would also

be an excellent reception area for convicts since there was
virtually no possibility of their escape. It was this aspect of the
scheme which most attracted officials.

For, while some loyalists found new homes for themselves in
Nova Scotia, the problem of what to do with the convicts in
Britain's overcrowded prisons remained.

Convicts had been transported from England since the days of
Queen Elizabeth, particularly to the American colonies where,
it was said, there was a shortage of servants, and, under an act
passed in 1718, contractors who offered to carry convicts to
America and hand them over to the colonial governor received
in return the right to sell the convict's services for the period of
his sentence.

This export from Britain ceased when the colonists established their independence, but the supply of convicted felons
sentenced to transportation from Britain, usually for repeated
offences, continued in abundance. This was not surprising in the
days when you could be banished for such offences as stealing
linen laid out for bleaching, setting fire to undergrowth (or
haystacks), disturbing fish ponds or making or selling fireworks.
There were many other less spectacular offences such as pick-
pocketing handkerchiefs, forgery, assault with stones, and, in
the case of women, being of ill-repute.

At first, the surplus felons awaiting a passage overseas were
confined on floating hulks in the Thames and elsewhere. But
this arrangement, unlike that of transportation, actually cost the
Government money as the contractors had to be paid for clothing
and feeding the prisoners. Not only that. There was a risk of the
convicts plotting a mass escape to the shore or of their giving
rise to some epidemic because of the unhealthy conditions of
their confinement. Something had to be done, and some new
place found. In 1779 Banks, the only public notability still alive
to have visited the new sub-continent, was called in to give
evidence before a committee of the House of Commons appointed
to look into the state of the gaols and the question of transportation.

Joseph Banks, Esquire [the evidence reads] being requested in
case it should be thought expedient to establish a colony of convicted felons in any distant part of the globe, from whence their

escape might be difficult, and where, from the fertility of the soil, they might be enabled to maintain themselves, after the first year, with little or no aid from the mother country, to give his opinion what place would be most eligible for such settlement, informed your Committee that the place which appeared to him best adapted such a purpose was Botany Bay, on the coast of New South Wales, in the Indian Ocean, which was about seven months' voyage from England; that he apprehended there would be little probability of any opposition from the natives. He was in this bay in the end of April and beginning of May, 1770 when the weather was mild and moderate; that the climate, he apprehended, was similar to that about Toulouse, in the south of France; the proportion of rich soil was small in comparison to the barren, but sufficient to support a very large number of people; there were no tame animals, and he saw no wild ones during his stay of ten days, but he observed the dung of what was called the Kangourous, which were about the size of a middling sheep, but very swift and difficult to catch; there were no beasts of prey, and he did not doubt but our sheep and oxen, if carried there, would thrive and increase; the grass was long and luxuriant, and there were some eatable vegetables, particularly a sort of wild spinage; the country was well supplied with water; there was an abundance of timber and fuel, sufficient for any number of buildings which might be found necessary.

And being asked, whether he conceived the mother country was likely to reap any benefit from a colone established in Botany Bay? he replied—"If the people formed among themselves a civil government they would necessarily increase, and find occasion for many European commodities; and it was not to be doubted, that a tract of land such as New Holland, which was larger than the whole of Europe, would furnish matter of advantageous return."

Banks' evidence did not produce any immediate response from the Government. The efforts of Matra and Young did.

In 1784 the law was altered to allow convicts to be transported elsewhere than to America. By 18th August 1786 a definite decision had been taken and Lord Sydney wrote to the Lords of the Treasury recalling that the gaols were now so overcrowded as to be a public danger and that efforts to find a suitable settlement area for them in Africa had failed. "I am therefore commanded," wrote Sydney, "to signify to your lordships his Majesty's pleasure that you do forthwith take such measures as may be necessary for providing a proper number of vessels for

2

the conveyance of seven hundred and fifty convicts to Botany
Bay together with such provisions, necessaries and implements
for agriculture as may be necessary for their use after their
arrival."

In December 1786 New South Wales was specifically named
as a place of reception for convicts. Three companies of marines
were to be sent with the fleet to keep order during the voyage
and on shore, and two years of provisions were to be supplied.
The Admiralty was asked to provide a warship and a tender to
convoy the vessels which the Treasury provided.

It cannot be said that there was any great publicity made or
even notice taken of these preparations. But there were several
good reasons for this. In the first place there was no point in
gratuitously informing the French and the Dutch of a proposal
to set up a new colony in a part of the world which they might
be interested in developing themselves.

And there were also critics at home. Some of them, humani-
tarians, were only too ready to argue that it was inhumane to
send convicts so far from home, to settle in some land which had
not yet been developed and might never be. There was also a
strong fear prevalent in Britain that the foundation of new
colonies led to the depopulation and weakening of the mother-
land. And the powerful East India Company might feel that its
interests would be prejudiced by any new settlement made in the
Far East.

So perhaps it was not surprising that the naval captain,
Arthur Phillip, chosen to lead the expedition, was far from being
a public figure. Indeed Lord Howe when he came to know of the
proposed appointment took little trouble to conceal his misgivings. He wrote to Lord Sydney on 3rd September 1786:

> The benefit of the King's service being our common object I am
> persuaded, my dear Lord, it will never suffer for want of our ready
> concurrence when a necessary facility can be rendered by us, on
> either part, to promote the advancement of it on any occasion.
>
> In the present instance, the settlement of the convicts, as you
> have determined, being a matter so immediately connected with
> your department, I could never have a thought of contesting the
> choice you would make of the officer to be entrusted with the
> conduct of it.

I cannot say the little knowledge I have of Captain Philips [*sic*] would have led me to select him for a service of this complicated nature. But as you are satisfied of his ability, and I conclude he will be taken under your direction, I presume it will not be unreason-able to move the King [George III] for having his Majesty's pleasure signified to the Admiralty for these purposes as soon as you see proper, that no time may be lost in making the requisite preparations for the voyage.

Phillip was then forty-eight years old and his record of service by no means unusual or outstanding. His father, Jacob Phillip, was a native of Frankfurt, Germany, and a teacher of languages. But his mother had previously been married to a naval officer and was therefore able to arrange in 1755 for Phillip to be accepted as a midshipman in the Royal Navy. Phillip saw service in the Mediterranean and the West Indies but after only eight years he retired on lieutenant's half pay to farm at Lyndhurst in the New Forest. At the age of thirty-six he volunteered to serve with the Portuguese in their war against Spain but in 1778 when Britain declared war against France he returned again to the Royal Navy. In September 1779 he was made commander of the fire-ship *Basilisk*; then in November 1781 he was ap-pointed post-captain of the frigate *Ariadne*, and in December 1781 captain of the *Europe*, a ship of sixty-four guns. In 1783 when peace was concluded he again went on half pay and was still unemployed when chosen to lead the First Fleet to Botany Bay.

As Governor, he was given a salary of £1,000 per annum in addition to his captain's pay of £500, together with an allow-ance of £20 a year for stationery and 5s. a day for a secretary.

But not everyone would have jumped at the offer.

In the first place, despite Lord Howe's assurances, the Admiralty was not enthusiastic about the affair. This was the first occasion on which the Admiralty had been asked to convoy convict ships and they were doubtless anxious that this should not be a precedent for future expeditions.

Secondly, the expedition was different from all others in as much as the Governor was not allowing the contractors to sell the services of the convicts to settlers but was himself assigning them. Consequently the contractors had no interest in seeing that the men they carried in their ships were likely to be useful in a new colony, and the prison officers in turn saw a golden opportunity of getting rid of the more useless prisoners by sending them to Botany Bay.

Yet from this material in six years Phillip laid the foundations of a commonwealth.

It would in many ways have been easier if the Dutch or the French had discovered Australia ahead of the British, for then, at least, there would have been something for the British to take over: roads perhaps, or well-trained natives. But the "Indians", as they were called, in Australia had shown no signs of wanting to co-operate with the white man, and were so ignorant that they did not know that plants grew from seeds or that a child was the result of sexual experience between a man and a woman.

For millions of years life itself had moved more slowly inside Australia than outside, and animals of the frog and toad family were still the most advanced type of life there at a time when primitive mammals were to be found elsewhere. About fifty million years ago the land-bridge which had previously connected Australia to Asia subsided into the sea and cut off the link between the two land-masses.

Australia, already remote from the main stream of evolution, became a museum of living fossils. The most interesting of these fossils is still the animal known to the early settlers as the paradox or watermole and to us as the duck-billed platypus. This lukewarm-blooded furry animal, with its sensitive rubbery bill and webbed feet, which lays eggs and suckles its young with milk served through enlarged pores, at first seemed so improbable that when a dead specimen arrived in London it was thought to have been cunningly sewn together by a native trickster.

Australia also has the finest collection—though not the monopoly—of marsupials, the animals that carry their young in pouches. (The pouch, by the way is really a form of compensation for a defect in the design of the reproductive organs of marsupials which makes it impossible for them to have "normal" size young. The offspring is in effect a premature baby which has just enough strength to crawl into its mother's pouch.)

The marsupials include not only many different types of

kangaroo and wallaby—some as small as a hare—but marsupial cats; marsupial mice; marsupial flying squirrels (which dive and then, when near the ground, glide upwards to their favourite branch); a marsupial "teddy bear", the koala; and the wombat, a marsupial badger whose pouch opens to the rear so that its young are not troubled by the earth, rocks and other obstacles encountered during digging operations. Among lower organisms Australia offers a special curiosity in the shape of twelve-feet earthworms, whose progress along their tunnels can be detected by loud sluicing noises.

In its vegetation, too, Australia is peculiar, as being dominated by a single family, the eucalyptus, known in Australia as "gums". Some five hundred kinds are known in Australia and only seven others outside it. There are red gums, white-wash gums, blue gums, black gums, silver gums, and gums with yellow, olive or red spots; iron-bark gums, woolly bark gums, scaly gums; there are lemon-scented gums, peppermint gums, honey-bearing gums and flame gums noted for their brilliant flowers. The mountain ash, three hundred feet high, is a "gum", so is the bush-like mallee.

But few of these facts were known to Phillip and his companions.

Preparations for the voyage were made with the same care and foresight that had lost Britain the American War of Independence. On paper, everything was provided for. Phillip was to be captain-general as well as Governor over the territory of New South Wales and his instructions prescribed the oaths that he was to take. He was allowed to appoint justices, to pardon and reprieve offenders, to declare martial law, to grant land, to guard lunatics, to appoint fairs and markets and many other privileges thought necessary to the well-being and good order of the colony. Instructions were also forthcoming as to where his ships were to call on their way to Australia, where they were to take on wine, seed grain, black cattle and sheep. The tools and clothing provided were to be accounted for to the Treasury and the stock was to be preserved as far as possible until enough fodder could be grown to make the farms self-supporting. Public worship was to be observed.

The three most important instructions were kept to the end.

Convicts who had earned their freedom were to be given land free of all fees and taxes for ten years, twelve months rations for themselves and their families, and tools and livestock necessary to set themselves up as small holders.

Phillip was also to send home a report as soon as possible on the conditions on which he thought land should be granted to members of the garrison who wished to stay on in Australia after their term of service had finished.

Finally the Government wanted no international trouble. There was to be no intercourse between the new settlement and those of the British East India Company or with islands traded with by other European powers. No ships large enough to allow private individuals to engage in such trade were to be built.

So much for the plans. In practice however the "suitable warship" provided by the Admiralty to accompany the fleet turned out to be *Sirius*, which had originally been designed as a merchantman for the East India Company. Before completion, she had caught fire and burnt down to the waterline. The Admiralty then bought the hulk at a knock-down price completed her with job-lot timber and used her for a victualler. For the purposes of the expedition she was returned to the dockyards and supposedly given a refit, equipped with twenty guns and called a frigate. She was small and slow. The armed tender *Supply* which was to accompany her was an equally poor sailer.

Six transports (*Alexander, Charlotte, Friendship, Lady Penrhyn, Prince of Wales* and *Scarborough*) and three supply ships (*Borrowdale, Fishbourne* and *Golden Grove*) were East Indiamen hired for the purpose.

Between them they had to carry and supply 600 male convicts, 250 female, 16 officers, 24 non-commissioned officers, 168 men and 40 wives. The ships, of course, were overcrowded. The convicts arrived with their clothes in rags and without needles and thread for repairing them. There were no overseers or superintendents to manage the convicts. No schoolmaster was provided and only one chaplain. The marines had no musket balls or cartridge paper for making ammunition. The armourers had no tools for maintaining the small arms. There was a lack of medicines, and of malt and other substances needed for

ill prepared

preventing scurvy. And Phillip learnt that plans had been made to feed the marines on Navy rations, that is, without flour.

In a letter dated 4th January 1787 Phillip wrote to Nepean: "I likewise beg leave to observe that the number of scythes (only six), of razors (only five dozen) and the quantity of buck and small shot (only 200 lb.), now ordered is very insufficient; and that twenty scythes, twelve dozen of razors at 12s. a dozen, and five of small shot, chiefly buck, in addition to the above is very necessary." As late as 11th January there were no surgeon's instruments aboard any of the transports.

The fleet sailed on 13th May 1787 after a wait that must have seemed interminable. (But, even so, a number of items were missing, among them the women's "cloathing" the ammunition for the marines, and the documents listing the convicts' crimes and their sentences, which had been delivered to the contractors and not apparently passed on). Some of the convicts had been aboard the ships waiting to sail for four months, with only limited spells in the fresh air on deck and the seamen had been complaining bitterly at being kept for so long on river pay which was less than they would have got at sea.

There was no common purpose. The Navy saw the expedition as just another job; the contractors were out to make money; the convicts when not apathetic were suspicious; and the marines who had volunteered for three years did so in many cases to avoid their creditors or their wives. They had no intention of obeying the Governor once they got ashore at the end of the voyage.

On June 3rd the First Fleet reached Teneriffe where the Spanish Governor was good enough to give a dinner at which ices were served.

On July 14th they crossed the Equator and ate the last of their English geese.

At the Cape they took on an extra bull, a calf, a stallion, three mares, three colts and rams, ewes, sows, boars, goats, poultry and plants, or cuttings of oranges, limes, lemons, vines, quinces, apples, pears, strawberries, figs, bamboos and sugar cane.

Many of those who sailed in the First Fleet would have agreed with the sentiments of David Collins the Judge-Advocate who, on leaving the Cape, wrote: "It was natural to indulge at this moment a melancholy reflection which obtruded itself on the mind. The land behind us was the abode of a civilized people; that before us was the residence of savages. When, if ever, we might again enjoy the commerce of the world was doubtful and uncertain."

The convicts gave little trouble on the voyage; they were usually handcuffed either to each other or to the side of the ship and loopholes had been provided for firing between decks if necessary to preserve order. On November 16th Phillip decided to split his fleet, taking the three fastest transports ahead with him so that huts, guard houses, stores and cattle sheds could be put up before the remainder of the prisoners arrived. Every day counted as all hay had been used up and the sheep were dying in spite of efforts to keep them alive with a mixture of flour and water.

On 4th January the leading ships sighted the coast of Tasmania and a fortnight later they anchored in Botany Bay.

2

Starvation Corner

A travel poster of Botany Bay as it is today with its parks, golf course, beaches and sprawling industries could hardly have been more misleading than the description of it which led the First Fleet to Australia to drop anchor in its waters in the hope of founding a settlement there.

The flowers which had impressed Sir Joseph Banks were there and perhaps the colonists chanced on the Golden Wattle blazing against the dark blue sky, the wax-like red Christmas Bells, the Swamp Heath and the Flannel Flower, as star-like as edelweiss. But the features that they were eager to find—deep, protected anchorages, fresh water, and land that they could cultivate were missing: there were salt marshes and scattered boulders in place of fertile meadows, and a kind of iron-grey growth instead of the vivid green grass needed by their starving sheep. It was a scene blighted of its natural colour in a frame of drooping ragged trees, standing aloof with their pale bark and leaves turned grudgingly edge on to the sun as if to preserve their precious moisture. And once out of sight of the long green rollers of the Pacific the landscape degenerated into a never-ending series of unfrequented silent glades among which the wanderer could lose himself in a few moments.

Phillip did not even bother to unpack the stores from his ships. He decided, instead, to disregard his orders to found a settlement at Botany Bay and to investigate the next opening up the coast, across the mouth of which Cook had passed years earlier.

He found there "the finest harbour in the world in which a thousand sail of the line may ride in the most perfect security", and chose one of the smaller creeks which had fresh water as well as a deep anchorage and which he named Sydney Cove after Viscount Sydney, to whom his report would in due course be sent.

The wonders of the harbour with its kingfisher-blue waters, its high wooded hills swooping down to the shore, its islands and its secluded bays, revealed only as the ships drew further inshore from the Heads, restored to the weary travellers the feeling that everything, after all, was going to be all right.

Phillip drew out a plan for the settlement and included in it a hospital, an observatory, a fort, a Government store, a public garden and private allotments. And on February 7th, three weeks after their arrival, he formally proclaimed the new state by reading his commission in the presence of the convicts and the marines who had marched to the assembly point with colours flying and the band playing.

But from the start it was a desperate enterprise. The expedition had to land in what was almost a forest. There were no overseers to control the convicts and the marines considered that their duties were to protect the colony and not to act as prison officers. Everything had to be hurried because the supply ships were on charter and the bill for them mounted every day.

The first essential was a permanent store for the rations. But the building was held back because no lime could be found to make the cement. So the walls had to be built of double thickness and held together with clay and the height was limited to twelve feet. Then there was a shortage of people to do the work. Some of the convicts were sick. Not more than a dozen of them knew enough carpentry to knock up a wooden shanty. The Governor himself had to be content with a portable canvas house which he had had constructed by Messrs. Smith of St. George's Fields, London, at a cost of £125. It was neither water nor wind proof, as a series of sharp thunderstorms, heralding the Australian winter, soon showed. Before there could be any cultivation, large numbers of well-established trees had to be cut down. But the trunks were good for nothing. The wood was found too heavy for boats and the gum with which it was veined caused it to split when subjected to any strain. There were no draught animals to cart away the fallen trunks and these had to be burnt where they lay. Then came the work of grubbing out the roots. Often the task was too much. On one occasion twelve men took five days to extract the fangs of a single specimen. Ordinary ploughing was out of the question; the undergrowth was spiny; and the mosquitoes and ants, like the popinjays, were found to be commonly of a wonderful greatness. Only eight acres were cleared in the first year. The work was so hard that the convicts preferred to lose their tools rather than carry it out. Australian trees, it was found, shed no leaves and therefore provided no leaf-mould to shelter seeds and seedlings from storm or drought during their early growth.

Within a week it became clear that the pioneers were going to have to live almost entirely on the rations that they had brought with them—salt beef, or pork, iron-hard ship's biscuits, flour, dried peas, and butter. The soil was inhospitable. There was no natural fruit: fish supplies were undependable and kangaroos soon learnt to keep at a safe distance from the shooting parties.

The colony had no botanist or even a knowledgeable gardener and the settlers had no idea of which plants were likely to do well in the new soil or at what time of year they should be sown.

Most of the seed had spoiled during the voyage out; the sheep died from eating the native grasses and the cattle escaped into the limitless ranges of the bush.

On the 15th May Phillip wrote to Sydney, "Your lordship will, I presume, see the necessity of a regular supply of provisions for four or five years; and of cloathing, shoes and frocks in the greatest proportion. The necessary implements for husbandry, and for clearing the ground, brought out, will with difficulty be made to serve the time that is necessary for sending out a fresh supply."

We have only to run through the "List of Articles most wanted in the Settlement" sent with Phillip's report of 9th July

1788 to see the straits to which the new colonists had been reduced. He asked for:

House Carpenter's axes
Chalk-lines (none sent out)
Felling Axes
Cross-cut saws
Pit saws
Saw setts
Files for cross-cut and pit saws (a considerable number as they
    soon wear out)
Gimlets, augers, chissels and gouges
Iron pots of 3, 4, and 5 gallons (much wanted at this time)
Billhooks
Scyths and reap-hooks
Nails, mostly of 18, 20 and 24 penny
Nails (spike), brads
Sheet and pig lead
Swan and buck shot
White and red paint
Oil for ditto
Canvas, No. 3,   6 bolts
        No. 4,   ,, ,,
        No. 6,   8 bolts
        No. 7,   ,, ,,
        No. 8,   6 bolts
Twine, one hundredweight
Sail needles
Copper nails for repairing boats
Iron in bars
Steel in ditto
Armourers' tools (none sent out)
Strong double tin plates
Stonemasons' tools
Trowels for bricklayers
Glass, not less than 10 inches by 8
Fifteen puncheons of red wine, for the use of the hospital
Hooks and fishing lines for the natives
Cloathing for the men and women convicts with a large pro-
    portion of shoes
Long frocks and strong jackets for the natives
Soldiers blankets for the convicts
Twelve turn-over carts

Wheel-barrows
Four timber carriages
Blacksmiths' hammers
Carpenters' ditto
Turkey stones for the carpenters' tools (none sent out)
Rope, of 1½ inch, 1 coil
Rope of 1 inch,   ,,   ,,

The "Indians" on the whole proved to be a great disappointment to Phillip, who had been ordered in his commission to
"endeavour by every possible means to open an intercourse with
the natives and to conciliate their affections, enjoining all our
subjects to live in amity and kindness with them".

Like the animals of the country they defied classification. They
could hunt men, and send news by smoke signal. They could
track so well that they could see from the bark of a tree whether
an opossum had climbed up it or down. At times they would
show Phillip's men where to find water and where to shelter in a
cave. At other times they would warn them off with a spear
thrown from afar. Only a few learnt even the vague roundabout
terms of pidgin English. There was no knowing how they would
act under any given circumstance. But one thing was clear, they
were not anxious to leave their families and live with the white
men. They expected a share of his fish but refused to work in
return.

This liking for fish led Phillip to believe at first that the
natives would be found only close to the coast; he did not
believe that anyone without a knowledge of agriculture would
find enough to live on in the interior of this inhospitable territory. He did not know that witchetty grubs found in the trees
and eaten raw were a favourite delicacy for the natives. But
later he found "Indians" inland too, always a nuisance, sometimes a menace; and always unfathomable.

The aborigines of Australia, then as now, relied on a dream-
world to justify and explain the past from which they had
evolved, the present they lived in, and the future to which they
were travelling. This dream-world often centred round an
animal or bird, sacred to them as tribal hero, a spirit who had
revealed to the wise men of the tribe their inheritance from the
past and who acted as a protector in the present. No native

would dare to hunt or kill the protector, who could make rain for him and even ensure the fertility of the tribe.

The paths, trees, stones and waterholes visited by these mythological heroes were as sacred to the natives as the Stations of the Cross to a devout Christian.

Such revelations, made known in dreams to the old men of the community, were passed on only to those young men who could be relied on to safeguard the traditions of the tribe. Young novices were admitted to full membership of the tribe only after they had undergone a complicated and exacting task designed to link their past to their future. This initiation symbolized the basic standards by which the tribe lived and might involve anything from two years' silence to having a front tooth knocked out. Bull-roarers (wooden clubs which when whirled round produced a formidable roaring sound) were used to warn off those not privileged to attend the final initiation ceremonies. Women who, even accidentally, witnessed these rites were put to death.

During his initiation a man might visit the dream-world of heroes from which he sprang and speak with hero-kangaroos and hero-serpents. And it was only in this dream-world that a father could find a child-spirit and direct it to the mother who was going to bring it into the world, for the natives saw no connection between love-making and children.

Marriage customs of the greatest complexity prevailed by which a man might not marry the daughter of his father's brother, but might marry the daughter of his father's sister, and by which a man's brother-in-law had the right to marry his brother-in-law's sister. Marriages between certain types of second cousin were favoured and young girls were frequently betrothed to old men before reaching puberty. The order in which presents are given between families would puzzle a diplomatic protocol expert.

So it was not surprising that our eighteenth-century colonists, the more educated of whom were looking in Australia for Rousseau's noble savage, could make little of these weird beings who rubbed white clay on their faces, stuck sticks through their nostrils and smelt of fish oil.

But there were other more practical causes of strife between the two communities. Because the Indians knew nothing of agriculture and had to live off the country there were no hedges and ditches, yet the boundaries between one tribe and the next were respected as if they had been marked out with an electric fence. Outside his own territory the native believed that he was no longer protected by his animal guardian and the old men, perhaps in order to avoid endless tribal strife, proclaimed that food from another's territory was poisonous and that it was better to starve than to eat it. Consequently, although the white men had usurped a large slice of the territory along the coast it was unthinkable for the natives there to transfer themselves inland. So they became an occupied race and a resentful one.

Believing their own traditions, they successfully resisted all efforts to teach them to grow their own food, and indeed could not understand why the white man wished to store so much provender without eating it, as they themselves would have done. From time to time they ambushed the colonists' cattle in some narrow gully—and the herd resolutely refused to return there in future no matter how tempting the grazing might be.

Just as the natives scorned agriculture, they adored hunting and were far more successful than Europeans, who frightened away most of the game with their guns. The aborigines were more subtle but more wasteful in their methods. In order to drive game they often set fire to the undergrowth, leaving even less for the cattle to feed on than there had been before.

Convicts could not be sent far into the bush in search of fresh pastures for fear of ambush and because of the temptation to escape.

The first gnawing doubts that food in the colony might not last until the next supply ship arrived from England began to appear towards the end of May. It was then that Lieutenant Ball, who had been sent on an expedition to Lord Howe Island, where turtle had been found earlier in the year, returned without a single ounce of turtle meat. The creatures had emigrated as is their habit.

In Sydney flour grew short; by September it was clear that almost none of the English wheat was going to sprout and that the weevils had got at the seed taken aboard at the Cape. The wheat crop on Norfolk Island, the colonies "branch" establishment to the north of New Zealand, had also failed. Phillip decided to send *Sirius*, the flagship of the expedition, to the Cape to fetch grain for the 698 men, 193 women and 42 children living on the Australian mainland.

In addition Captain John Hunter of the *Sirius* was to bring back twelve baskets of garden seeds, some coarse thread, leather for shoe repairs, barrels of tar, tin saucepans, and sugar, sago, raisins and spices for the hospital.

In May of the following year, 1789, *Sirius* was back again at Sydney Cove, but she had been able to take on only four months' supply of flour for the settlement in addition to her own provisions. Food by then was so scarce that a night watch of twelve trusty convicts had to be set up to put a stop to the plundering of private gardens and fowl runs. Hungry pigs and horses followed their masters' examples and broke into the gardens to eat what they could find there. Six marines were put to death for breaking into the Government stores. In September the butter gave out and, later the same year, rats destroyed large quantities of flour and rice in the storeroom. Some of what still remained had been contaminated by oil and tar which had been put aboard the storeships and had to be thrown away.

In November the men's rations had to be cut to two-thirds of the normal in the hope of making them last till June. Rats and crows were eaten as delicacies, and seven officers dined off the side-bone of an emu.

On three days a week all boats were sent out to fish. More and more convicts were moved from the mainland to Norfolk Island where the soil was said to be better, and their departure served to depress considerably the spirits of those left behind.

On March 27th the general ration was reduced to 4 lb. of flour, $2\frac{1}{2}$ lb. of salt pork and $1\frac{1}{2}$ lb. of rice per head per week.

Among the more perceptive members of the colony was Captain Watkin Tench, a Welsh officer whose agreeable and vivid style and good-hearted sense of humour ultimately brought him many readers at home when his diary was written up and published as *A Complete Accounty of the Settlement at Port Jackson in New South Wales*. But even his optimism and his hopes for the future began to dwindle. Of the early days of the year 1790 he wrote:

Our impatience of news from Europe strongly marked the commencement of the year. We had now been two years in the country, and thirty two months from England, in which long period no supplies, except what had been procured at the Cape of Good Hope by the Sirius, had reached us. From intelligence of our friends and connections we had been entirely cut off, no communications whatever having passed with our native country since the 13th of May, 1787, the day of our departure from Portsmouth. Famine besides was approaching with gigantic strides, and gloom and dejection overspread every countenance. Men abandoned themselves to the most desponding reflections, and adopted the most extravagant conjectures.

Still we were on the tiptoe of expectation. If thunder broke at a distance, or a fowling-piece of louder than ordinary report resounded in the woods, "a gun from a ship" was echoed on every side, and nothing but hurry and agitation prevailed. For eighteen months after we had landed in the country, a party of marines used to go weekly to Botany Bay to see whether any vessel, ignorant of our removal to Port Jackson, might be arrived there. But a better plan was now devised, on the suggestion of captain Hunter. A party of seamen were fixed on a high bluff, called the South-head, at the entrance to the harbour, on which a flag was ordered to be hoisted, whenever a ship might appear, which should serve as a direction to her, and as a signal of approach to us. Every officer stepped forward to volunteer a service which promised to be so replete with beneficial consequences. But the zeal and alacrity of captain Hunter, and our brethren of the Sirius, rendered superfluous all assistance or co-operation.

Here on the summit of the hill, every morning from daylight until the sun sunk did we sweep the horizon, in hope of seeing a sail. At every fleeting speck which arose from the bosom of the sea, the heart bounded and the telescope was lifted to the eye. If a ship appeared here, we knew she must be bound to us; for on the shores of this vast ocean (the largest in the world) we were the only community which possessed the art of navigation, and languished for intercourse with civilised society.

To say that we were disappointed and shocked, would very inadequately describe our sensations. But the misery and horror of such a situation cannot be imparted, even by those who have suffered under it.

Vigorous measures were become indispensable. The governor therefor, early in February, ordered the Sirius to prepare for a

3

voyage to China; and a farther retrenchment of our ration, we were given to understand, would take place on her sailing.

But the Sirius was destined not to reach China. Previous to her intended departure on that voyage, she was ordered, in concert with the Supply, to convey major Ross, with a large detachment of marines, and more than two hundred convicts, to Norfolk Island; it being hoped that such a division of our numbers would increase the means of subsistence. She sailed on the 6th of March. And on the 27th of the same month, the following order was issued from head-quarters

"Parole—   Honour
"Counter sign—Example

"The expected supply of provisions not having arrived, makes it necessary to reduce the present ration. And the commissary is directed to issue, from the 1st of April, the undermentioned allowance, to every person in the settlement without distinction. Four pounds of flour, two pounds and a half of salt pork, and one pound and a half of rice, per week."

On the 5th April news was brought, that the flag on the South-head was hoisted. Less emotion was created by the news than might be expected; every one coldly said to his neighbour, "the Sirius and Supply are returned from Norfolk island". To satisfy myself that the flag was really flying, I went to the observatory, and looked for it through the large astronomical telescope, when I plainly saw it. But I was immediately convinced that it was not to announce the arrival of ships from England; for I could see nobody near the flag-staff except one solitary being, who kept strolling around, unmoved by what he saw. I well knew how different an effect the sight of ships would produce.

The Governor, however, determined to go down the harbour, and I begged permission to accompany him. Having turned a point about half way down, we were surprised to see a boat, which was known to belong to the Supply, rowing towards us. On nearer approach, I saw Captain Ball make an extraordinary motion with his hand, which too plainly indicated that something disastrous had happened; and I could not help turning to the governor, near whom I sat, and saying, "Sir, prepare yourself for bad news". A few minutes changed doubt into certainty; and to our unspeakable consternation we learned that the Sirius had been wrecked on Norfolk Island. . . . Dismay was painted on every countenance, when the tidings were proclaimed in Sydney. . . .

At six o'clock in the evening, all the officers of the garrison, both civil and military, were summoned to meet the governor in council; when the nature of our situation was fully discussed; and an account of the provisions yet remaining in store laid before the council by the commissary. This account stated that, on the present ration the public stores contained salt meat sufficient to serve until the 2nd July; flour until the 20th August; and rice or pease in lieu of it, until the 1st of October.

Several regulations for the more effectual preservation of garden property, were proposed, and adopted: and after some interchange of opinion, the following ration was decreed to commence immediately: a vigorous exertion to prolong existence, or the chance of relief, being all now left to us.

"Two pounds of pork, two pounds and a half of flour, two pounds of rice, or a quart of pease, to every grown person, and to every child of more than eighteen months old."

"To every child under eighteen months old, the same quantity of rice and flour, and one pound of pork."

(When the age of this provision is recollected, its inadequacy will more strikingly appear. The pork and rice were brought with us from England: the pork had been salted between three and four years, and every grain of rice was a moving body from the inhabitants lodged within it. We soon left off boiling the pork, as it had become so old and dry, that it shrunk to one half in its dimensions when so dressed. Our usual method of cooking it was to cut off the daily morsel, and toast it on a fork before the fire, catching the drops which fell on a slice of bread, or in a saucer of rice. Our flour was the remnant of what was brought from the Cape, by the Sirius, and was good. Instead of baking it, the soldiers and convicts used to boil it up with greens.)

The immediate departure of the Supply, for Batavia, was also determined.

Nor did our zeal stop here. The Governor being resolved to employ all the boats, public and private, in procuring fish which was intended to be served in lieu of salt malt, all the officers, civil and military, including the clergyman, and the surgeons of the hospital, made the voluntary offer, in addition to their other duties, to go alternately every night in these boats, in order to see that every exertion was made; and that all the fish which might be caught was deposited with the commissary.

The best marksmen of the marines and convicts were also selected, and put under the command of a trusty serjeant, with directions to range the wood in search of kangaroos; which were ordered, when brought in, to be delivered to the commissary.

And as it was judged that the inevitable fatigues of shooting and fishing could not be supported on the common ration, a small additional quantity of flour and pork was appropriated to the use of the gamekeepers; and each fisherman, who had been out during the preceding night had, on his return in the morning, a pound of uncleaned fish allowed for his breakfast.

On 17th April, the Supply, Captain Ball, sailed for Batavia to hire a Dutch boat loaded with provisions. We followed her with anxious eyes until she was no longer visible . . . and all our labour and attention were turned to one objection—the procuring of food. . . .

The distress of the lower classes for clothes was almost equal to their other wants. The stores had long been exhausted, and winter was at hand. Nothing more ludicrous can be conceived than the expedients of substituting, shifting, and patching, which ingenuity devised, to eke out wretchedness, and preserve the remains of decency. The superior dexterity of the women was particularly conspicuous. Many a guard have I seen mount, in which the number of soldiers without shoes, exceeded that which had yet preserved the remnants of leather.

Nor was another part of our domestic economy less whimsical. If a lucky man, who had knocked down a dinner with his gun, or caught a fish by angling from the rocks, invited a neighbour to dine with him, the invitation always ran "bring your own bread". Even at the Governor's table this custom was constantly observed. Every man when he sat down pulled his bread out of his pocket, and laid it by his plate.

The insufficiency of our ration soon diminished our execution of labour. Both soldiers and convicts pleaded such loss of strength, as to find themselves unable to perform their accustomed tasks. The hours of public work were accordingly shortened; or rather, every man was ordered to do as much as his strength would permit: and every other possible indulgence was granted.

In proportion, however, as lenity and mitigation were extended to inability and helplessness, inasmuch was the most rigorous justice executed on disturbers of the public tranquillity. Persons detected in robbing gardens, or pilfering provisions, were never screened: because as every man could possess, by his utmost exertions, but a bare sufficiency to preserve life, he who deprived his neighbour of that little, drove him to desperation. No new laws for the punishment of theft were enacted; but persons of all description

were publicly warned, that the severest penalties, which the exist-
ing law in its greatest latitude would authorise, should be inflicted
on offenders. The following sentence of a court of justice, of which
I was a member, on a convict detected in a garden stealing potatoes, will illustrate the subject. "He was ordered to receive three
hundred lashes immediately, to be chained for six months to two
other criminals, who were thus fettered for former offences, and to
have his allowance of flour stopped for six months." . . .

Further to contribute to the detection of villainy, a proclamation,
offering a reward of sixty pounds of flour, more tempting than the
ore of Peru or Potosi, was promised to any one who should appre-
hend, or bring to justice, a robber of garden ground. . . .

At length the clouds of misfortune began to separate, and on the
evening of the 3'd of June, the joyful cry of "The flag's Up",
resounded in every direction.

I was sitting in my hut, musing on our fate, when a confused
clamour in the street drew my attention. I opened my door, and
saw several women with children in their arms running to and fro
with distracted looks, congratulating each other, and kissing their
infants with the most passionate and extravagant marks of fond-
ness. I needed no more; but instantly started out, and ran to a hill,
where, by the assistance of a pocket-glass, my hopes were realised.
My next door neighbour, a brother officer, was with me; but we
could not speak; we wrung each other by the hand, with eyes and
hearts overflowing.

Finding that the Governor intended immediately to set off in his
boat down the harbour, I begged to be of his party.

As we proceeded, the object of our hopes soon appeared:—a large
ship with the English colours flying, working in, between the heads
which form the entrance of the harbour. The tumultuous state of
our minds represented her in danger; and we were in agony. Soon
after, the governor, having ascertained what she was, left us, and
stept into a fishing boat to return to Sydney. The weather was wet
and tempestuous; but the body is delicate only when the soul is at
ease. We pushed through wind and rain, the anxiety of our
sensations every moment redoubling.

A few minutes [of pulling] completed our wishes, and we found
ourselves on board the Lady Juliana transport, with two hundred
and twenty five of our countrywomen, whom crime or misfortune
had condemned to exile. We learned that they had been almost
eleven months on their passage, having left Plymouth, into which
port they had put in July 1789. We continued to ask a thousand

questions on a breath. Stimulated by curiosity, they inquired in
turn; but the right of being first answered, we thought, lay on our
side. "Letters! letters!" was the cry. They were produced and torn
open in trembling agitation. News burst on us like the meridian
splendour on a blind man. We were overwhelmed with it; public,
private, general and particular. Nor was it until some days had
elapsed, that we were able to methodize it, or reduce it into form.
We now heard for the first time of our sovereign's illness, and his
happy restoration to health. The French Revolution of 1789, with
all the attendant circumstances of that wonderful and unexpected
event, succeeded to amaze us.

A general thanksgiving to Almighty God, for his Majesty's
recovery, and happy restoration to his family and subjects, was
ordered to be offered up on the following Wednesday, when all
public labour was suspended; and every person in the settlement
attended at Church where a sermon, suited to an occasion, at once
so full of tratitude and solemnity, was preached by the Reverend
Richard Johnson, chaplain of the colony. [And no wonder! For the
Lady Juliana, unfamiliar with the harbour stood in so close to the
North Head that only the set of the tide prevented her from being
wrecked.]

All the officers were afterwards entertained at dinner by the
Governor. And in the evening, an address to his Excellency,
expressive of congratulation and loyalty, was agreed upon; and in
two days after was presented, and very graciously received. . . .

We were joyfully surprised on the 20th of the month [June] to
see another sail enter the harbour. She proved to be the Justinian
transport, commanded by Captain Maitland; and our rapture was
doubled on finding that she was laden entirely with provisions for
our use. Full allowance, and general congratulation, immediately
took place.

Of course the troubles of the colony were by no means over.
For the *Juliana* and the *Justinian* merely helped to make up the
loss of an earlier supply ship, the *Guardian*, which struck an
iceberg 400 miles from the Cape of Good Hope and was all but
wrecked.

As late as the autumn of 1792, Governor Phillip was writing
that when the supply ship *Atlantic* arrived from Bengal, the
settlement had only thirteen days' flour and forty-five days' maize
in store at the ration then issued, which was down to $1\frac{1}{2}$ lb. of
flour and 4 lb. of maize per man per week.

Also, as Phillip pointed out: "The ground which the military may cultivate will be for their own convenience, and nothing from that quarter or from the officers in the civil department can be expected to be brought into the publick account. Providing houses and barracks for the additional number of officers and soldiers, rebuilding those temporary ones which were erected on our first arrival,[1] which must be done in the course of another year, as well as building more stone houses and huts for the convicts as they arrive, will employ a considerable number of people; and works of this kind will always be carrying on . . ." (i.e. not everybody could help to grow food).

Also, the quality of labour was poor. Phillip wrote:

Experience, Sir, has taught me how difficult it is to make men industrious who have passed their lives in habits of vice and indolence. In some cases it has been found impossible; neither kindness nor severity have had any effect; and tho' I can say that the convicts in general behave well, there are many who dread punishment less than they fear labour; and those who have not been brought up to hard work, which are by far the greatest part, bear it badly. They shrink from it the moment the eye of the overseer is turned from them.

The public farm at Rose Hill goes on well. I hope that next year a very considerable quantity of ground will be sown; but, sir, this settlement has never had more than one person to superintend the clearing and cultivating ground for the public benefit or who has ever been the means of bringing a single bushel of grain into the public granary. . . .

I wish, sir, to point out the great difference between a settlement formed as this is and one formed by farmers and emigrants who have been used to labour, and who reap the fruits of their own industry. Amongst the latter few are idle or useless, and they feel themselves interested in their different employments. On the contrary, amongst the convicts we have few who are inclined to be industrious, or who feel themselves anyways interested in the advantages which are to accrue from their labours, and we may have many who are helpless and a deadweight on the settlement. Many of those helpless wretches who were sent out in the first ships

---

[1] Many of these had twigs stretched over the glassless windows in place of lattices.

are dead, and the numbers of those who remained are now considerably increased. I will, sir, insert an extract from the surgeon's
report, who I directed to examine these people.

"After a careful examination of the convicts, I find upwards of
one hundred who must ever be a burden to the settlement, not
being able to do any kind of labour, from old age and chronical
diseases of long standing. Amongst the females there is one who
has lost the use of her limbs upwards of three years, and amongst
the male two who are perfect idiots."

Such are the people sent from the different gaols and from the
hulks, where it is said the healthy and the artificers are retained.
Sending out the disordered and helpless clears the gaols, and may
ease the parishes from which they are sent; but, sir, it is obvious
that this settlement, instead of being a colony which is to support
itself, will, if the practice is continued, remain for years a burden
to the mother country.

Of the 930 males sent out by the last ships, 261 died on board,
and fifty have died since landing. The number of sick this day is
450 and many who are not reckoned as sick have barely strength to
attend to themselves.

The only real surprise in this report of Phillip's is its mild-
ness.

The contractors who ferried the convicts from England to
Australia had no claim on the prisoners once these were landed,
and therefore no real interest in seeing that they arrived at Port
Jackson alive. On the contrary, if a convict died on the voyage,
the contractor saved the rations that he would otherwise have
eaten, unless, as sometimes happened, his fellow convicts succeeded in propping the body up in an attitude sufficiently lifelike
to deceive the guard who handed out the food.

It was not unusual for the convicts to be cooped up in hutches,
six feet square, fettered with irons which had been designed, not
so long before, for the slave trade. Many arrived in Australia
almost without having drawn a breath of fresh air since leaving
England. Some died in the boat while being rowed ashore; other
weaklings expired when the stronger prisoners tore the blankets
and food from their hands.

The colonists too were in a prison of a kind. It was difficult
for them to break loose from the coast towards the Blue Mountains where, if they had only known it, they could have found all

the timber and limestone they could use. For them the exploration of the interior was the key to disenchantment. As Tench put it:

The first impression made on a stranger is certainly favourable. He sees gently swelling hills, connected by vales which possess every beauty that verdure of trees, and form, simply considered in itself, can produce: but he looks in vain for those murmuring rills and refreshing springs, which fructify and embellish more happy lands.

Nothing like those tributary streams, which feed rivers in other countries, are here seen: for when I speak of the stream at Sydney, I mean only the drain of a morass; and the river at Rose Hill is a creek of the harbour, which above high water mark would not in England be called even a brook. Whence the Hawkesbury, the only fresh water river known to exist in the country, derives its supplies, would puzzle a transient observer. He sees nothing but torpid unmeaning ponds (often stagnant and always still, unless agitated by heavy rains) which communicate with it. Doubtless the springs which arise in Caermarthen mountains may be said to constitute its source. To cultivate its banks within many miles of the bed of the stream (except on some elevated detached spots) will be found impracticable, unless some method be devised of erecting a mound, sufficient to repel the encroachments of a torrent, which sometimes rises fifty feet above its ordinary level, inundating the surrounding country in every direction.

The county between the Hawkesbury and Rose Hill, is that which I have hitherto spoken of. When the river is crossed, this prospect soon gives place to a very different one; the green vales and moderate hills disappear, at the distance of about three miles from the river side; and from Knight Hill and Mount Twiss, the limits which terminate our researches, nothing but precipices, wilds, and deserts, are to be seen. Even these steeps fail to produce streams. The difficulty of penetrating this country, joined to the dread of a sudden rise of the Hawkesbury, forbidding all return, has hitherto prevented our reaching Caermarthen mountains.

Nevertheless it was already clear that the colony could not stand still and was, in fact, moving slowly forward. Before he landed at Port Jackson Phillip had been given power both to free convicts before their sentences had been completed and to grant them lands. The first convict to be "emancipated" was John

Irving, a surgeon's assistant, who was given his freedom on
14th July 1790. Others soon followed.

And there were also convicts whose sentences had expired.
Phillip turned one of them, James Ruse, into a pioneer farmer by
starting him off with an acre and a half of cleared ground and
with enough help in clearing the heavy timber off another five
acres. He was also given two sow pigs, six hens, enough grain
to sow his ground for the first year, a hut, tools, rations from the
public store for fifteen months and a promise of a grant of thirty
acres complete if he made a success of his holding. Ruse took
over his farm on 30th March 1791.

Phillip Schaffer, a convict superintendent, sent out from London in response to Phillip's request, resigned his post about the
same time to become Australia's first civilian settler. He was a
widower with a daughter. Schaffer was granted 140 acres on the
north side of the creek leading to Parramatta, and was allowed
daily rations for eighteen months, a hut, two acres of ground
cleared of timber, help from four convicts for eighteen months,
tools, seed grain for the first year and two sow pigs.

In August 1789 Phillip had also received authority to grant
land to non-commissioned officers, privates and others. Two
seamen, Robert Webb and William Reid, both late of the *Sirius*,
were the first to step forward.

Authority to grant land to officers staying on after their tour
of duty was sent by Dundas to Governor Phillip in July 1792,
although the document did not arrive until after Phillip had left
the colony for good.

Phillip himself would have liked more settlers. As early as
July 1788 he reported that fifty farmers sent out with their
families could do more than a thousand convicts in a year to
render the colony independent of the mother country for provisions. In September he again asked for settlers to be sent out
and was prepared to assign convict labour to them; and in
October of the same year he wrote again to Lord Sydney: "It
must, my Lord, be settlers, with the assistance of the convicts,
that will put this country in a situation for supporting its
inhabitants."

And so it was no accident that before Governor Phillip retired
in December 1792 because of ill health and went home to die in

obscurity in Bath, there were three types of Australian settler, free civilians, ex-convicts and the military. They were destined all of them to quarrel for generations with each other, with their rulers on the spot and with the Government at home, which was so indifferent, apparently, to their fate.

3

Mutineers Defeat Governor Bligh of the Bounty

Even in Phillip's time there were quarrels between the Governor and the officers sent out for the protection of the colony. The marines who sailed to Australia in the First Fleet declared that their privileges and duties were set out in a letter from the Admiralty to the commanding officers of marines at Portsmouth and Plymouth. They refused to bow to the Governor's will or to protect its food supplies from night raiders. They were not civilians and few of them had any thought but to finish their term of duty and go home.

In due course, therefore, they were replaced by a body of men raised specially for permanent service in that remote territory under the name of the New South Wales Corps. (Three guineas was offered for each recruit, the only stipulation being that he should be sound in mind and body, not less than 5 feet 4 inches in height and between the ages of sixteen and thirty.) The first contingent of the Corps arrived in June 1790.

And it was not long before they were just as discontented as their predecessors.

Thus Captain Hill who landed at Sydney off the transport ship *Surprize* wrote a month later:

> To enter no further into the detail of our miserable existence,
> I will give you a just account of how I am situated, which is prefer-
> able to many by my being second Captain in the Regiment and

consequently entitled to a second choice of quarters. Here I am, living in a miserable thatched hut, without kitchen, without a garden, with an acrimonious blood by my having been nearly six months at sea, and tho' little better than a leper, obliged to live on a scanty pittance of salt provision, without a vegetable, except when a good-natured neighbour robs his own stomach in compassion to me; not a mouthful of fresh meat to be obtained, and if, rarely, such a thing should present itself, not to be purchased but at an exorbitant price (eighteen pence per lb.). Fish is by no means plentiful, at least, they are not caught in abundance—not enough to supply the sick; but, should one be offered for sale, t'is by far too dear for an officer's pocket. Tho' I have been here so little time, yet, when my salt ration has been set before me unaccompanied by either vegetable, vinegar, or other thing to render it palatable or wholesome, I have felt the contention between hunger, etc., as described by Sterne of the pannier's ass. A soldier should endure all hardships cheerfully when the service requires it, but when they are occasioned by ignorance, incompetency, injustice or oppression, he has a right to complain. With a wish to preserve my health as much as possible from the inroads of scurvy and counteract the effects of the diabolical morsel I am daily obliged to eat, I purchased some wine, being a vegetable juice and obtained it as a favour—port wine at forty shillings the dozen, and sherry at fifty. I had also the offer a few days ago, of three small pigs, very poor and not old enough for roasters; my mouth literally watered at the sight of them, but the price of fifteen shillings each was too great for my purse; I therefore had the resolution to withstand the powers of appetite, which were very acute. Soap is from three to four shillings the pound; bad Irish salt butter, eighteen pence; sugar, two shillings; flour, when any can be bought, a shilling; teas exorbitantly dear. So that from a principle of saving, and induced by a laudable motive (I hope), I have journeyed thus far to live miserably and yet to spend every farthing of my income, which would have supported me very comfortably, if not genteely in England. In America, the officers and settlers had grants of land in proportion to their rank; but those of the marines who are now here, and have borne every hardship, have no such thing, neither is there any intention of giving each their portion. In my humble opinion nothing can be more impolitic.

Two years later Major Francis Grose, Commanding Officer of the Corps wrote home to Matthew Lewis, Under-secretary at war, in the same strain:

Sir, I think it requisite to request your interference in behalf of the officers and soldiers who are doing duty at this place. Unwilling as I always shall be to complain, I, but with little reluctance, set about the subject of this letter, being confident that the Secretary of State will be better pleased to remove the grievance than to hear it has happened. I need not inform you that the necessaries of life are not often to be purchased, and that the ration allowed by Government is the soldier's chief and almost only support. How whenever it happens that a short allowance is issued to the felons, the soldiers' ration is also reduced, and that without the smallest difference or distinction—the captain of a company, and the convict transported for life, divide and share and share alike whatever is served out. Our numbers are too much reduced by unwholesome food and bad quarters to make the saving a matter of much moment, even in the greatest scarcity—nor can I imagine it was intended we should so equally partake of whatever miseries assail the colony; and what makes our situation the more unpleasant is that the Governor does not feel himself authorized to indulge with grants such as would wish either for comfort or amusement to cultivate a small quantity of ground. I have frequently applied to Governor Phillip on this business, who, in answer to my representations, assures me he has more than once written to the Secretary of State, that unfortunately he has never received any reply whatever. . . .

In this predicament the officers decided to take matters into their own hands. Between them they subscribed more than £4,000 in shares of £200 in order to charter the whaler *Britannia* from its master and owner, Captain Raven, and send her to the Cape for the comforts that they needed.

Phillip was reluctant to allow the ship to go. He was afraid of quarrelling with the East India Company who had an official monopoly of trade in the Far East. He said that more provisions were expected to arrive in the settlement before the *Britannia* could make the double journey to the Cape and back and he offered to use official transport ships under his control for fetching private goods ordered by the military.

But Grose and the officers would have none of this and *Britannia* duly sailed for the Cape; she even carried some official mail aboard her.

This was where the Governor and the military parted company. The despatch of the *Britannia* was the first step towards the formation of a state within a state which led a few years later to the overthrow of the Governor by a military junta who ruled the colony in his stead.

When Phillip left Australia, Grose stepped into his shoes as lieutenant governor, and a new era began in which the army played an increasingly important part.

Grose did not hang about, waiting for instructions for a new policy to come from home. On his own initiative he discontinued the arrangement by which the Government itself grew the grain needed to feed the colony. Instead, he gave land to officers, other ranks and to civilians. And by altering the convicts' official hours of work, he made it possible for the new landowners to employ convicts, fed and clothed by the Crown, for clearing and cultivating their new estates. Even better; he agreed that the Government would be responsible for buying what was grown.

In his report home he wrote:

> I have allotted to such officers as have asked one hundred acres of land, which, with great spirit, they, at their own expence, are clearing. Whether their efforts result from the novelty of the business, or the advantages they promise themselves, I cannot say, but their exertions are really astonishing; and I absolutely expect, if they continue as they begin, that in the space of six months the officers will have a tract in cultivation more than equal to a third of all that has ever been cleared in the colony. As I am aware they are at this time the only description of settlers on whom reliance be placed, I shall encourage their pursuit as much as is in my power.

In the same letter, he also notified the Right Hon. Henry Dundas that he considered it expedient while on a reduced ration to make "some little distinctions between the convicts and the civil and military people, which difference will, of course, be discontinued whenever full allowance to the whole can with safety be issued".

It was under Grose, too, that the military became more and more interested in the business of importing spirits—mainly rum—and selling it to colonists and convicts alike.

In his first despatch to Dundas, Grose reported that the *Hope*, an American ship employed in collecting skins and carrying them to China, put in to Sydney for wood and water, and that

her Master had announced that he had a quantity of both spirits
and provisions for sale. The Master, Grose reported, was
willing to sell the provisions only if the spirits were bought as
well, and he, Grose, mindful of the risks of farming in Australia
and of the hazards facing supply ships from England, decided to
purchase 200 barrels of cured beef, 80 barrels of pork, 44 barrels
of flour which brought the stores up to seven months' supply
at the full ration.

Seven thousand five hundred and ninety-five gallons of spirits
at 4s. 6d. per gallon were also bought with a view to passing
them on to the non-commissioned officers and soldiers of the
New South Wales Corps, although Grose did not yet know
whether he was to issue it as a free allowance or deduct it from
their pay. For the time being the spirits were charged for, but
they were nevertheless in great demand, and within little more
than a month the Commissary had disposed of £405 worth—
about one third of the consignment. The call was so brisk that
when, shortly afterwards, the *Bellona* arrived from England
carrying more rum, this was sold off at 5s. a gallon "in order to
prevent extortion by sea captains".

In the beginning there was no desire on the part of the New
South Wales Corps to establish themselves commercially as
wine and spirit merchants. Still less did they want to make a
living out of the debaucheries of their fellow men. But in a
world built round a ration store which dispensed only salt beef
and pork, rum was a short cut to paradise. It enabled the
colonists to shut out for a moment the picture before them of
muddied tracks, uncleared tree stumps, rude huts, and human
depravity.

Officially the sale of rum to convicts was banned. But in
practice it was the one inducement which made them work, and
wise employers included regular dispensations of rum or other
liquor in the day's time table, deducting an appropriate amount
(usually twice what they paid for the rum) from the convicts'
wages.

The convicts who were allowed in their spare time to hire
themselves out to work earned sufficient liquor to keep them
happy by night as well as by day. Soon night bonfires lit up the
tracks winding above the shore, and the area known as "The

The First Fleet in Botany Bay

Arthur Phillip

Lachlan Macquarie

William Bligh

John Macarthur

Rocks" became notorious for its scenes of vice and debauchery. Patrols took care to walk in pairs when they ventured down its steep and treacherous pathways in search of criminals or deserters.

So, for the officers, the trade in rum and gin became first an aid to good farming and then, in the case of some officers, a substitute for it. The whole of the military in New South Wales came to be nicknamed the Rum Corps and many of the officers took to living with convict women. To this way of life John Macarthur, who was to be the father of Australia's wool trade, was a notable exception.

Macarthur was of Scottish descent (his father had fought for Bonnie Prince Charlie) but he had settled in Devonshire. There he married a west-country girl, Elizabeth Vale. At the age of twenty-two he sailed in the Second Fleet to New South Wales in January 1790 as a subaltern, taking his wife and young son with him.

This alone would have distinguished him from his fellow officers, for the presence of his family enabled him to lead a wholesome existence in circumstances which led others to give themselves up to drink and loose living. In addition he was a man who sought responsibility. He had played the leading part in chartering the *Britannia* for the enterprise that had caused Governor Phillip so much misgiving.

Grose soon singled out Macarthur and promoted him for service at the Government settlement at Parramatta about seventeen miles inland, at a time when Parramatta looked like becoming the capital of the colony. He was appointed Paymaster of the Regiment and given the use of the Regimental Funds. He was allowed to control the victualling. He was further appointed Inspector of Public Works and was able in consequence to choose both the position of his house and of the land attaching to it. He selected a site on a peninsula on the eastern edge of Parramatta. Within two years he had increased his farm from its original 100 acres to 250 acres, with 100 acres under wheat, maize and potatoes. The farm also supported two mares, two cows, 130 goats and more than a hundred hogs. A man and half a dozen greyhounds provided him with 300 lb. of meat, mainly kangaroo and wild duck, every week.

4

Here indeed was one of the makers of Australia. From his portraits alone one might have guessed that Macarthur was a man of strong individuality and character. The face is lean and bony with no hint of self-indulgence; the expression non-committal, the regard intense and the jaw stubborn. A man, in short, who knew his rights and was determined that they should be respected. It was not perhaps surprising in an age when the cult of personality was intensively pursued, that Macarthur should meet and clash with other individuals as self-willed as himself, both inside and outside his official sphere. Thus he had quarrelled with Captain Gilbert who was in command of the ship which was to take him to New South Wales and had challenged him to a duel. He had quarrelled, too, with his commanding officer Captain Nicholas Nepean, as also with Governor Phillip, though in each of these instances there was something to be said in his favour. Later he was to challenge and wound Colonel Paterson, his commanding officer in New South Wales. Obviously conditions in the colony were not conducive to an atmosphere of peace and contentment. There was no relief from the same faces, the same scenery and much the same problems day after day. There was also a natural cleavage between the New South Wales Corps, to which Macarthur belonged and the civilians who affected to control it. This cleavage became wider when Britain again declared war on France, for new recruits were needed at home and the New South Wales Corps had to make up its strength with ex-convicts who had their own private grudges against the civil establishment.

For example, in one typically small-town quarrel, a soldier left his sentry box in order to give a comrade his opinion of John Baughan, a master-carpenter under whom he had served as a convict. Baughan who was working in a nearby hut, slipped out of it unobserved, picked up the musket which the sentry had unwisely left there, and reported, gun in hand, to the Sergeant of the Guard. The sentry was punished and his comrades, in revenge, raided and destroyed Baughan's hut.

Then the Governor, Captain John Hunter, a superannuated naval officer who had succeeded Grose, took a hand. His sense of direction and powers of navigation were strictly reserved for the ocean wave and he seems to have had no hesitation in attacking publicly the whole reputation of the New South Wales Corps. This in turn brought Macarthur on the scene. He succeeded in settling the case out of court with a handsome apology but clashed sharply with one of the magistrates who tried to persuade Baughan to prosecute after all.

A further quarrel ensued between Macarthur and Richard Atkins, the civilian who had succeeded him as Inspector of Public Works. Macarthur accused Atkins, with justice, of drunkenness and indecent exposure. Angry letters were sent by Macarthur direct to the Duke of Portland, the Colonial Secretary, and Hunter in turn accused Macarthur of interfering with the good government of the colony. He charged the New South Wales Corps as a whole with encouraging indolence, indiscipline, confusion and licentiousness and held the officers responsible for the "destruction of all order, the almost total extinction of every spark of religion, the encouragement of gambling" not to speak of robbery, murder and other species of crime. A body of military men with their own discipline and *esprit de corps* were unlikely to submit tamely to criticisms of this kind from any Governor. Moreover all these reports were almost the direct opposite of what Portland had heard of the Colony from Grose. They contradicted Macarthur's forecast, that he hoped within the next eighteen months to be able to support himself without any cost to the Government and believed that any industrious farmer in the colony would be capable of doing the same.

Portland was also highly perturbed by Hunter's free-handed spending on grain, bacon, and public works, and wrote calling on Hunter to correct "that fundamental and destructive error by which the public expenses of your Government have grown to such enormous bulk". The wretched Governor seemed incapable of controlling the Corps and equally incapable of ceasing to accuse them in his reports to Portland of ruining the economy and morals of the colony.

On the 5th November 1799 the military won their first victory. Hunter was recalled and replaced by another naval officer, Captain Philip King. But King was not the man to heal the breach between the civil and the military. Gout and other infirmities shortened his temper, and his sense of dissatisfaction was increased when he found that many of his subjects on the

colony were better off than he himself. He began to send away
the ships that called from across the world bringing spirits to
match the colony's now world-famed thirst.

King had a blazing row with Macarthur over the conduct of a
naval officer, and with the officers of the New South Wales
Corps over their judgement of the case. And Macarthur fought
a duel with his commanding officer when the latter refused to
give up dining with Governor King. Macarthur was arrested
and sent home to answer for his conduct. King in turn was
severely reprimanded for not having settled the issue himself
and Macarthur seized the chance to show the people who
counted at home that he could provide wool from his Spanish
sheep at the very time when England, cut off from the Continent
by Napoleon, most needed it for her newly invented textile
machinery. His opinions were sought and treasured by a special
Committee of the Privy Council on Trade and Plantations.

King in the meantime had been quite unable to come to terms
with the officers of the New South Wales Corps. In May 1803
he asked for permission to come home and Lord Hobart, who as
Minister for War now administered the colony, was pleased to
treat this request as a resignation.

Next year Macarthur was back in New South Wales. And he
brought with him a letter from the Colonial Secretary asking the
Governor to grant him not less than 5,000 acres in perpetuity
in order to increase and improve the breed of sheep in New
South Wales. He was even invited by King to stay at Government House. He had become an Esquire with his own ship and
friends at Court.

But it was inevitable that he should quarrel with the King's
successor in a continuation of the old struggle between the
civilian authorities and the army.

For the man chosen to succeed King was the ex-Navy Captain
William Bligh, notorious even in the Navy of those days for his
overbearing manner, for the fluency of his vituperation and
abuse and the malignancy with which his volleys of curses were
delivered. Bligh had commanded the *Bounty*, the ship sent in
1787 to collect bread-fruit plants from Tahiti for introduction
to the West Indies. He was the central figure in the mutiny on
that vessel. On 28th April 1789 Bligh with eighteen men was

cast adrift off the Tonga Islands in a 23-feet open boat with only a small stock of provisions and without a chart, while the mutineers sailed away first to Tahiti and then to Pitcairn Island. Surviving almost incredible risks and hardships, Bligh managed, in forty-one days, to sail his little craft to the Dutch island of Timor—a distance of 3,618 miles.

Most of the mutineers sailed on to Pitcairn island where they remained undiscovered for nearly twenty years. But a few stayed on in Tahiti, and were recaptured and brought to trial in England.

Three of them were executed at Portsmouth and Bligh was promoted from lieutenant to commander and then to post-captain. But it might well have occurred to the Admiralty to ask themselves whether the price for good order and discipline was too high.

Perhaps, by the time it came for Bligh to go out as Governor of New South Wales, the Admiralty had answered that question to its satisfaction, for their lordships made clear that from the day he took up his new role, Bligh would be leaving their service for good.

But Bligh's quarter-deck manner stayed with him and it was not long before he had a blistering row with Macarthur. Undoubtedly the scene for this was set by an occurrence for which Bligh was in no way responsible—namely the flooding of the Hawkesbury River which lost the colony much of its grain and a large part of its meat supply. Prices rose sharply and Macarthur's reputation fell because what the colonists now wanted was not wool but something they could eat on the spot. And so it was perhaps not altogether surprising that when Macarthur broached his plans for increasing the size of his flocks and the pastures needed to support them, the Governor's reaction was unfavourable. "What have I to do with your sheep, sir?" he roared. "What have I to do with your cattle? Are you to have such flocks of sheep and herds of cattle as no man ever heard of before? No, sir, I have heard of your concerns, sir. You have got five thousand acres of land, sir, in the finest situation in the country, but by God you shan't keep it." Two other similar outbursts followed.

Bligh resented almost everything which met his eyes in his

new domain. He affected to despise the New South Wales
Corps because of their "intercourse" with the freed convicts,
both men and women. He dishonoured agreements made between the settlers and Government departments at home. He
was tyrannical and contemptuous of any legal niceties, taking
the view that, in New South Wales, he made the laws and be
damned to those that did not obey them. He requisitioned men
from the New South Wales Corps to act as his bodyguard without bothering to inform its officers, and sneered at them publicly
as ex-convicts. There was a memorable scene after the Governor
fancied that some of the garrison had laughed in church at a
dress worn by his daughter. And eventually the Governor wrote
home recommending that the Corps be sent home in a body—
regardless of the fact that many of them, knowing that they had
been recruited for permanent service, had married and taken to
farming. And worst of all, after having illegally received several
grants of land from the outgoing Governor, Bligh refused to
make grants of land to others who wished to develop it. He
tried to put an end to the liquor trade. But he associated himself
with black market merchants and appointed them to positions of
trust. He seized Macarthur's property without a warrant and
allowed his bailiff to default on obligations to him.

And he began to demolish one by one the dwellings of those
who had offended him on the pretext that they were unsuitably
placed or that they caused obstruction, including of course
Macarthur's own partly constructed enclosure.

He had Macarthur himself arrested for not paying for the
upkeep of a vessel that the Government had seized from him.
And finally he fell foul of the Court of officers whom he had
selected to try Macarthur and declared that they were no Court.

From then on, soldiers of the Corps themselves mounted
guard to protect Macarthur from the wrath of the Governor.
On the morning of 26th January two constables acting on
Bligh's orders seized Macarthur and threw him in the common
gaol on the pretext that he had jumped bail. Bligh accepted a
memorial from the Judge-Advocate accusing the officers who
had attempted to shield Macarthur of having usurped the powers
of the Government and of having encouraged rebellion and
"perhaps treason" in the colony.

The officers knew then that there was only one way to protect themselves and they took it. It was decided to put Bligh under arrest on the grounds that insurrection and a massacre would be likely if they did not do so. Lieutenant-Colonel George Johnston, whose superior officer Colonel Paterson, lieutenant-governor of the colony, was stationed in Tasmania, himself assumed the title of lieutenant-governor and issued a warrant for the release of Macarthur from prison on bail. The die was cast.

That evening a posse of soldiers with colours flying and fixed bayonets, marched in the setting sun to seize Bligh. The port had circulated twice round the Government House dinner table when the screams of the Governor's daughter told Bligh that the crisis had come. Bligh hid himself behind a bed in a servant's room, where the rebels discovered him. They called on him to resign his authority and placed him under house arrest.

That night the tyrant's effigy was burnt on bonfire after bonfire to the sound of bell-ringing and military salutes. A week later Macarthur was acquitted of the charges which the Governor had tried to bring against him, while Bligh was told that his staff had admitted to helping the Governor to subvert the course of justice and deprive innocent men of their property, their liberty and lives. Macarthur was made Secretary—equivalent to Chief Administrator—of the Colony.

Bligh remained under guard and was eventually transferred to the military barracks while the rebels took care to send home lurid instalments of a serial narrating the Governor's more discreditable transactions and personal indiscretions (including illicit liaisons with women of the town), which had come to their knowledge from examining the Governor's private papers.

Whitehall realized that whatever might be the rights and wrongs of the case, Bligh had lost all authority over the colonists. They appointed a new Governor, Lachlan Macquarie. Macquarie was told for form's sake to reinstate Bligh in his post for twenty-four hours (but he was to have no power to exercise any of his functions). Then the ex-Governor was sent home. So was the whole of the New South Wales Corps. Johnston was court-martialled in England and cashiered—a nominal punishment only—and was allowed to return to Australia. Macarthur was kept away from the settlement, under threat of prosecution if he returned, for nine years and by the time he was back in New South Wales the cold war between the civilian machinery and the military had ended.

Australia indeed was already so prosperous that it was no longer much of a hardship for regular army troops to be stationed there. And those that came out were henceforth put firmly under the Governor's control.

A problem of quite a different nature had arisen.

4

Macquarie the Magnificent

Never before had the world heard of a penal settlement quite like the one in New South Wales.

It was an open prison in which, for many years, there were for the normal prisoner no cells. There were no walls; no bars; nowhere to escape to. Old lags as they arrived felt the irons struck from their legs. Often their new clothes were un-marked with the broad arrow and were better probably than any they had worn in freedom at home. In their new land the men wore blue jackets and black pantaloons or in some cases dyed military uniforms. Only those who had committed fresh crimes after landing were condemned to wear a black and white "magpie" uniform decorated with the letter "R" for Rogue.

Married convicts were allowed to bring their wives with them and those that were not already married were encouraged to become so. Female sinners were pardoned if they could find themselves respectable husbands. Women convicts who were not married and unlikely to find a suitor frequently entered domestic service, but, in a settlement where men greatly out-numbered women, a girl required no outstanding talents to become the mistress of an officer or even of a highly placed Government official.

The convicts mixed perforce with the middle classes of the

colony who like them were excluded by the custom of the day from social contact with their betters.

The convicts enjoyed the same rations as civilians. They shared the same dangers and many of the same hardships, and in ability and bravery many showed themselves the equal of their jailors.

On arrival they were told to find their own lodgings, and because the Government contributed nothing towards the rent or towards the support of their dependents, they were allowed to pay their way by working for whom they pleased after 3 p.m. when their day officially ended.

Even in the days of Governor Phillip they acted as patrolmen (because the Government had sent none) and as their own overseers. Later, as more and more convicts arrived and the difficulty of disciplining them (and the expense of employing them on Government work) increased, it was found convenient to issue them tickets of leave allowing them to earn their living (including support for their families) independently and pretty well as they chose.

Some were given conditional freedom, provided that they had spent a period of years working for the Government, and a growing number became free on completing the sentences for which they had been transported, which more often than not was seven years.

In 1792 at the end of Governor Phillip's term of office, convicts still under sentence accounted for four-fifths of the population. By the end of the century the proportion was little more than a third, and ten years later the freed men and the children of the colony easily outnumbered the prisoners. Thus the make-up of the people of the colony changed almost from season to season.

Of course the main concern of the Home Government was to make sure that the convicts they had got rid of with so much difficulty and expense did not return home, and Australia's greatest Governor, Lachlan Macquarie, who succeeded Bligh, was the first man to draw the logical conclusion of this official preoccupation.

His conclusion was that if the former convicts were to be kept in Australia, they should be encouraged to stay there voluntarily. For this purpose it was necessary to let bygones be bygones and to remove from ex-convicts the disabilities from which they formerly suffered. Then, if Australia offered them a future, they would be ready to seize it.

Macquarie set out these ideas in a despatch to Lord Castlereagh in the spring of 1810:

I was very much surprized and Concerned, on my Arrival here, at the extraordinary and illiberal Policy I found had been adopted by all the Persons who had preceded me in Office respecting those Men who had been originally sent out to this Country as Convicts, but who, by long Habits of Industry and total Reformation of Manners, had not only become respectable, but by many degrees the most Useful Members of the Community. Those persons have never been Countenanced or received into Society. I have, nevertheless, taken upon myself to adopt a new Line of Conduct, conceiving that Emancipation, when United with Rectitude and long-tried good conduct, should lead a Man back to that Rank in Society which he had forfeited, and do away, in as far as the Case will admit, all Retrospect of former bad Conduct. This appears to me to be the greatest Inducement that Can be held out towards the Reformation of the Manners of the Inhabitants, and I think it is consistent with the gracious and humane Intentions of His Majesty and His Ministers in favour of this Class of People.

Macquarie, like many another of history's great men got his job by accident. A new Governor, Miles Nightingall, a son-in-law of the Chairman of the Court of Directors of the East India Company, had been chosen to succeed Bligh. But Nightingall had second thoughts about going to Botany Bay and produced every possible excuse—including rheumatism—to save himself from taking up the appointment. Macquarie, who had originally been appointed Lieutenant-Governor, merely because the 73rd Regiment which he commanded was to replace the New South Wales Corps, found himself unexpectedly in the top post.

It was to be expected that the outlook of New South Wales' first military Governor would be different from that of the Spartan captains who had preceded him. He was, first of all, a clansman from the Hebrides, a landowner and wealthy into the bargain. He had married well. His manners were courteous and dignified. Most of his military career, apart from a comparatively uneventful campaign in Canada and the United

States, had been served in India and Ceylon where he had first marvelled at and then grown accustomed to the magnificence of the Indian rulers. He had witnessed the wealth of European "nabobs" in the employ of the Company, and had himself been lavishly rewarded with prize money at the conclusion of several campaigns fought on the Company's behalf. His regiment, like others on service in India, had lived in style, with fine horses, numerous servants and a first-rate cellar. Then, just when he was expecting to be allowed some service at home after a quarter of a century in and around the tropics, the regiment was ordered to Botany Bay to the back of beyond where roads were unknown, houses unnumbered and where pigs and naked savages wandered the streets.

No wonder Macquarie determined to introduce to New South Wales something of the life that he had known in Madras, Bombay and Seringapatam. No wonder, either, that having acted as Deputy Adjutant in the first Indian army to serve outside Asia, he had a sense of what was fitting and proper as well as the ability to carry out his ideas with organization and method.

During his term of office the streets of Sydney were named and in some cases paved, the houses numbered and fenced, washing was banned from the Tank Stream on which the city's water supplies depended. Divine worship was encouraged on Sundays and regular marriage any day of the week. The Governor seldom travelled without an imposing bodyguard. A permanent police force was formed. The Bank of New South Wales was founded in 1817. An official port office was set up and standard weights and measures. To encourage horse breeding, the Governor laid out a race course in what was afterwards known as Hyde Park, and decreed that all dogs were to be tied up during race week, during which two balls were held under the Governor's patronage.

After high tea, eaten between four and five in the evening, the Regimental Band, following the Governor's orders, played in Hyde Park, while the fashionable ladies and gentlemen took their evening stroll. Many of the men were in uniform and others dressed in the coats, ruffles, wing collars and knee breeches of the Englishman of the day.

There were private parties, subscription dances and picnics.

And as the fear of starvation receded for good, the capital, if we may so call it, began to wear a smile. A fountain was installed. An obelisk marked the centre of the city and showed the orientation of the main features of the colony.

Thus Sydney by the wish of those who ruled it, gradually became no more a penal settlement or Devil's Island as the King's Ministers had once planned, but, instead a station to which convicts under sentence prayed fervently that they might be transported.

Macquarie determined that it should remain so. He discouraged the lash and he encouraged the convicts in his care to make the best of their abilities in their own interest and those of the colony.

"Let punishment be as severe as may be necessary to effect the grand object," he wrote. "But when that which the law has ordained has been fulfilled, for the sake of mercy and justice there let it terminate. . . . My principle is that when once a man is free, his former state shall be no longer allowed to act against him: let him then feel himself eligible for any situation which he has by a long term of upright conduct, proved himself worthy of filling."

And this policy was followed from the very moment that the prison ship had docked in Sydney Cove. Before the prisoners were even landed the Governor's Secretary and the Chief Superintendent of Convicts went aboard the transport vessel. The prisoners were mustered in the presence of the Captain and Surgeon. They were asked about their treatment and interviewed so that they might be assigned to the most suitable employment. Thus T. Henshall, transported for coining, became the colony's first Master of the Mint charged by Macquarie with the job of converting a cargo of Spanish dollars into Australia's first currency. And Francis Greenway, a bankrupt west-country architect who had been sentenced for counterfeiting another's signature on a contract, was given a ticket of leave immediately on arrival and appointed acting Government Architect and Assistant Engineer with a salary, a horse and a convict servant for himself and a house and rations (including coal) for himself and his family. Some convicts had already made their mark under earlier Governors. Dr. Halloran, an ex-convict, had established the colony's most fashionable school. Andrew Thompson, transported in Phillip's time for rick-burning at the age of twenty-six became Chief Constable of the Hawkesbury River district, and James Meehan, one of the Irish rebels, had done all the important Government survey work for about six years before Macquarie took office.

Simeon Lord who had arrived in 1791 with a seven-year sentence, owned two houses by the time he was freed, and operated as an auctioneer, shipowner and as merchant in such things as pearls, sandalwood, seal-skin, whale blubber and hats. Michael Robinson, sentenced for blackmail, had become the colony's acknowledged Poet Laureate, for which he received a fee of two cows per annum; and William Redfern, a surgeon's mate when he took part in the Nore mutiny, had been called on to act as medical adviser to Bligh himself and had been given the King's Commission as the colony's Assistant Surgeon. Isaac Nichols, an ex-convict, became the colony's first port-master.

All these men grew up with the colony and prospered with it. And Macquarie realized that their prosperity could be his own security. For the convicts represented a class entirely beholden to the Governor for their advancement. Their abilities and accomplishments made him independent of the army which had threatened to become a state within a state. Independent, too, of the settlers who not only held the country to ransom with their high prices but intrigued at home against the Governor.

Macquarie visualized a nation of small yeoman farmers of the kind that had proved successful throughout England and Scotland, the only difference being that the yeomen of New South Wales would consist largely of time-expired convicts.

It was not to be expected that landowners and farmers would submit without protest to the Governor's policy. They argued, and here they were right, that the soil of Australia was unsuited to the kind of small mixed arable or pasture farm on which a man would be expected to produce wheat and diary products as well as meat off the same estate. They disapproved of the Governor's enthusiasm for new public buildings, stables, barracks and churches which had to be built with labour that would otherwise have been assigned to the settlers. They complained about the expense in words that Whitehall was only too glad to accept.

They disagreed with the Governor's view that convicts were more easily controlled in the city than in the countryside and insisted that it was far better for the convicts to be dispersed over the countryside where they could help to get home the harvest. Instead, Macquarie built barracks for the convicts, and, as compensation for the expense, kept them working until sunset instead of putting them at the disposal of the settlers after 3 p.m.

The settlers had yet another grievance. They resented competition from emancipated convicts or emancipists as they were called, for the top administrative jobs. One settler, the Rev. Samuel Marsden, a successful wool farmer, refused to read the Governor's proclamations publicly from the pulpit. Other settlers grew indignant when asked to sit next to emancipists at the Governor's table or to consult with them in the management of the community. These "exclusivists" declared that it was intolerable that the Governor should act as if the convicts rather than the settlers were the true founders of the colony. Thus Macquarie was drawn into a quarrel even with his own soldiers.

The real clash between the Governor and the exclusives came when Jeffery Bent, President of the Colony's newly established Supreme Court, refused to sit because two emancipist solicitors were to be permitted to practise there. The Court remained closed for more than a year, and the leading figures of the colony sent a petition, highly critical of the Governor, to the House of Commons, an action to which he in turn took the strongest exception.

There was trouble, too, over the American ship *Traveller* which sailed into Sydney in the early days of 1816 carrying tea and sugar both of which the colony badly needed. The Governor announced her arrival with full publicity but the chaplain of the 46th Regiment, the Rev. Benjamin Vale, acting on his own initiative (though with the knowledge and consent of the Acting Crown Solicitor, Joshua Moore), arrested the ship and claimed her as a prize. Macquarie, angry and embarrassed, ordered Vale to be court-martialled, and dismissed the Acting Crown Solicitor from his post.

But, alas, the wind of change had reached London, and Bathurst, the Minister for the Colonies who had supported

Macquarie on most issues in the past, criticized him not only for court-martialling a clergyman who had not been accused of scandalous or immoral conduct, but also censured Macquarie for questioning the right of the citizens of New South Wales to petition Parliament.

Bathurst also said that former convicts could be allowed to practise in the Courts only when no free qualified solicitors could be found.

The fact was, of course, that the policies which the Home Government had been prepared to support in 1810 no longer held good even five years later.

The growing prosperity of Australia, as we may now begin to call the colony, made it a near-paradise for the felons who were sent there and the settlement had therefore lost its value to the Home Government as a deterrent against crime. Indeed it had become attractive to free men demobilized and unemployed after the end of the Napoleonic war, for wheat prices at home had slumped 40 per cent in two years and farmers were selling up and dismissing their labourers. Respectable citizens who could not be expected to submit to the iron discipline needed to run a prison settlement began to think of emigrating to Australia.

Men of substance and capital were needed to exploit the resources of New South Wales and the newcomers would not be the kind to be beholden to the Governor. They were not to be expected to sit at the Governor's table alongside ex-convicts. And if pushed too far they might, the Home Government feared, not only repudiate the Governor's authority as Bligh's had been repudiated, but might revolt and even enter into war against the mother country as the former American colonies had so recently been doing.

Thus autocratic Governors, such as were wished on Australia in its earlier years, were becoming unfashionable.

Other developments in the colony itself changed the whole picture. In 1813 the Australians had broken through the barrier of the Blue Mountains—a wall which had hitherto confined the settlement to a narrow coastal strip about forty miles deep.

There were, of course, all kinds of reasons why the feat had not been performed before. One was that the explorers never

Arrival of Government gold conveyance at the Colonial Treasury,
Sydney 1851. From a sketch by Marshal Claxton

A Government jail gang in Sydney around 1830

The squatter's first home

Gold washing on Summerhill Creek near the site of Hargreaves' gold
discovery of 1851, by G. F. Angas

knew whether they would find enough food in the mountains to sustain them. They therefore had to carry enough to feed themselves and their horses there and back. Water supplies were uncertain. They might find none or, equally, there was the danger that they might get cut off from Sydney by floods on the Hawkesbury River which was capable of rising twenty feet in a single night.

Above all there was the character of the barrier that was to be crossed. Most travellers, in the days before Macquarie, were obsessed with the idea that they were dealing with a conventional range of mountains and that somewhere there would be a pass through them. But valley after valley led nowhere. In fact the explorers were facing what was really a table land and the way to cross it was to look not for valleys but for the high ground.

The first group to realize this was a party of three adventurers led by Lieutenant Lawson, an officer with surveying experience. With him were Gregory Blaxland, one of the rebel farmers who had helped to overthrow Bligh, and William Charles Wentworth, farmer and son of the Colony's principal surgeon. They set out from Emu Island on 18th May 1813 with four servants, four horses and five dogs, starting up through a ridge of forest with good grazing and water. They came to a zone of bush where the brushwood was so thick that they had to cut a path through it before they could carry their gear. And their route lay across ridges of sharp granite and quartz which cut the horses' feet. It took them nearly three weeks to travel a distance of not much more than fifty miles over rugged hills to the far edge of the table land.

Here the travellers were confronted with an almost perpendicular precipice dropping more than six hundred feet into a forested glen. The horses were tired and the men were almost starving. They were suffering from enteritis. Their shoes were cut to pieces and their clothes in rags. They had no food for the journey home. They had to lead the horses in the dark down the steeply falling escarpment in the hope that they would find water at the foot. And there *was* water waiting for them, and also grass, as green as the Vale of Clwyd in North Wales, after which the valley was afterwards named. It was the first fresh

5

grass that the horses had had for more than ten days. Lawson,
Blaxland and Wentworth decided to make this the turning point
of their journey, for it had been undertaken purely on their own
initiative.

Later that year Macquarie sent out one of his assistant surveyors, George William Evans, to mark out the new route.

Evans went further than the Lawson, Blaxland, Wentworth
expedition and was able to scale the range on the far side of the
valley and reach fertile green valleys and rivers filled with duck
and trout, together with uninterrupted grazing in gently-rising,
well-watered dales, "covered with the finest grass and intermixed with the White Daisey as in England." "The soil is
exceeding rich," Evans wrote in his journal, "and produces the
finest grass intermixed with variety of herbs; the hills have the
look of a park and Grounds laid out."

Macquarie next organized a road-building party of forty to
open up the country. It was headed by William Cox, the
Principal Magistrate of Windsor, New South Wales. They
made a thorough job of it. The brushwood which had torn
Evans' clothes to ribbons was cleared. The swamps which he
had probed for water were cleared. Trees were cut down and
rooted out, and the ridges of granite and quartz which had cut
the horses hoofs and worn out men's shoes were covered with
gravel well rolled in.

So quickly was the work done—it took only six months—that
Governor Macquarie himself was able to drive over the route
early in 1815 to found Bathurst, the first Australian city west of
the Blue Mountains. The new settlement was founded on
Bathurst Plains through which the Macquarie River—the first
main river to be discovered on the western side of the watershed
—flowed. Convicts who had helped in this pioneer work were
granted their freedom.

Macquarie wrote in his published report:

> The Governor here feels much pleasure in being enabled to
> communicate to the public that the favourable reports, which he
> had received of the country to the west of the Blue Mountains have
> not been by any means exaggerated. The difficulties which present
> themselves in the journey from hence, are certainly great and
> inevitable; but those persons who may be inclined to become

permanent settlers there, will probably content themselves with visiting this part of the colony but rarely, and of course will have them seldom to encounter. Plenty of water and a sufficiency of grass are to be found in the mountains for the support of such cattle as may be sent over them; and the tracts of fertile soil and rich pasturage, which the new country affords, are fully extensive enough for any increase of population and stock which can possibly take place for years.

Within a distance of ten miles from the site of Bathurst, there are not less than 50,000 acres of land clear of timber, and fully one half of that may be considered excellent soil, well calculated for cultivation.

Although timber was less plentiful and neither coal nor lime-stone had yet been discovered there was plenty of game. "The two principal rivers contain a great quantity of fish," the report added, "but all of one denomination, resembling the perch in appearance and of a delicate fine flavour, not unlike that of a rock-cod; this fish grows to a large size, and is very voracious. Several of them were caught during the Governor's stay at Bathurst, and at the halting place of the Fish River. One of these caught weighed 17 lb. and the people stationed at Bathurst stated that they had caught some weighing 25 lb."

This winning of the west added greatly to the riches of the colony but also the difficulties of the Governor. It made impracticable Macquarie's ideas of a nation of small ex-convict farmers dependent for their livelihood on the good will of the Governor. The big sheep farmer was the man of the moment. He alone could make the most of the new pastures, and he would want to take the convicts out of the care of Macquarie into the far west in search of the golden fleece.

The breakthrough in Australia also stimulated the appetites of the Treasury in London. Officials there had long suspected from the increasing prosperity of the colony and from the wealth of public buildings being thrown up there that untold amounts of revenue must be going to waste and that the colony instead of needing subsidies should be providing an old-age pension for her British parent.

And so Whitehall in its wisdom sent out a special Commissioner, Mr. Thomas Bigges, to report on the state of the colony and to make suggestions for its future. His report, by no means complimentary to Macquarie, ran to 300 solid pages and was filled with rumour, prejudice, unsworn testimony and inaccuracies.

The immediate result was that Macquarie's successor, Sir Thomas Brisbane, was ordered to take away convicts assigned to Government overseers and clerks, and transfer them to the more prosperous farmers who had resources to employ them and money to support them. In this way the Government saved the expense of maintaining the convicts but became still more dependent on the crops produced by the settlers.

The less immediate result was that the home Government swung over to the idea firstly that free settlers, preferably rich ones, were of greater benefit to the prosperity of the country than convicts, secondly that new immigrants of this kind would lead to the colony becoming self-supporting as Governor Phillip had once hoped, and thirdly that prison settlement discipline and justice by military court were unsuited to a colony that was to develop along these lines.

Australia was to be treated as an investment instead of as a scrap-heap.

5

Growing Pains

It was certainly true that Sydney was now less of a convict
outpost than a commercial capital. A Chamber of Commerce was
founded in 1825 and also the Turf Club; street lighting was
installed a year later. A museum, and a library (combined with
the hospital dispensary) were established in 1827.

As P. Cunningham, a naval surgeon, wrote in his book *Two
Years in New South Wales*, published in 1827:

> Where, thirty-eight years ago, not an ear of grain was cultivated
> we now see fifty thousand bushels advertised—for the mere annual
> consumption of one of our distilleries—while four steam-mills, ten
> water mills, eighteen windmills and two horse mills furnish us
> with an abundance of excellent flour from our own wheat, and
> thirteen breweries provide ale and beer from our various descrip-
> tions of colonial grain. Now we have four vessels constantly
> whaling; six sealing; two employed as regular packets between
> Sydney and Newcastle and between Sydney and Port Dalrymple
> besides irregular traders to all these places, and a number of small
> craft coasting to the Hawkesbury, Illawarra and other points. . . .

Cunningham's general description of the colony conveys an
atmosphere far removed from that of a penal settlement:

> An elegant light-house of white freestone, with a revolving light,
> built upon the southern side of the entrance to Port Jackson, and

called Macquarie Tower, points out, both by day and night, the precise situation of the harbour. Beside the light-house is a signal post and a telegraph, to communicate to Sydney everything relative to ships leaving or approaching the port. The coast-line here consists of high mouldering cliffs of whitish sandstone, which arrest strongly the attention of the stranger; whilst the country in the vicinity, clothed in a livery of evergreen shrubs, presents a pleasing and refreshing picture to the eye, so long habituated to the dreary and boundless expanse of sea, spread out daily in desert magnificence. The stunted appearance of these shrubs, however, and the patches of white sand scattered among them, impress on the mind no high idea of the fertility of the soil from which they draw their subsistence. You enter Port Jackson between two high bluff points, named the North and South Heads, about three quarters of a mile apart; and proceeding onwards, the sweet natural scenery of our queen of harbours gradually expands upon your view. You steer nearly west to Sydney, which is distant five miles; the first glimpse you have of its situation being the tall and slender spire of St. George's church, shooting up into the clear horizon before you. The shores onwards are bold, and often precipitous—agreeably varied in the general outline by romantic little bays, which, with their white sandy beaches, open irregularly to the right and left as you sail along. On each side, the land, broken and moderately high, terminates toward the shore in narrow ridges, covered with native shrubs in perpetual summer verdure among which rocks of varied hues peep here and there abruptly out, while slender streams of water, gurgling down the narrow valleys between the ridges, just reveal themselves at intervals, and retire again from view. To the left as you steer up the harbour, you first open the pilot houses, with their clean whitewashed walls and small fairy gardens, perched at the bottom of a snug little sunny bay; then the pretty cottage called the Retreat, formerly the residence of Sir Henry Brown Hayes; and next the beautiful eastern fashioned mansion of our excellent naval officer, Captain Piper, which, with its tastefully ornamented lawn and delightful grounds, cannot fail to impress the stranger very favourably as to the wealth and height of improvement to which the colony has, in its short but prosperous career, attained. . . . Sydney Cove is formed by two ridges running out into the harbour; the one to the left terminating in Bennilong's Point, on the low extremity whereof stands Fort Macquarie, with its castellated martello towers; and that to the right, in Dawes Point, with a fort bearing that name, which in like manner occupies its extremity. Down the hollow between these ridges, a small rill trickles slowly into the head of the Cove, in the rocky sandstone bed of which tanks have been cut to retain the water during the summer droughts—an arrangement which proves of material service to the town's people. Along this hollow for upwards of a mile in a westerly direction, extends our main thoroughfare [George Street], which all the other streets either run parellel to or intersect at right angles—the town thus occupying the whole of the hollow, and creeping up the gradual ascents on each side. The ridge on the left is successively crowned by the lofty looking buildings of the horse barracks, the colonial hospital, the convict barracks, and a fine Gothic Catholic chapel, beyond which lies the promenade of Hyde Park, flanked towards the town by a row of pretty cottages, and towards the country by a high brick-walled garden appertaining to the Government. On the ridge to the right of the Cove, rows rising above rows of neat white cottages present themselves, overlooked by the commanding position of Fort Phillip, with its signal post and telegraphic appendages. . . . A few hundred yards from the head of the Cove, toward the left, stands the Governor's house, with its beautiful Domain in front, ornamented by large trees of the finest and most varied foliage, scattered singly or in clumps; with a fine belt of shrubbery closing in the back-ground. . . . Between the Domain and the Cove, an agreeable walk has been formed, chiefly in the solid rock and fenced off from the domain by a freestone wall, which, being level at its top with that portion of the enclosure approaching the Point, the interior attractions may be thus pleasantly viewed; and it is in consequence of this circumstance, together with the prospect it commands of the shipping in the harbour and its communicating with the other fine walks around, that this promenade has become the favourite of our Sunday pedestrians and fashionables—along which they pour, to enjoy the cool evening sea breeze among the delightful scenery bordering the shores of the harbour beyond. . . . Near the harbour, where the ground is very valuable, the houses are usually contiguous, like those of the towns in England; but generally speaking, the better sort of houses in Sydney are built in the detached cottage style—of white freestone, or of brick plastered and whitewashed, one or two stories high, with verandas in front, and enclosed by a neat wooden paling, lined occasionally with trim-pruned geranium hedges; they have, besides, a commodious garden attached, commonly decked out with flowers, and teeming with culinary delicacies. Into the enclosure immediately around the house, the dogs are usually turned out at night, to ward off rogues,—and uncompromising diligent watchmen they certainly are, paying little of that respect to genteel exterior which their better-bred brethren in England are so apt to demonstrate. . . . Although all you see are English faces, and you hear no other language but English spoken, yet you soon become aware you are in a country very different from England, by the number of parrots and other birds of strange note and plumage which you observe hanging at so many doors, and cagefuls of which you will soon see exposed for sale as you proceed.

Of course the prisoners have not been banished from the streets for, as Cunningham notes:

The Government gangs of convicts, also marching backwards and forwards from their work, in single military file, and the solitary ones straggling here and there, with their white woollen Paramatta frocks and trousers, or grey or yellow jackets with duck overalls (the different styles of dress denoting the oldness or newness of their arrival) . . . with perhaps the jail gang straddling sulkily by in their jingling leg-chains, tell a tale too plain to be misunderstood.

But the author soon returns to more pleasant themes:

Sydney is most abundantly supplied with fish which are caught with hooks and lines, chiefly towards the heads of the harbour, by the native blacks, and disposed of to the retailers, who hawk them about the town; the sounds of "Fish O", "Hot Rolls, all hot" and many other English cries, often chiming in agreeably upon your ear "right early in the morning", agreeably, I say, from their recalling to your remembrance, in these unmusical strains, scenes you have so newly forsaken. King-fish, mullet, mackeral, rock cod, whiting, snappers, bream, flat-heads and various other descriptions of fishes, are also found plentifully about. Mud oysters are brought over from Botany Bay, where they are abundant, and by fitting yourself out with a few slices of bread and butter, and other requisites, and taking a pleasant stroll around any of the romantic shores of our beautiful harbour, you may quickly secure a cheap and most delicious lunch from the sweet and finely flavoured rock oysters wherewithall its tide rocks are crusted, and which are collected by poor individuals and sold shelled at a shilling a quart. . . .

The pleasure-walks and drives in the vicinity of Sydney constitute not the least of its attractions, the delightful promenade round the Government Domain we have already noticed. Turning to the left in your onward course down the cool shady carriage drive, called Mrs. Macquarie's round which winds round the long, narrow and closely wooded point facing Garden Island, your pleasurable feelings will be still more sensibly excited. The abrupt shores are here romantically diversified with huge masses of rock, scattered irregularly along them, or jutting out in shelving cliffs affording an agreeable retreat from the rays of the noon-day sun, where you may revel in the luxury of the cool sea-breeze, and enjoy the variegated marine prospect spread out before you. Fronting the beach, at the extremity of this point, is a commodious seat, hewn out of the rock, which projects like a pulpit canopy over you, and at the back whereof is an inscription recording the year of its formation, and under whose auspices it was executed.

The south-head road, is however, the grand equestrian resort, along which gigs with well dressed people and spruce dandies à cheval, may be seen careering. Sunday is here, as everywhere else, the great gala day, when all the various equipages are most profusely shown off; when the animating bustle here displayed, the clouds of starting dust scattering abroad from behind the carriage wheels and the heels of the horses, and the passing smiles and congés of the different groups hurrying backwards and forwards, present a very lively picture. The road terminates at the tall and airy light-house, perched upon the bold headland forming the southern entrance to the harbour, and overlooking the whole southern ocean spread out in boundless expanse before you. Midway, a road to the left carries you to a rising ground named Bellevue, level at top, and commanding an extensive view of the ocean, and all the surrounding wild natural scenery. The country on the route will afford few charms to the mere agriculturalist, alive to no other attracting save the fertility of the soil; but to the admirer of untamed nature, in all her primeval variety, this spot, where low undulating hills (of rock and sand) lie scattered about in disorderly array, garnished with shrubs in liveries of the freshest green, and flowers of the liveliest hue, cannot fail to impress its beauty on the heart too deeply to be readily forgotten.

Abundance of gigs may be hired in Sydney at fifteen shillings a day, and riding horses at ten shillings, so that you may readily visit every spot worth seeing in the vicinity. A four-horse stage-coach runs twice a day and a caravan once, between Sydney and Paramatta (a distance of fifteen miles) and another coach twice a week to Liverpool (twenty one miles), while a third proceeds from

Paramatta to Windsor (twenty three miles) three times a week also, so that you may thus travel thirty-six miles into the interior westerly, and twenty one miles southerly, by stage-coaches alone. . . . The Golden Fleece, a commodious two storey brick inn with a green lawn before it, surrounded by a carriage way railed in at front, with a gate at each corner (to admit of each entrances and exits) is the Paramatta head-quarters of the Royal Mails; and possesses everything requisite to tempt you to stay another day to survey the lions of the place. Most of the houses in Paramatta are built of brick or white freestone; but no inconsiderable number are clapt board buildings, all roofed, as in Sydney, with iron-bark shingles, which ultimately assume so completely the leaden hue of slate, that it would be no easy matter to tell the difference at a little distance.

A few years later Charles Darwin, the scientist, wrote on entering the harbour (Sydney), "We were astounded with all the appearance of the outskirts of a great city in numerous windmills, forts, large stone white houses, superb villas etc. Imperial Rome in her ancient grandeur would not have been ashamed of such an offspring."

But it would have been wrong to imagine the colony in 1820 as being "ripe for development". Out of 1,840 buildings then standing, fewer than one in seven were of bricks. A still smaller number were built of stone and the remainder were either of wood bark or dried mud. There was no public transport inside Sydney, and those who had no horse walked. The plough was almost unknown in parts of the colony; fields were furrowed by hoe; reaping and threshing by hand.

Tobacco, soap, sugar, tea and clothing had to be imported. Hats made from the plaited leaves of the cabbage tree could still be seen even in George Street.

Throughout the 1820s, Sydney's water supply depended on tanks in the lumber yard, on private wells, and on what could be brought in barrels from swamps and lagoons near the town. A piped supply was not fully installed until 1837, and even then a man had to be employed to signal a warning by hand from the Sydney reservoir to the pumping station several miles away when enough water had been received. Only one in eight children went to school. At the end of 1819 the colony had a civilian population of just over 30,000 counting women and

children. Of these 156 were concerned with the management of
the colony and just under two thousand had come to New
South Wales as free settlers. Troops and military staff accounted
for 1,275. Fifteen thousand, four hundred and fifty had arrived as
prisoners but had later earned freedom and the remainder,
12,700, were either convicts still serving sentence or the children
of convicts.

The women, who made up less than one third of the total,
were in the worst position. In earlier days when a ship arrived in
Sydney Cove with women aboard, every man with resources
sufficient to maintain a housekeeper was allowed to select from
their number any one that he approved of (and many a hovel was
thereby doubtless turned into a home). But Commissioner Bigge
soon put a stop to that. It was he who ordered Macquarie's
successor, Governor Brisbane, to see that the rusty mooring
chains sunk in the middle of Sydney Cove be replaced by new
ones so that ships with convicts aboard could lie out there out
of touch with the shore.

No tickets of leave were to be handed out to any women. In
future on arrival any applications for servants were to be made
through the Colonial Secretary. Women convicts were also compelled to land in the dresses provided for them by the Navy
Board—even though the Navy petticoats were so short that for
modesty they had to wear their own clothes underneath.

In Macquarie's day women who had not been assigned had
been sent to the Female Factory at Parramatta, which consisted
of a long room over the gaol used for spinning, a few sheds, and
the upper floor of a small house. Girls without bunks slept on
the floor of the shed alongside the heaps of greasy wool. The
cracks between the boards of the floor were so wide that it was
impossible to clean the floor without soaking those below with
water. It was also impossible to prevent assignations between
men and women convicts from being made and kept.

Macquarie under pressure had built a new factory, well lit and
rainproof, for the women on Emu Plains, on the other side of the
water, but the women missed the male companionships of their
old abode, and with so much talent out of circulation the colony's
population increased but slowly. In 1826 Governor Darling,
realizing that early marriage was the best policy, decided that

female convicts employed by the Government who earned enough to live out in lodgings should have two days' leave a week; one more than the single men. When this incentive failed to reduce the number of women in the factory the Governor decided in 1829 to hand out tickets of leave to all well-behaved women after a short period of probation.

He also contemplated passing legislation compelling husbands to take back their wives from the factory once the sentence for which they had been sent there had been served. He asked that in the meantime no more women should be sent out to Australia for a year.

It was still a man's world down under. And during those years between 1820 and 1830 it was not romance that men looked for but land.

In April 1824 a group of M.P.s, financiers and capitalists met in the chambers of Mr. John Macarthur Jr. in Lincoln's Inn, London, in order to form a £1 million Company to develop agriculture in New South Wales. Parliament approved of the Australian Agricultural Company almost at once. It was granted a Royal Charter and was given permission to take up one million acres of land, provided that it employed as many convicts as free men on its estates. (This was not difficult since the convicts, as Macquarie had said years previously, were far more experienced and reliable than the average free immigrant.) The agreement provided that after five years the Company should pay a quit rent of 30s. per 1,333 acres, but even this would be remitted if the Company could show that it had maintained the equivalent of a thousand convicts for the whole of the five-year period. In addition the Company ran its own immigration scheme under which skilled mechanics were lent their passage money on terms of easy repayment.

Meanwhile the Governor was plagued to dole out more land. As Brisbane wrote to Lord Bathurst in England in November 1823:

Not a cow calves in the colony but her owner applies for an addition grant [of land] in consequence of the increase of his stock. Every person to whom a grant is made receives it as the payment of a debt; everyone to whom one is refused turns my implacable enemy. Seated in this situation, I cannot but call to mind the

French King, who exclaimed from a similar feeling "by every gift that I bestow, I create one ungrateful person and ten enemies. . . ." I do trust that Your Lordship will take under your most serious consideration the weight of odium, which must overwhelm every Governor without the establishment of some efficacious check to the applications which are hourly crowding for land. If Your Lordship determine on the permanence of the old clearing and cultivating clauses, perhaps You would not think it inadvisable to fix an invariable proportion of land to be cultivated in every grant: (at present the proprietor of thirty acres engages to cultivate a third, but of two thousand a twentieth): to render the species of cultivation demanded definite; (at present it may be grain or it may be grass); to make the conditions of clearing less unequal; (Newcastle is a thick forest; Argyle a British nobleman's park; at Bathurst there is scarcely a tree. . . .)

Faced with these problems the Home Government began to consider more favourably the idea of outright sale of Crown lands. This would save the authorities in New South Wales from collecting the quit rents charged for Grant Land.

It would make sure, too, that those buying the land were capitalists and would produce immediate revenue. But even this arrangement was not so advantageous as it might have appeared at first sight. For if the new owner had to pay for his land instead of getting it under grant, he would have less money for stocking it. Moreover the surveyors were so overworked that it was impossible for them to determine the real value of what they were offering for sale, and equally impossible for the settlers to wait until the area in which they were interested had been surveyed. Some officials argued that if all lands were sold and none granted, then the crown would have nothing in reserve. But others pointed out that if the grant system were continued, no one would think it worth while to buy land. Eventually, both sales and grants were continued of land before it had been surveyed.

Fresh efforts were made to satisfy the current land hunger by new explorations. In 1824 Hamilton Hume, a farmer who had formerly worked for the Government, and William Hovell, a retired sea captain, made the first overland journey from the east side of the Blue Mountains to Australia's southern coast

passing near the site of Canberra and ending up to the east of the
Port Phillip inlet not far from the future Melbourne.

They used bullocks as pack horses, swam across rivers, were
bitten to distraction by mosquitoes, harassed by bush fires and
were reduced to feeding their dogs on boiled flour. But they got
home safely and the convicts who went with them were freed.
The same year, Brisbane was founded (though it was chosen,
because of its remoteness, as a suitable convict settlement—
which it remained for fifteen years).

But all this was mere nibbling at the edges of a vast continent.
What was needed were pioneers ready to face the interior.
And long before Queen Victoria's day they began to appear.

In 1827, Allan Cunningham, who had already spent ten years
exploring as a botanist, discovered the Darling Downs of
which he was able to report that

> . . . the lower grounds, thus permanently watered, present flats,
> which furnish an almost inexhaustable range of cattle pasture at all
> seasons of the year—the grasses and herbage generally exhibiting,
> in the depth of winter, an extraordinary luxuriance of growth.
> From these central grounds rise downs of a rich, black and dry
> soil, and very ample surface; and as they furnish an abundance of
> grass, and are conveniently watered, yet perfectly beyond the reach
> of those floods, which take place on the flats in a season of the rains,
> they constitute a valuable and sound sheep pasture.

That same year, Charles Sturt, the eldest of the thirteen
children of an English judge, arrived in Australia as a captain
in the 39th Regiment with no special love for his military duties
and an immense interest in the possibilities of exploration. He
fell in love with Sydney where he found "a climate so soft and
enchanting that few have left it but with regret". He was given
the task of finding out whether the rivers that flowed westwards on the far side of the Blue Mountains drained into an
inland lake or sea. His first trip, which he began in January
1828, was undertaken during a drought so severe that in some
pools dead frogs made the slime undrinkable. Elsewhere the
men had to squeeze the mud of a river bed through cloth in order
to get a few drops to drink. Sturt discovered a new river which
he named the Darling after the new Governor. He did not realize

that it was the main channel draining the plains of Central Queensland. He was unable to follow it far because its waters were salt, and had no idea whether it found its way to the coast or faded away in some inland swamp.

In his report he confessed to failure:

It is impossible for me to describe the nature of the country over which we passed, for the first eight miles. We rode through brushes of polygonum, under rough-gum, without a blade of vegetation, the whole space being subject to inundation. We then got on small plains of firmer surface, and red soil, but these soon changed again for the former; and at 4 p.m. we found ourselves advanced about two miles on a plain that stretched away before us, and bounded the horizon. It was dismally brown; a few trees only served to mark the distance. Up one of the highest, I sent Hopkinson, who reported that he could not see the end of it, and that all around looked blank and desolate. It is a singular fact that during the whole day we have not seen a drop of water or a blade of grass.

To have stopped where we were, would, therefore, have been impossible, to have advanced, would probably have been ruin. Had there been one favourable circumstance to have encouraged me with the hope of success, I would have proceeded. Had we picked up a stone as indicating our approach to high land, I would have gone on; or had there been a break in the level of the country, or even a change in the vegetation. But we had left all traces of the natives far behind us; and this seemed a desert they never entered— that not even a bird inhabited. I could not encourage a hope of success, and therefore gave up the point; not from want of means, but from a conviction of the inutility of any further efforts. If there is any blame to be attached to the measure, it is I who am in fault, but none who had not, like me, traversed the interior at such a season, would believe the state of the country over which I had wandered. During the short interval I had been out, I had seen rivers cease to flow before me, and sheets of water disappear; and had it not been for a merciful Providence, should ere reaching the Darling, have been overwhelmed by misfortune.

Next year he was able to solve the mystery of Australia's waterways by taking an enormous gamble. He wanted to explore the Darling but he reckoned that another river, the Murrumbidgee, whose waters were known to be sweet, would lead in the same direction as the Darling, and decided that it would be better to follow it instead of the larger river. He also calculated that at some point the Murrumbidgee would lead into a larger water course which would float him downstream to its mouth, perhaps even to the sea. So he took with him the frames and timbers for building a strong 27-feet whaler and, when he thought that he had got far enough, he picked a team of six men, sent back the others with the bullocks and drays and continued his journey by boat. Then in his own words:

The general appearance of the Murrumbidgee from the moment of our starting on the 13th, at a late hour in the afternoon, had been such as to encourage my hopes of ultimate success in tracing it down, but about three o'clock we came to one of those unaccountable and mortifying changes which had already so frequently excited my apprehension. Its channel again suddenly contracted, and became almost blocked up with huge trees, that must have found their way into it down the creeks and junctions that we had lately passed. The rapidity of the current increasing at the same time, rendered the navigation perplexing and dangerous. We passed reach after reach, present the same difficulties, and were at length obliged to pull up at 5 p.m. having a scene of confusion and danger before us that I did not dare to encounter with the evening's light; for I had not only observed that the men's eyesight failed them as the sun descended, and that they mistook shadows for objects under water, and vice versa, but the channel had become so narrow that although the banks were not of increased height, we were involved in comparative darkness, under a close arch of trees, and a danger was hardly seen ere we were hurried past it almost without the possibility of avoiding it. The reach at the head of which we stopped, was crowded with the trunks of trees, the branches of which crossed each other in every direction, nor could I hope, after a minute examination of the channel, to succeed in taking the boat safely down so intricate a passage.

We rose in the morning with feelings of apprehension, and uncertainty; and, indeed, with great doubts on our minds whether we were not thus early destined to witness the wreck and the defeat of the expedition. The men got slowly and cautiously into the boat, and placed themselves so as to leave no part of her undefended. Hopkinson stood at the bow ready with poles to turn her head from anything upon which she might be drifting. Thus prepared, we allowed her to go with the stream. By extreme care and attention on the part of the men we passed this formidable barrier.

Hopkinson in particular exerted himself and more than once leapt from the boat upon apparently rotten logs of wood, that I should not have judged capable of bearing his weight, the more effectually to save the boat. It might have been imagined that where such a quantity of timber had accumulated, a clearer channel would have been found below, but such was not the case. In every reach we had to encounter fresh difficulties. In some places huge trees lay athwart the stream, under whose arched branches we were obliged to pass; but, generally speaking, they had been carried root foremost, by the current and therefore presented so many points to receive us, that, at the rate at which we were going, had we struck full upon any one of them, it would have gone through and through the boat. About noon we stopped to repair, or rather to take down the remains of awning, which had been torn away; and to breathe a moment from the state of apprehension and anxiety in which our minds had been kept during the morning. About one we again started. The men looked anxiously out ahead, for the singular change in the river had impressed on them an idea that we were approaching its termination, or near some adventure. In a sudden, the river took a general southern direction, but in its tortuous course, swept round to every point of the compass, with the greatest irregularity. We were carried at a fearful rate down its gloomy and contracted banks, and, in such a moment of excitement had little time to pay attention to the country through which we were passing. It was however observed that chalybeate springs were numerous close to the water's edge. At 3 p.m. Hopkinson called out that we were approaching a junction, and in less than a minute afterwards we were hurried into a broad and noble river.

It is impossible for me to describe the effect of so instantaneous a change of circumstances upon us. The boats were allowed to drift along at pleasure, and such was the force with which we had been shot out of the Murrumbidgee, that we were carried nearly to the bank opposite its embouchure, whilst we continued to gaze in silent astonishment on the capacious channel we had entered; and when we looked for that by which we had been led into it, we could hardly believe that the insignificant gap that presented itself to us was, indeed, the termination of the beautiful and noble stream whose course we had thus successfully followed. I can only compare the relief we experienced to that which the seaman feels on weathering the rock upon which he expected his vessel would have struck—to the calm which succeeds moments of feverish activity, when the dread of danger is succeeded by the certainty of escape.

Sturt and his party had reached what is now the Murray River which carried him to the sea not far from the site of the future city of Adelaide. But he and his men had to row more than a thousand miles upstream against the current to get home.

Sturt himself had become blind by the time he arrived back in Sydney and did not recover his sight for several months.

About the same time as Sturt was striking across to South Australia, other pioneers were looking towards the west. The Colonial Office had taken alarm at the news that the French had sent several vessels on voyages of exploration there, and in 1817 Lieutenant Philip Parker King was sent on the first of a series of survey trips to King George's Sound, the most southerly point of Western Australia, to the Swan River, the waterway leading to the sites of Perth and Fremantle, and many other points further north. The survey was duly made but in 1825 the French sent two vessels to make a further reconnaissance and Bathurst felt forced to act. He told Governor Darling to establish settlement at Western Port near the Port Phillip inlet, and to forestall the French by other settlements further west. The British flag was accordingly hoisted near St. George's Sound on Christmas Day 1826 and the western territory added on to New South Wales. Early in 1827 Captain Stirling was sent to make a more thorough exploration of the Swan River. His report, delivered in April, declared that the soil was better than any seen east of the Blue Mountains, that there was fresh water and but few trees to clear. The Admiralty, however, took the view that there was little to be gained by such an isolated settlement and that it would be more profitable to develop other areas further east. The Swan River project was turned down, but later the same year the scheme was revived, reconsidered and grudgingly adopted. On 2nd May 1829 H.M.S. *Challenger*, commanded by Captain Fremantle, arrived at the Swan River and took formal possession in the name of His Majesty.

But this was only the start. The previous autumn, a syndicate headed by Mr. Thomas Peel, a relative of Sir Robert Peel, was formed in London to finance and establish within a period of four years a settlement in Western Australia of 10,000 emigrants from England, Scotland and Ireland, together with cattle and provisions. In return the Syndicate asked for grants of up to four million acres of land valued at 1s. 6d. per acre, from which they would allow 200 acres to every male emigrant. The object of the settlement would be to grow cotton, tobacco, sugar, flax and to breed horses, cattle and pigs.

The Home Government was prepared to encourage a scheme of this kind (provided that other people found the money for it) but not on such a large scale; they reduced the grant from four million to one million acres. Whitehall stipulated that those wishing to go would have to pay for their own passage and maintain themselves when they got to the colony. They must form themselves into parties in which there were at least five women to every six men. In return for this the settlers would get the freehold of forty acres of land for every £3 they spent on stock, farming tools, or other items needed to bring the land into production. In addition, anyone who paid for the passage of a labourer was entitled to another 200 acres of land. It looked like easy money. The first colonists arrived at the beginning of June.

Then the troubles began.

Cold weather had set in, and with it came storms and heavy seas. The Swan River itself was suitable only for shallow draft vessels and one ship had already grounded and damaged herself through going too close to the mainland. Captain Stirling, who had been put in charge of the settlement in Western Australia with the rank of Lieutenant-Governor, decided that it would be safer to land the stores off shore on Garden Island a little to the south of Swan River and build warehouses there. It was three months before sites for two cities on the mainland were chosen, one on the south side of the river at Fremantle and the other on the north side at Perth. Meanwhile vast quantities of land were doled out to people who were quite unable to bring such areas into cultivation. No preparations had been made to receive the settlers and there were no roads to take them to their properties or to bring back any produce they might have raised. They lived through the winter in huts set up on the beach. Many of the labourers who had agreed to serve deserted or were dismissed and sailed for Sydney where conditions were easier. Those that occupied their properties were separated from the Governor and from each other. Mr. Peel, who alone of the original syndicate persisted in his support for the scheme, had no one to help erect the houses he had brought with him. Stock perished because there was no one to look after the animals. One man had to leave a seventy-guinea piano to rot on the beach. Tools rusted away before they could be used.

In 1830 there were four thousand people on the settlement. By 1832 the number had fallen to 1,500. A few settlers lived on but their dream of a free colony, pioneered without convict labour, had to be abandoned. In 1849 they surrendered, asked for convict labour, and became a penal colony. Transportation to Western Australia was not abandoned until 1868.

Elsewhere, however, as the proportion of free colonists increased, the Governor's powers diminished. From 1823 he was compelled, before passing any legislation, to consult a Legislative Council and listen to its advice. Six years later the Council was strengthened and the Governor was required to obey it instead of merely taking account of its rulings. In June 1825 Van Diemen's Land—now Tasmania—was detached from New South Wales and made into a separate colony. Then came the order of August 1826 that, in future, there should be trial by jury for all crimes and misdemeanours and in civil cases if either side requested it.

These irritations were particularly galling to Sir Ralph Darling who had become Governor of New South Wales in 1825. Sir Ralph was an old soldier who had commanded a regiment during the disastrous retreat to Coruña and had reached the rank of major-general two years before Waterloo. Then he joined the Horse Guards Staff. He was a stickler for discipline and was soon weeding out emancipists one and all from Government service. Shortly after he arrived in Sydney he became deeply concerned about the criticisms of his administration which were constantly appearing in Australian newspapers. It should be explained that, until 1824, the Colony's only newspaper bore the title of the *Sydney Gazette and New South Wales Advertiser*. It was published by authority of the Governor and survived largely on a diet of Government proclamations and hand-outs. That very year, however, a rival, independent newspaper called *The Australian* was founded—without the Governor's permission. In 1826 it was joined by *The Monitor*.

Sir Ralph, however, was not the kind of man to stand idly by in the face of such irregularities. He tried to introduce a system of licences for newspapers (the licences could of course have been withdrawn at the Governor's pleasure). He pressed for all articles to be signed so that their authors could if necessary be proceeded against in person, and he demanded the banishment of any newspapermen convicted of "blasphemous or seditious libels".

Sir Francis Forbes, the Chief Justice of the Colony, maintained, however, that these measures were in contradiction of the laws of England and refused his assent to them. A proposal for a vicious stamp tax on newspapers was referred to Whitehall and rejected. The Governor's temper was not improved by these reverses.

In November 1827 at a Turf Club dinner, one of the Governor's Chief Tormentors proposed a silent toast (usually accorded to dead soldiers) to the Governor while the band played "Over the Hills and Far Away". Darling dismissed all Government servants who had attended the meal and founded a rival club under his own patronage.

Finally there was the celebrated case of two privates, Joseph Sudds and Patrick Thompson, of the 57th Regiment, who stole a length of cloth from a shop in Market Street because they felt that even the life of a convict would be preferable to one of military service. They were duly sentenced to seven years' "transportation" but the Governor decided, as a warning to other would-be-deserters, to vary the sentence to one of seven years with the road gang, and for good measure had them fitted with leg irons, chains, and iron collars fitted with two spikes of iron. Those worn by Sudds were said to be "light". They weighed 13 lb. 12 oz. Sudds fell ill and died, and the fact that he was already a sick man when arrested hardly excused the chief surgeon for his failure to inform the Governor of this material fact. For the papers—and for all those opposed to the Governor's policy, the Sudds-Thompson case provided a splendid opportunity to attack Darling, and W. C. Wentworth urged that the Governor should be impeached on a charge of murder or some other equally grave crime.

Eventually the battle between the Governor and his charges

was solved in part by the usual remedy of recalling the Governor, but even more by the colonists themselves, who started to spread over their continent in a human explosion which took them far beyond the reach of bumbledom into regions where, with official cries of protests growing fainter and fainter, the Australian outback legend really began.

6

When Free Men Flowed Out-back

And now it was time for most of Australia to forget her sordid past and to break free from her dependence on convict labour.

On Friday, 21st August 1829, a London newspaper, the *Morning Chronicle*, published the first of eleven "Letters from Sydney", in which a colonist, apparently disillusioned by his own experiences, discussed the obstacles facing any settler emigrating to Australia.

In fact, the author, Edward Gibbon Wakefield, had never visited Australia, still less farmed there, and his "letters" had been composed in prison, where he was serving a three-year sentence for abducting an heiress. But the articles were clearly and attractively written; their analysis of the problems was penetrating, and their conclusions logical.

Wakefield (who later became a reformed character and a respected public figure) argued that convict labour, though it helped pioneer settlers, was undesirable in the long run. Life and property, he argued, were less secure in a colony composed largely of criminals and ex-criminals, and the disparity in the numbers of men and women led to drunkenness and immorality. Furthermore the Governor, so long as he remained a jailor-in-chief, could never grant free settlers the liberties that they desired and were entitled to expect. Wakefield believed, in addition, that the Government system of handing out grants of land would have to be discontinued if convict labour were to be replaced by that of free citizens, since no one, as long as he could get land under grant for himself for next to nothing, would be content to work for anyone else (even though his passage from England might have been paid by his would-be-employer).

Accordingly, Wakefield proposed that land should no longer be allotted under grant, but should, instead, be sold to selected couples at a price high enough to pay for the passages of more free immigrants. Free citizens, he felt, deserved self-government, and this principle was enthusiastically adopted later in both New Zealand and Canada.

Wakefield was soon able to convince a group of influential English businessmen that South Australia was the right spot for his new system. Land grants were ended there in 1831 and a South Australian Association was formed two years later to develop the territory discovered by Sturt. British Members of Parliament backed the new Association, and a bill promoting Wakefield's scheme was successfully piloted through the House of Commons. The Duke of Wellington gave his support in the House of Lords.

The bill declared that no convicts were to be sent to South Australia. A fund was to be set up to promote the emigration of free citizens. It was to be financed by selling land at not less than twelve shillings an acre (this was nearly two and a half times the current price in New South Wales). Families, it was decided, should emigrate as one unit, and if possible the numbers of men and women should be equal. Free passages would be given only to those under thirty.

As usual with a venture that was really worthwhile, Whitehall accepted no responsibility whatever, but threatened to take over the colony lock, stock and barrel if there were not twenty thousand people in it by the end of twenty years; in the meantime the scheme was to be administered on behalf of the Association by eight commissioners. After this send-off Colonel William Light, the Government Surveyor-General, selected a site on a barely navigable creek as the location of the capital.

The feelings of the promoters can well be imagined when they read an account given by T. Horton James in his guide-book *Six Months in South Australia—with advice to emigrants—to*

*which is added a Monthly Calendar of Gardening and Agriculture
adapted to the Climate and Seasons*, which appeared in 1838.

Having sung the praises of two havens, Port Lincoln and
Victor Harbour, James turns to the one actually chosen by the
Surveyor-General:

> The only other harbour worth mentioning in the colony is Port
> Adelaide, which is well enough for small vessels, after they are
> inside, being secure from accident, but in any other respect it is
> totally unfit for general purposes of commerce, and will never come
> to anything, as no amount of expenditure could make it available
> except for the trifling domestic trade in Mangrove ashes for the
> future soap makers of the Colony. Without even those first requi-
> sites of wood and water, and without even ballast, how can it be
> expected to succeed? This place can be looked upon only as a mere
> make-shift for the present 'till Port Lincoln and Victor Harbour
> shall be established.
>
> It is very disagreeable to be compelled to speak in this decided
> tone of the unsuitableness of Port Adelaide, because it seems to
> imply a censure upon Colonel Light, the Surveyor-General of the
> Colony, in whose discretion it rested, where to select the site of the
> first town; but the author considers it of far more importance to
> speak the truth in order that any impediments to the prosperity of
> the Colony may be remedied, if not removed. . . .

Of the climate he wrote:

> In the latter end of March, April, September, and October, the
> temperature is delightful—neither hot nor cold—you do not
> perceive whether there is any fire in the room or not or whether
> the window is open or shut; but from the latter end of November,
> all December, January, February and part of March, the heat is
> oppressive and almost intolerable. I have seen the thermometer in
> these uncomfortable months, in a dark room nearly closed up, and
> with a thick roof of thatch over it, as high as 96 degrees—not once
> but a dozen different days; and if the instrument is hung upon a wall
> in the direct beams of the sun, it rises to 140 degrees. This is a
> degree of heat I never remember to have felt in any part of the
> tropics even, it dries up everything, not merely the few running
> streams that in winter come from the mountains, but all garden
> vegetation; and so pulverises the dust in the camp at Adelaide, that
> it is reduced to an almost impalpable powder, and penetrates every
> article of clothing, from its extreme fineness; whilst as much caution

is requisite in stepping across the road, as if a person were going through the muddiest part of Piccadilly or Whitechapel.

Of course the tiny little Torrens all but vanishes before such a sun; in the few places where it runs at all, there would be plenty of room for the whole of it to run through an Irishman's hat; and a far better river is made every day in the London streets when the parish turncock opens a plug. There are, however, several pretty good holes which have too much water in them to be entirely exhausted by the sun's heat, and it was on account of these water holes that the town was placed in this unfortunate situation.

The eastern wind, which is the cool and constant wind in summer, blowing through the Bass' straits, over the great lake, and which becomes a strong sea breeze at Port Lincoln and Encounter Bay, is never felt, with its refreshing coolness, at Adelaide, because the township is placed close under the West side of Mount Lofty; and it is the absence of this summer or sea breeze which occasions an excessive heat as now described. . . . And as the few wells about the settlement of Adelaide become dry and the water scarcer, the more you want it for washing; and the fine particles of lime-stone dust carried up in numerous whirlwinds about the plains, fall into one's eyes, and a three months' attack of ophthalmia is the frequent consequence. Half the people you see have got bad eyes, the dandies even wearing veils; but it may be very reasonably doubted whether they do not produce more harm than good. This is the only drawback to the colony and would never have been experienced had the gallant Colonel had much experience in the new Colonies, or even had he followed the intentions of the Commissioners.

The informal welcome to be expected by the immigrants is then described in greater detail:

The scene is beautiful at almost any season, but especially in the Spring, about September, October and November. After sailing up the gulf, a pilot is seen making fast for the ship from Holdfast Bay, and is presently alongside and on the quarter deck. When the usual salutations and enquiries have been mutually exchanged between Captain Lipson and the passengers, the old gentleman takes charge of the vessel, and points out the entrance of the harbour, calling out to the man at the wheel, "starboard a little" and then "port". In about half an hour, two white buoys or beacons are seen ahead very close together, and between them is the narrow entrance. One of the sailors is now ordered into the chains, with the hand-lead to ascertain the depth of water. While he is crying out "by the

mark three—quarter less three", the passengers are looking over
the sides of the ship at the bottom, which is seen distinctly, and
presently bump, the vessel strikes upon the mud and sand. This is
the bar of Port Adelaide. The gentlemen whisper to each other that
the ship is aground—still there is nothing going on more than
usual, no hurry or noise—many don't believe it—they felt no
shock. The captain frowns, whilst the pilot thinks nothing of it, but
walks about, calm and unruffled, as if he were in his own parlour;
the sails are not even clued up, because the pilot thinks she will
float again in the course of an hour or two, and, the bottom being
soft, there is no damage to be apprehended—that every ship
touches more or less on entering the port, but they are always got
off again, and so on. The careful captain, however, who has brought
the ship all the way from England in danger, and not carried away
either a rope yarn, or a studding sail boom, is not a little annoyd
at having the matter treated so coolly and wonders that the pilot,
knowing the ship drew fourteen feet water, should attempt going
over the Bar with barely thirteen feet on it. The pilot then gets
out of it by saying, the tides are very irregular in the Gulf, particularly with northerly winds, and there the discussion stops. While
the ship is on the bar, waiting for the evening tide, the passengers
are mostly below, packing up their trunks and portmanteaus, sup-
posing that it will be all right at six o'clock, and that running a ship
aground is nothing, when you are used to it. And sure enough about
sun-set, or a little before, the flood tide is making, and with the
help of the southerly wind, the good ship is afloat again—the yards
are squared, and you are gliding pleasantly along up the narrow and
muddy creek, with shoals on either side. Presently, the ship has to
cross a second bar, near Snapper Point, and the sailor is ordered
again in the chains to heave the lead. He sings out "quarter less
three" and soon after you are in deep water. There is here a turn
in the creek, and as it is dark and the wind against you, the old
gentleman is preparing to bring up for the night. The royals and
top-gallant sails are first stowed, when orders are given to stand
by the anchor. The topsail halyards are eased down, and all sails,
except the jib and mizzen, are taken off the ship. The pilot then
cries out "Let go the anchor" and away the noisy chain rattles
through the holes. You are now welcome to South Australia though
there will be no going ashore 'till the morning, for you are still
eight or nine miles from the landing place. At break of day the
passengers are roused from their berths by the noise of the windlass
pawls, and the usual bustle in getting a ship under weigh; and one

by one they appear on deck, to take a view of the land; but the scene is changed from yesterday, they are now sailing up a narrow, dirty ditch, fringed on both sides with odious mangrove trees, and nothing to be seen on either of the low swampy shores but the dwarf tea trees or melaleuca. You occasionally get a view of the hills far away to the left. They are the Mount Lofty range, which were yesterday seen on the right, and a little of the ardour of the first announcement of land is beginning to subside. The shores resemble the worst parts of the coast of Essex below the Nore, and at high tide the little mangroves are half covered with the water. You look out for a landing place in vain, though the ship now anchors again, and you are at the end of your voyage. The boat is lowered to put the passengers ashore, and you see two or three small vessels at anchor higher up the creek, which the pilot says have lately arrived from Van Diemen's Land with sheep, potatoes, flour, etc. etc. It is now ten o'clock and unless you make haste, you are informed, there may be some difficulty in landing, as the tides are here very unaccommodating, being always low water in the middle of the day, which is a phenomenon not yet satisfactorily explained. You ask if this is Port Adelaide, and the answer is yes! You step into the boat with a number of other passengers, carpet bags, band boxes, and parcels, and four hands from the ship shove off, and pull up the creek. The landing place is about a mile higher up, and you already see the bottom, and in a few minutes you stick fast in the mud. Here all four sailors push the boat along with the oars, but the tide is falling fast, and no one can say where the deep water is, as the bottom is as plain one side of the boat as it is on the other. The good-natured sailors, now seeing there is nothing else to be done, step out of the boat into the water, trowsers and all, and succeed in pulling the boat along a considerable way; but presently she is again stuck as fast as ever on the shelly bottom. What is to be done?—Which is the landing place? The iron store is seen about a quarter of a mile off, and the passengers now must all get out and walk as the sailors have done. But it will be too deep! It will be up to our knees, exclaims a lady, with new shoes and silk stockings: never mind, you must either do that or wait till dark: so here goes, and out they spring, ladies and all, bonnets, boxes, and baggage of all kinds under their arms, while the sailors are carrying the heavy matters. Young ladies and children are seen on the sailors' backs, and shoes and stockings are being carried in their hands, whilst the muddy bottom occasionally gives way under the feet of the adults, and, long before they reach the landing place, they run a risk of falling in the water, not to say suffocating in the mud. One comfort, however, is there is nobody to look at you. The shore is an uninhabitable swamp, and the few people who are living in the wigwams at Port Adelaide, are too busily engaged in landing boards and rolling up casks, to take any notice of a party of ladies and gentlemen up to their knees in mud trying to reach the shore. This is at last managed, without the loss of either life or limb, but it is certainly anything but pleasant. Arrived on the dry land, the party wash the mud off their legs, and put on the shoes and stockings. Then, carrying their trunks as well as they can, the sailors having all gone back to look after the boat and get her afloat, they all walk up the side of a little canal, as it is called, which brings them to the only spot of land at the creek free from inundations, which is called the Sand Hill, where one or two grog shops, made of branches of trees, are seen, a few native blacks stark naked, and a large iron store painted white, belonging to the Commissioners. This is Port Adelaide! Port Misery would be a better name: for nothing in any other part of the world can surpass it in every thing that is wretched and inconvenient. Packages of goods and heaps of merchandize are lying about in every direction as if they had cost nothing, Stacks of what were once beautiful London bricks are crumbling away like ginger-bread, and evidently, at each returning tide, half covered with the flood; trusses of hay, now rotten, and Norway deals, scattered about as if they had no owner—iron ploughs and rusty harrows—cases of door frames and windows that had once been glazed—heaps of the best slates, half tumbling down—winnowing machines broken to pieces—blocks of Roman cement, now hard as stone, wanting nothing but the staves and hoops—Sydney cedar and laths and shingles from Van Diemen's Land in every direction; whilst, on the high ground, are to be seen pigs eating through the flour sacks, and kegs of raisins with not only the head out but half the contents; onions and potatoes apparently to be had for picking up. The sight is disheartening. What with the sun and the rain— the sand and the floods—the thieves with four legs and the thieves with two—the passengers hug themselves at the recollection that *they* have brought no merchandize for sale, glad enough to be able to take care of themselves. The sooner they get out of this horrid little hole the better, so they enquire if there is any coach to the town—they are answered by a careless shake of the head, and so, like good settlers, they determine to set off and walk, carrying their light parcels with them and leaving the heavy things with a friend who refuses to go any further. They ask for a drink of water, before starting—there is not such a thing to be had; but the bullock carts are expected down every minute with the usual supply! What, no water? exlaims our passenger. No, sir, but the Commissioners are sinking a well, though they have not yet found any but salt water; but they are going to dig in another place, shortly, we understand.

Away they start for the city of Adelaide, and after ten minutes rough walking though the loose sand which is fatiguing enough, they gain the firm and beaten road, with the cheerful hills before them, glad enough to have overcome their morning troubles. Though very warm, the walk is agreeable, and out of a cloud of dust before them, they soon descry a dray or two each drawn by a long line of bullocks. They perceive by the splashing of the water from the open bungs, that the casks contain the daily supply for the port, and the drivers very cheerfully give them all a drink: this enables them to walk on with renewed spirits, over the naked plain, and, tired and dusty, in about seven miles more, they reach another iron store, the property of the Commissioners, where they now begin to see a few marquees and huts, and people walking about. They step across the "Torrens" [river] without knowing it, and enquire for the Inn. They are directed to the Southern Cross Hotel, then kept by a German Jew of the name of Levy, considered the best house in the settlement, and here we will leave them for the present, hungry, thirsty, fatigued—covered with dust and perspiration—and with feelings of shame and disappointment at being so taken in!

There were many other reasons why the colony got off to a bad start.

The landowners, instead of settling down to cultivate their estates, stayed in Adelaide itself, and busied themselves with land speculation, encouraged by the Commissioners themselves who promised that the price of land would be raised some time soon from 12s. to £2. The labourers, unemployed, decamped as soon as possible to New South Wales where they hoped to be able to buy land of their own more cheaply. And much of the pioneering had to be entrusted to emancipated convicts who sailed over from Van Diemen's Land. Thus in its early days the colony produced very little from its own resources and had to import food from Sydney. By 1840 its expenditure was nearly six times its revenue, and, the following year a new Governor, Captain George Grey was sent to put things right. He introduced a regime of unheard of austerity. The Commissioners were sacked *en bloc* and not replaced. Government relief works which had been introduced to provide employment were cut to the bone and the remaining labourers were at last forced to seek work where they rightfully belonged—on the land. Government expenditure was halved and speculators who had hoped to make fortunes were compelled to sell out to genuine farmers. Miraculous changes then occurred; within four years the Colony was producing more food than it needed. Then, one day, a carter who was bringing his team down a hilly side on the Mount Lofty Range noticed a piece of glistening rock kicked up by the log which was being towed behind the dray as a brake. The rock proved to be a sample of rich silver lead ore—and there was enough of it to support a mine. Rich copper ore was found further north and by 1849 the Colony became self-supporting. A year later it was granted self-government.

Melbourne (formerly known as Bearbrass) became Melbourne about the same time as Adelaide became Adelaide—that is, just before Queen Victoria came to the throne. And it, too, had a far from auspicious launching ceremony.

The inlet of Port Phillip, leading to the site of Melbourne, had been surveyed in 1802 by John Murray on orders of Governor King. Then the area was forgotten for twenty years until the arrival of Hamilton Hume. A convict settlement was established there in 1826 as an experiment and withdrawn two years later.

But in the meantime a young Australian, John Batman, had become interested. Batman, then twenty-seven, had been born in Parramatta and apprenticed there to a wheelwright. But he did not fancy his prospects in competition with cheap convict labour and emigrated to Van Diemen's Land. There he married a convict lass and acquired some fame by capturing single-handed the Tasmanian Bush Ranger (bandit) Matthew Brady, who had been bold enough to offer a reward of twenty gallons of rum in return for the Governor's body.

Batman had heard from the sealers who used Port Phillip that the land there was fertile and in 1827 he applied to Governor Darling for permission to settle there. His application was rejected. Other pioneers applied in 1833 and 1834 and were also refused. But in November 1834 Edward Henty and his sons ignored the ban and settled at Portland Bay, while, almost at the same time, a group of merchants in Van Diemen's Land formed the Port Phillip Association to buy land from the natives and commissioned John Batman to act on their behalf. Batman sailed into Port Phillip in May 1835, explored the Yarra (the river on which Melbourne stands) recording in his journal the understatement, "This will be the place for a village". He signed a "treaty" with eight chiefs, purchasing 600,000 acres to the north and west of the Yarra in return for 40 pairs of blankets, 130 knives, 42 tomahawks, 62 pairs of scissors, 40 looking-glasses, four flannel jackets, four suits of clothes, 18 red shirts, 250 handkerchiefs and 150 lb. of flour, and a yearly tribute or rent.

"The parchment the eight chiefs signed this afternoon," Batman wrote in his journal, "delivering to me some of the soil of each of them, as giving me full possession of the tracts of land. This took place alongside of a beautiful stream of water, and from whence my land commences, and where a tree is marked four ways to know the corner boundary."

Then, while Batman was back in Hobart trying to persuade the local Governor to recognize his "treaty", a third rival party sailed into Port Phillip and settled on the very spot that Batman had chosen for his "village".

Meanwhile, in Sydney, Governor Bourke had been getting worried about all these wildcat settlements.

Although they were a good deal nearer to Hobart than to Sydney, he felt that he should control them since they were on the mainland. And since he did not feel equal to setting up a separate police force there, he decided to ban all settlement and to proclaim all the settlers as trespassers on Crown Property.

But, as often happened in such cases, the result of this proclamation was the very opposite of what the Governor had intended. For those who had previously held back in deference to the rights of the Port Phillip Association and the other pioneers, now considered that they had just as good a claim to the lands around Port Phillip as those who had got there before them. They flocked over and set themselves up without a single official to help or hinder them or register their holdings.

So in May 1836, Bourke, seeing that his ban was totally disregarded, bowed to the inevitable and sent a police magistrate to reconnoitre on the community of defiant squatters, which by then numbered 177. Six months later Bourke sent over a permanent magistrate and, in March 1837, he arrived himself and gave what he alone could provide—permission to establish a lawful township with the official title of Melbourne.

By 1838 Melbourne had its own paper, *The Advertiser*, its own club, and its own racing. A "ferry" consisting of a boat and two men was already in service between Melbourne and William's Town on the opposite side of the river. "Parties from Melbourne are requested to raise a smoke and the boat will be at their service as soon as practicable; the least charge is five shillings and two shillings each when the number exceeds two," a notice said.

By June 1839 the city boasted seventy-seven warehouses, shops and offices. Settlers flocked in not only from Van Diemen's Land and New South Wales but direct from London. Land prices rocketed and a Mr. Ebden who had acquired three blocks of land on Collins Street for £54, sold it not three years later for £10,250. Property auctioneers did so well that they were able to offer their clients free lunches of ham served with beer, brandy and even champagne.

Next year, Melbourne's citizens felt so sure of themselves that they were able to start agitating for separation from New South Wales, and some ten years later, final victory came with the establishment of the new Crown Colony of Victoria, with Melbourne as its capital.

The path to independence in Australia was smoothed by a growing feeling at home that transportation no longer served the needs either of the colony or the mother country. In November 1837 a Select Committee of the House of Commons was appointed to inquire into "transportation, and its efficacy as a punishment, its influence on the moral state of society in the Colonies and how far it is susceptible of improvement".

James Backhouse, a Quaker from York who travelled and preached in New Zealand and Africa as well as in Australia, played an important part in influencing public opinion against

7

transportation. His journal, published in 1838, no doubt helped
to create a receptive atmosphere for the proposals put forward
by the Select Committee of the chain gangs that helped to build
the Colony's roads. Backhouse wrote:

> About five miles from our lodging place, we visited an ironed-
> gang, and three miles further along the road a second, and had
> religious interview with the men. There are about sixty men in
> each: both are under the charge of Lieutenant Campbell. They are
> lodged in huts upon large open areas by the road-side, without any
> stockade. When not at work, they are kept on the spot by a military
> guard, who are ordered to fire upon any who may attempt to
> escape, and not stop when called it. We were informed that they had
> no Bibles nor other books, and that their only religious instruction
> consisted in prayers read by the officer or serjeant in charge on
> First-days. A few of the prisoners lodge in moveable caravans on
> block wheels, which when stationary are banked up with earth.
> These have doors, and iron barred windows on one side: four or
> five men sleep in each end of them on the floor, and as many more
> on platforms. They are not less crowded than the huts, and are
> unwholesome dormitories: many of the men sleeping in them
> become effected with scurvy.

In a joint report to the Governor dated 19th January 1837,
Backhouse and his colleague, George Washington Walker,
wrote:

> Although the convict population of New South Wales is kept
> under a considerable degree of subjection and discipline, yet the
> measure of reformation among them, evinced by the adoption of
> better principles, is exceedingly small. This need not excite sur-
> prise when the paucity of the means employed for their reformation
> is considered in connection with the facilities for obtaining strong
> drink, that are placed in their way notwithstanding the regulations
> prohibiting the sale of spirituous liquors to prisoners. The oppor-
> tunities open to them, from the vast number of licensed public-
> houses, and of places where spirits are sold covertly, are available
> to a large proportion of the prisoners, who are constantly com-
> mitting petty theft to enable them to gratify their propensity for
> strong drink.
> In visiting the various penal establishments of the colony, and
> observing the limited means made use of for moral and religious
> instruction, we must conclude that restraint rather than reformation

has been the object of the British Government in the institution of the penal discipline of New South Wales. . . .

The frequency of flagellation in some of the ironed-gangs, as well as in other stations of prisoners, including the Hyde Park barracks, Sydney, is a subject deserving notice; for as a punishment, flagellation is generally admitted to have a degrading effect. In some of the ironed gangs, this punishment has, on an average, been administered four times round to each man, (many of the cases being of fifty lashes each), in a period of less than eighteen months. And we have been informed that upwards of one thousand men have been flogged in the Hyde Park barracks within the same period. . . .

We have visited most of the prisons in the colony, and would respectfully state our conviction, that not one of them is on a plan calculated to promote reformation. In the whole of them prisoners are congregated in considerable numbers in day-rooms, in most of which they also sleep; and in many instances side by side on the floor, or on platforms, and but few in hammocks. None of the prisons have any adequate provision for solitary confinement, and in some of them the cells are so few that prisoners sentenced to solitary confinement have to wait a considerable time in the common rooms for their turns, otherwise more than one person would have to be in a cell at the same time.

Some of the prisons do not effectually exclude communication between the male and female prisoners, as for instance, those at Port Macquarie, Newcastle and Liverpool. That at Maitland is sometimes so crowded as to render it necessary for some of the prisoners occasionally to spend the night in the yard, to avoid suffocation. That at Campbell Town, under the Court House is unfit to place human beings of any description in, even for an hour, however small their numbers may be; the effluvium from it renders the court-house above untenable, if the windows be closed; and with the number occasionally placed in it, their health must be seriously endangered. Many of the prisons in the interior have no airing courts, and it would be difficult to describe, in a few words, the contamination which must be the inevitable result of placing a number of persons, without employment, in association often for several months at a time in such places. . . .

The addition of tread-mills to gaols, or of other means of furnishing employment to the prisoners confined in them is much to be desired. But we would remark that when the sentence to a treadmill, or to solitary cells, is lengthened out to a great number of days, it materially diminishes the salutary effect. In the former the stiffness induced at first begins to subside after a week's exercise; and at the expiration of a fortnight, many persons of the labouring class would leave the treadmill with less disgust than at the expiration of a week. Persons often sleep a considerable portion of the first two or three days in solitary confinement, but want of exercise soon renders them wakeful and they then begin to feel their situation painfully, but the human mind, as well as body, quickly accommodates itself to circumstances, and a large proportion of persons would be released from this punishment, also, with less abhorrence of it, at the end of a month, than at the end of a week.

On the same principle, the female prisoners in the factories at Parramatta and Bathurst, and in the gaols at Newcastle and Port Macquarie, being generally kept without employment, (as was the case when we visited those establishments) become inured to idleness, often in such a degree as not to be again recovered to industrious habits.

In concluding these observations, we take the liberty of stating our conviction, that the undue measure of punishment that is yet attached to many offences by the British law, has a direct tendency to frustrate one of the chief ends designed, viz. the reduction of crime. . . . And however ideas of human expediency may have led to the adoption of a scale of punishment more severe than is sanctioned by the Divine law, experience has not only proved the hopes founded on such measures to be fallacious, but that in proportion as this sacred standard of human action has been departed from, the consequences have uniformly been injurious.

The Select Committee concluded in its report published in August 1838 that transportation did not deter, and so far from reforming the prisoner, further corrupted him, as well as the society in which he passed his life after release.

Henry Parkes, afterwards Prime Minister, wrote when he landed almost penniless in Australia in 1839, "I have been disappointed in all my expectations of Australia except as to wickedness; for it is far more wicked than I had conceived it possible for any place to be or than it is possible for me to describe to you in England."

The Select Committee further decided that the system was not susceptible to reform but would have to be replaced, and suggested that sentences of compulsory labour should be served in penitentiaries at home or, if abroad, in places where there were no free settlers. The Committee conceded that Norfolk Island and the Tasmanian Peninsula would be suitable for this purpose since they were isolated from the rest of the territory. Soon after the report had been published, the Home Government decided to abolish transportation to New South Wales and the system of assigning convicts to private masters there. The special convict prisons there were gradually wound up.

One more effort was made to return to the bad old days in 1849 when Mr. Gladstone, then Colonial Secretary, suggested that, in order to relieve the pressure on Tasmania, which since 1840 had received all the long-term prisons, transportation to New South Wales should be revived, provided that for every convict a free immigrant should be sent out; for every man a woman; and that the convicts should as far as possible be separated from each other. In addition Whitehall began to send out offenders who had already served their term of punishment in England and who wanted a chance to reform in a new land. At first these "exiles" were welcomed both in Port Phillip and in Sydney, but later the Home Government began to include not only those who had completed their sentences but those who were on "ticket of leave". Both Sydney and Melbourne refused to allow the ships carrying this new cargo to unload and the Governor Fitzroy wisely decided to send the ships on to the scattered areas near Moreton Bay where labour was desperately needed. (The farmers of New South Wales might still have welcomed the return of the convicts but the townsmen feared competition from "cheap labour".)

In 1852 Van Diemen's Land along with all other Australian territories was excused from having to take further convicts and four years later blotted out its past by changing its name to Tasmania. Western Australia which had needed convict labour so desperately during its early years was able to do without it from 1868 on. Thus the question of whether any Australians today have convict ancestry is now somewhat academic. If they have, it is a most encouraging sign for the future of the human race.

7

Days When the World was Wide

The land hunger which had existed in Australia during the twenties was nothing to that which prevailed there in the thirties and forties, when the prosperity of the country was seen to depend on the comfort and security of its sheep and cattle. Australia was not a land on which sheep could be closely folded during the day as they can be in Britain, with perhaps a crop of kale for sustenance. On the contrary, over Australia's skimpy terrain each sheep needed as much as three acres. And even then the flock could not stay long in the same area before the nourishment to be got from the herbage was balanced by the energy needed to seek it out. Then came the trek to the next waterhole —perhaps many miles away. And in the meantime the stock would have increased. In three good seasons a flock might double its numbers.

How was the Crown to grant enough land to satisfy this wool-clad "population explosion"? Darling had tried to limit settlement to the nineteen countries lying within roughly 150 miles of Sydney. But there was no way of preventing sheep and their owners from crossing this frontier into the unprotected Crown lands beyond. In vain Whitehall called them trespassers and outlaws. In vain the Colonial Office trumpeted that it was as presumptuous for a sheepfarmer to drive his flocks into the wilderness, without Queen Victoria's permission, as it would be

for a Berkshire farmer to fatten up his oxen on the lawns of
Hampton Court.

These words fell on stony ground (had not Charles Darwin
himself said Australia "can never become an agricultural country
since the climate is so dry and the soil light, that the aspects
even of the better parts is very miserable"?) and a local spirit
of defiance began to question whether the Crown could be
allowed to hold up indefinitely the future prosperity of its
subjects.

Even before Queen Victoria came to the throne Governor
Bourke, who held the reins from 1831 to 1837, argued against
the policy of restriction.

He maintained that the colonists would not be wealthy unless
they were allowed to keep sheep and the sheep would not be
healthy unless they were allowed to wander. "Our wool is our
wealth," he said, "and I am disposed to give the sheep ample
runs."

Governor Gipps who succeeded Bourke took the very same
line. He said that curbing the wool men and their flocks was like
trying an Arab by drawing a circle round him in the sands of the
desert. In each case starvation would be the only result.

The Crown had begun in 1824 to ease matters by selling land
as a result of Bigge's recommendations but, as we have seen,
the authorities continued also to make grants of land in lieu of
pensions and for other good reasons. In 1831, however, Whitehall finally decided to cease all grants. One reason for this was
that it was laborious and unprofitable to collect the quit rents
charged by the Crown on granted land. Another reason was the
British view that at all costs the land must be developed and that
this could best be done by transferring Crown Land to those who
had enough capital to buy it. Furthermore if land were sold, it
might be possible, by raising and lowering the price, to control
the rate at which it passed out of the Government control. This
reasoning, like so much other official thinking, was fallacious.

A uniform reserve price of 5s. an acre subject to auction was
fixed in 1831, but few of the sheep-men were willing or able to
offer this kind of money when they could trespass for nothing.
By 1836 the number of illegal squatters had increased to the
point where no Government had any chance of prosecuting

them. Bourke therefore decided to recognize their existence and
at least make a little money out of them. He issued licences
which allowed the squatter an unlimited run in return for a fee
of £10.

But this was too good to last. Governor Gipps replaced the
£10 "unlimited" licence with one allowing the holder to graze
on a hundred acres of unused Crown land for one year; there
was no guarantee that he would be allowed to keep it after the
twelve months had ended.

If the Crown decided to sell the run the luckless squatter stood
to lose all the buildings, dams, fencing and provision fields that
he installed—unless he could get to the Land Office before anyone else and pay his deposit.

The squatters soon became ready to strike a bargain with the
Government in return for security of tenure. They were prepared to pay a contribution towards the cost of bringing new
immigrants to Australia and to the expense of policing the areas
allotted to them. After much agitation the Home Government
agreed that they should be granted fourteen-year leases after
which they should be allowed to buy a block of 324 acres to
enclose their homestead.

From then on, squatting became respectable. Some of the
squatters were men of substance in Sydney whose sons or
employees went pioneering. Some were men who had come
from England with capital to invest. Of them Governor Gipps
said in 1846, "Among the squatters of New South Wales are
the wealthiest of the land, occupying, with the permission of the
Government, thousands and tens of thousands of acres, young
men of good family and connections in England, Officers of the
Army and Navy. Graduates of Oxford and Cambridge are also
in no small number amongst them."

But for success one had to be ready to forget the cosy ways of
the old country.

"In searching for a suitable grant, it is a great point to fix
upon a place where the land *round* it is all so indifferent that no
new settler is likely to place himself near you, for a considerable
period at least, enabling you thus to have a free run for your
stock for miles without being encroached on; it being a good
maxim to consider near neighbours as bad neighbours, in first

settling," wrote P. Cunningham, a surgeon in the Royal Navy who had spent two years in the colony.

A horse, slung with canvas bags for changes of clothes etc., slung over behind the saddle with a blanket under to wrap yourself up in at night, and a light cord round the horse's neck to tether him by, furnish your personal equipment while on this quest; and if pushing into a country at a distance from settlers, a pack-horse with provisions ought to accompany you. A steady white man who is a good bush-ranger, and a black native, complete your train. The note of the bell-bird, tinkling like a dull sheep-bell announces in our drouthy wilds the welcome presence of water (a very useful thing to know); and toward this sound you may confidently proceed.

The settlers are generally hospitably disposed, and in these jaunts you are always welcome to such fare and such accommodation as they have it in their power to give. A tinder-box, or powder flask, conjures up a fire when you bivouac in the forest, while a few slips of bark, peeled from a tree, shelter you from the cold and the wet; and with a good fire at your feet, and tin of hot tea before retiring to rest, you may sleep comfortably enough.

Those who wanted something more elaborate faced almost unsurmountable difficulties. Richard Howitt who with his brother Geoffrey bought a run of ninety-five acres offered at the Government sale in Melbourne on 10th June 1840 wanted to take it over at once:

Our weather-boarded cottage had been prepared by my nephew in Melbourne, ready for putting up on the farm, when we could get it conveyed there. To engage a drayman and dray for that purpose, we had canvassed the town and its suburbs for days and days in vain. At length, after a fortnight's incessant search, we found a person from the country willing to cart up the house, four miles, four loads of it, for six pounds. This he did with his dray and oxen in four days.

When we reached the location—and the roads are none of the best, to say nothing of the Merri Creek, the bed of a torrent, full of rough stones, then partially flooded—we found ourselves in a wild open country, our cottage to be the only one for miles. To get out house materials to their intended site, was a task of no small difficulty, the face of the land being covered with growing trees or with partly burnt timber, boughs, and with rank kangaroo grass. After many pauses, grave considerings, turnings and backings, with considerable skill and patience in the driver and aided by especially good fortune, load after load was conveyed to the spot safely. Only we had one accident on the way, and small accidents become great privations under some circumstances. What the sea, that remorseless element, had spared to us of glass and tea-things were, by one unfeeling jolt of the dray amongst the rocks, thrown, and the basket holding them, to the ground in pitiable ruin. The fragments lie to this day under a monstrous gum tree by the road-side.

Then came the work of developing the run. Although the bounds of the run might be unfenced, yet it was essential to have a stock-yard and protection for the homestead:

> Wet as the weather was [wrote Howitt] we commenced bringing down our fencing materials from the forest where they were being split ten miles further up the river. And through what kind of country we had to bring them! Along the sides of sloping hills, and through the marshes, and deep break-neck ravines. Our first attempt was unfortunate; something about the pole of the cart broke, and off the bullocks set in a gallop—crash went the wheels against a tree, and the cart was broken, the team all at liberty. The bullock driver declared it to be useless trying again, for not one of the four bullocks were leaders. Two more bullocks were bought after nearly a week's inquiry, and a dray was borrowed. Again and again, when the weather would permit us a load was got down. I walked up the ten miles and home again, that if any accident happened, I might be at hand to render any assistance. Day after day I went; for if I did not go I had no rest at home through apprehension. Sometimes at the gullies or ravines, we had to unload the cart for it to get over, and when over to reload it. On some occasions we had the bullocks down; and then there was great danger of their necks being broken.

One cannot help feeling, as one reads this heart-rending story that the Howitts were not the stuff of which successful settlers were made—indeed after five years they returned to the home country.

More practical was the advice given by Dr. James Bennett Clutterbuck who practised from 1840 onwards for nine years in the Melbourne area.

> The least expensive mode is generally adopted in the erection of a bush dwelling:—no otium cum dignitate obtains in such quarters.

The exterior of the building is usually composed of large slabs of wood; the floor is made of mud, or boards of such inequalities of surface as would render any attempt to "trip it lightly on fantastic toe" a rueful and hazardous affair. The dwelling of the squatter is in most instances infested day and night by mosquitoes. The only effectual mode of even temporarily getting rid of these unpleasant intruders is subjecting them to the effluvia of ignited animal manure, which effectually answer the desired end of causing their speedy retreat. The bushman has become so accustomed to this mode of dealing with these, his numerous companions, and so habituated to the fumes arising from this altar of incense, that he and his family appear to be insensible to disagreeables of this kind.

The construction of an Australian hut is a fertile means, amongst others, of prolonging the state of bachelorship; few young men having the courage to lead an accomplished young lady from the hymeneal porch to within the precincts of a villa of so truly rustic a character.

This kind of hut would have a roof of bark weighted with heavy logs and tied down with ropes and hide (nails were useless as the bark shrank too much), holes for windows, with bark for shutters, a log for a chair and a tallow candle to read by in the evenings. Others, made of turf, were still more primitive and to begin with many squatters slept under their drays.

The choice of food was equally limited. It is true that in stations that were already well established a host might offer his guests luxuries such as jugs of cream, fresh butter, juicy melons, and game at table together with log fires, linen sheets and the rest. Elsewhere the traveller would more probably encounter boiled mutton or cold corned beef enlivened at times with a species of chutney formed by mixing jam and Worcester sauce or its equivalent. Tea, in which large quantities of dark brown sugar had been dissolved, was served scalding hot and usually without milk, though occasionally some would be provided by a ewe who had lost her lamb.

Then there was "damper". The best damper was made from a mixture of flour and water, seasoned with a little salt, kneaded to a flat round cake about three inches thick and cooked on the ashes of a fire. In extreme cases stale damper, soaked in strong tea, and sprinkled with sugar, was accepted as "pudding".

An existence anything like that of England was not to be

thought of away from cities or stations that were already prospering.

Sleep came quickly in the evenings, and those who were not playing cards, whittling wood or plaiting a new whip fell asleep over a book.

A visit to town might take a full month and many squatters had to content themselves with one trip only each year. Life in the cities was expensive, though the contrast between town and country was less extreme than it is today. For example the tracks leading to Sydney were still so bad in 1840 that carts found difficulty in reaching the centre of the city. In Melbourne you needed a horse to jump the gutters and at least one coach was wrecked when its wheels were smashed by a tree stump embedded in one of the main streets.

Naturally those who concentrated on their sheep rather than on themselves did best. They were able to occupy larger runs before coming up against the livestock of their neighbour, and the increase in the size of their flocks provided the largest slice of their profits.

But success was not automatic. It was easy to be swindled by ex-convicts and hard not to lose sheep through scab, drought, flood or bush fire or from attacks by the black man or by dingoes, and many were ruined by a fall in wool prices.

Capital was needed, for it might take a score of men, two or three bullock teams and a dozen saddle horses to manage a large flock of sheep in pioneer country.

Skilled labour was scarce. It was difficult to secure the shepherds who were so vital for watching the folds at night.

Of course there was a great deal more to sheep farming than sleeping in the watch-hut to protect the sheep from dingoes and the spears of the natives, and seeing that the hurdles did not blow down. They needed special attention at lambing and for some time before that. Animals had to be "dressed" for scab, as well as washed and sheared. The wool had to be carted away and stores brought up. In addition, the run and its water supplies had to be maintained.

Travel was still an adventure, for although there were tracks from each station leading towards the nearest town, there might be none between one station and another. Few landmarks were to be seen in that landscape of mauves, olives and ochres and the sun was often too high to steer by. Even when using a compass, it was difficult to hold a straight course across river, forest and mountain or to be sure whether you had reached or over-reached your destination. Hoof-marks were often the only sign-posts.

In 1837 Horton James wrote:

Another day of solitary travelling twenty-five miles to Kiamba; passed a deserted station on the road, that any person, one would think, might have been contented with. Not a man, beast, nor habitation of any kind, was seen all day, nor anything of man's handy work. All day was one glare of heat, and the water holes near Manton's station, were so thick and muddy, that the horse would hardly taste. But a little before sunset and going down the pass to Kiamba, some cool drops of rain began to fall, the mountains echoed again to the rebounding thunder, and the storm concluded in torrents of big rain. Wet to the skin, and knowing that I had run out, by the time of day, my twenty-five miles, I was on the lookout for wheel tracks, in order to find the hut before dark. This is rather a severe job to a perfect stranger, with no other direction than this: "after you have rode twenty-five miles, you will see some marks of a dray's wheels; then turn off to the right and in about two miles, off the road, you will find Smith's bark hut in the bush." A small hut is not easy to find in an immense forest just at the close of evening, nor is it easy to know when we have gone exactly twenty-five miles, where there are neither huts nor inhabitants for the whole day's journey. But habit and observation make everything easy, if you add self-possession, for without this essential ingredient, young practi-tioners in the bush could often lose themselves, and perhaps their lives also. In these wild solitudes of New South Wales, a country which produces nothing of itself calculated in the smallest degree to support the life of man, the idea will intrude occasionally on the lone traveller, of his utter loneliness and helplessness—and how little he can perform in case of accident and how little he can endure.

The cautious man moving alone through hostile country would cook his meal shortly before dark, then stamp out his fire and leave the track for a secluded spot on which to bed down. Then the horse bell would be muffled and the traveller would rig up a primitive tent of cheese cloth so that no attacker could be sure whether his intended victim was asleep or wide awake and ready to fire.

But travel in Australia could be fun too:

On I went [wrote Richard Howitt nearly ten years later], and without any concern saw the sun gradually go down, the dark to gather round me, miles from any habitation, and the moon and stars grown bolder and brighter. Pleased I was when I saw not far from the road the old cold ashes, and I soon warmed them with a new fire.

I set up the cast-down poles—one end in a forked tree—the other resting on the ground. These I thatched over with the ready-cut branches of the wild cherry-tree; and had soon a very snug house. My bed I next made of branches of a shrub, very myrtle-like, and of heath. Then, with the fire blazing brightly at my feet, with the carpet bag for a pillow, wrapped warmly in my blanket, the laughing jackass merrily bade me good night and I slept soundly at intervals—waked sometimes by the melancholy howl of a wild dog, or a rustle amongst the leaves of my house of perhaps a snake or a kangaroo rat—to hear a little way from me in the trees—plop-plop— the noise of the flying squirrel going from bough to bough; and the sharp gutteral noises of opossums. Then what a hush amidst a gently breeziness would come over the wilderness? Soft as feathers was the dray and balmy atmosphere—the moon hanging how amazingly near me, like a large pearl, and the stars as near like intense fiery rubies!

And for the young at heart Australia was heaven. In *Old Melbourne Memories* Ralph Boldrewood wrote:

At sunrise I awoke much fresher than paint and walking to the door of the tent . . . looked out upon the glorious far-stretching wild. What a sight was there, seen with the eyes of unworn, undoubting youth! On three sides lay the plains, a dimly verdurous expanse, over which a night mist was lifting itself along the line of the river. The outline of the Anakie-You Yangs range was sharply drawn against the dawn-lighted horizon, while far to the north-east was seen the forest-clothed summit of Mount Macedon, and westward gleamed the sea. The calm water of Corio Bay and the abrupt cone of Station Peak, nearly in the line of our route, formed an unmistakable yet picturesque landmark.

The cattle, peacefully grazing, were spread over the plain, having been released from camp. The horses were being brought in; amongst them I was quick to distinguish my valuable pair; Old

Watts, the campkeeper, a hoary retainer of Yering—who gave his name to the affluent of the Yarra so called—was cooking steaks for breakfast. Everything was delightfully new, strangely exhilarating, with a fresh flavour of freedom and adventure.

After breakfast, we saddled up and, mounting our horses, strolled on after a leisurely fashion with the cattle. I was riding, as became an Australian, a four-year-old colt, my own property, and bred in the family. A grandson of Skeleton and Satellite, he was moderately fast and a great stayer. Mr. Donald Ryrie rode a favourite galloway yclept Dumple—a choice roadster and clever stock-horse, much resembling in outline Dandie Dinmont's historic "powney". He and I were sufficiently near in age to enjoy discursive conversation during the long, slightly tedious, driving hours, to an extent which occasionally impaired our usefulness. When, in argument or narrative, we permitted "the tail" to straggle unreasonably we were sharply recalled to our duty. Our kind-hearted choleric leader then adopted language akin to that in which the ruffled M.F.H. exhorts the erring horsemen of his field.

Ah me, what pleasant days were those! A little warm, even hot, doubtless. But we could take off our coats without fear of Mrs. Grundy. There was plenty of grass. "Travelling" was an honourable and recognized occupation in those Arcadian times. "Purchased land" was an unknown quantity. Droughts were disbelieved in, and popularly supposed to belong exclusively to the "Sydney Side". The horses were fresh, the stages were moderate, and when a halt was called at sundown, the cattle soon lay contentedly down in the soft, thick grass. The camp fires were lighted, and another pleasant, hopeful day was succeeded by a restful yet romantic night.

Alone it was even more fun:

A few more days' easy travelling took us nearly to our journey's end. We reached the bank of the Merai, at Grasmere, the head station of the Messrs. Bolden, and there not many miles from the site of the flourishing township of Warrnambool, we drafted our respective cattle, and went different ways—Mr. Ryrie's to his run, not far from Tower Hill, and mine to appropriate some unused country between the Merai and the sea.

Here I camped for about six months, and a right joyous time it was in that "kingdom by the sea". I remember riding down to the shore one bright day, just below where Warrnambool now stands. No trace of man or habitation was there, "nor roof nor latched door". As I rode over the sand hummock which borders the beach, a draft of outlying cattle, basking in the sun on the farther side, rose and galloped off. All else was silent and tenantless as before the days of Cook.

I took up my abode provisionally upon the bank of the Meria, which, near the mouth, was a broad and imposing stream, and turned out my herd. My stockman and I spent our days in "going round" the cattle; shooting and kangaroo-hunting in odd times—recreation to which he, as an ex-poacher of considerable experience, took very kindly. The pied goose, here in large flocks, with duck, teal, pigeons, and an occasional wild turkey, were our chief sport and sustenance. Old Tom looked after the cattle; they needed all his attention for a while, displaying, as they did, a strong desire to march incontinently back to the banks of the Merai.

In two or three weeks the hut was up. How I admired it! The door, the table, the bedsteads, the chairs (three-legged stools), the washstand, were all manufactured by Joe Burge, out of the all sufficing "slab" of the period. A wooden chimney with an inner coating of stone-work worked well without smoking. The roof was neatly thatched with the tall, strong tussock-grass, then so abundant.

We ought to have made the most of those days—of the time which came "before the gold". We never saw their like again. Then we tasted true happiness, if such ever visits this lower world. Everyone had hope, encouragement, adequate stimulus to work—hard work which was well paid, leading to enterprise, which year by year fulfilled the promise of progress.

Nobody was too rich, no one was wealthy enough to live in Melbourne. Each man had to be his own overseer, had to live at home. He was therefore, friendly and genial with his neighbours, on whom he was socially dependent. No one thought of going to Europe, or selling off and "cutting the confounded colony" and so on. No! there we were "adscripti glebae" as we thought from a dozen or so to a score of years. It was necessary for all to make the best of it, and very cheery and contented nearly everybody was.

Yes, paradoxically the golden age in Australia may indeed have dawned before the discovery of gold and may have ended at this very point in our story.

8

Golden Dawn

In April 1851 Edward Hargraves, an Australian prospector, rode into Sydney with samples of gold taken from a pool to the north-west of Bathurst. Within a month four hundred others like him were madly washing panfuls of New South Wales earth near the rocks of Summer Hill Creek, the site of the Ophir mine. An historic "rush" had begun.

This was not the first time that the Colony had yielded nuggets. James McBrien, the Government surveyor, had found gold in the Fish River near Bathurst in 1823. Count Strzelecki, the explorer, had found traces of gold in 1839 at Hartley, in the Blue Mountains, and so had the Rev. W. B. Clarke at Bathurst, two years later. But the authorities feared that the convicts would stage an uprising if the news leaked out. "Put it away, Mr. Clarke," cried Governor Gipps, as the Reverend produced a glittering sample of his discovery. "Put it away, or we shall have our throats cut." The Governor's secret was fairly safe so long as only a few enlightened men, relative amateurs as far as mining was concerned, knew of it.

But the authorities were forced into action by the California gold rush of 1849. For groups of enterprising Australians had already set off across the Pacific to make their fortunes in the United States, and there was little doubt that in due course they would return to Australia knowing where to look for gold and

how to mine it. The Governor, therefore, decided to take the
revolutionary step of engaging a Government geologist.

Certainly when Hargraves, who had once fished for bêche-de-
mer off the north coast of Australia, returned to Sydney in
January 1851 after a trip to California, he knew exactly where
to look and what to do. Early in February he rode across the
Blue Mountains to Bathurst and on to Guyong. When he left
the inn, he took with him as guide John Lister, the eighteen-
year-old son of the licensee, and made for the wilderness to the
north-west in search of creeks and ponds in which the barriers
of rock over which the waters flowed could be expected to have
held back the heavy particles of gold. Almost at once Hargraves
found what he was looking for at the junction of Summerhill
Creek and Frederick's valley. Taking a shovelful of earth he
swilled it round in a pan, adding water until all the "mud" had
vanished and only the slate, rock and heavier particles remained.
Sure enough there at the bottom of the dish was a small nugget
of gold. Hargraves washed five more panfuls and all but one of
them glittered. "My boy," he cried, turning to Lister, "this
means that I shall be a Baronet, you will be knighted, and my
old horse will be stuffed, put in a glass case and sent to the
British Museum."

Another young prospector, James Tom, now joined the party
and the three explorers made surveys over an area stretching
for nearly three thousand square miles. Again and again they
found samples that "coloured". The problem was how best to
exploit their finds. Naturally the gold belonged to the Crown
but Hargraves at first thought that it would be not too difficult
to strike a bargain with officialdom, by which he should receive a
reward in return for his disclosing where the gold was to be
found. But the authorities for once knew a good thing when they
saw it, and Hargraves was told that he must not hold them to
ransom but tell all and rely on their good nature to reward him
adequately. To this after some weeks' haggling he finally agreed.
In May the Government geologist confirmed his discoveries and
if Hargraves did not become a baronet, he was rewarded with
£10,000 and an appointment as a Land Commissioner.

Soon the creeks all over the Blue Mountains were being prospected. Gold fever began to spread throughout Australia when

it was learned that Dr. Kerr's aboriginal shepherd had picked up a nugget weighing 106 lb. Men hurried away from the newly established colony of Victoria in order to return to New South Wales, and Melbourne was in danger, in the very year that it had gained independence from Sydney, of becoming a ghost city. Its citizens offered a reward of £200 to anyone finding gold on the Victoria side of the border. The money was claimed almost at once by a prospector who found gold only sixteen miles outside Melbourne at Anderson's Creek. Other finds were made at Clunes, Buninyong, Ballarat, Mount Alexander and on an almost inexhaustible field at Bendigo.

And now Victoria's gold rush soon became even more desperate than the earlier mad gallop to New South Wales. It was more disruptive too because Victoria had a smaller population than New South Wales and therefore fewer labourers to spare for prospecting. There were more than a hundred gullies and lakes to be examined within a few miles of Bendigo alone and everyone wanted to be there. Farmers sold up and left; traders shut shop and made for the hills; there was no one to shear the sheep; army officers, clergymen and even the police joined in the hunt. For who would not give up their ordinary job for the chance of earning £30 a day?

The more knowledgeable set out in a cart with their possessions including clothes, stores, blankets and a tent secured safely under a tarpaulin. But there were others who left the shelter of the city without knowing how to make themselves at home in the bush. They had no horse and found their swag (the bushman's portmanteau cum bed-roll in which their possessions were wrapped) too heavy. They brought no canvas tent with them, and were incapable of lighting a fire in the open or of knocking together a hut. They were soon on the sick list.

The Government, when informed of a new gold strike, were prepared to provide a Gold Commissioner a "gold tent" where treasure could be deposited under armed guard, and a magistrate to settle disputed claims. But it might be some time before a policeman appeared on the scheme or for that matter a blacksmith or a priest.

Typhoid often arrived ahead of the doctor.

The very lives of the diggers were none too secure during the earlier and more profitable years of gold mining. Some of the most vicious ex-convicts sailed across from Tasmania to join in the fun. Bushranging became so profitable that those engaged in it could afford to stay in comfort at an inn without pitching their tents before stealing the diggers' horses.

The going was tough. The prospectors concentrated on first the rivers and creeks for gold that had accumulated there, and this was all very well as long as the water held out. But in the dry season the "washing stuff" had to be loaded into a bucket and carted to the nearest creek at a charge of perhaps a shilling for every bucket. Eventually there might be as many as 20,000 people working on a single field, each with a minute claim measuring 10 feet square.

The hours were long and anyone with hopes of success was wise to begin work at the crack of dawn so that he would be in time to deposit his treasure safely in the gold tent before dark. And those who failed to work their claim for a single day through ill-health or shortage of water stood the risk of having it snatched away—quite legally—from them by someone else prepared to take over.

Later the gold reefs had to be sought below ground, perhaps at a depth of 150 or 250 feet, with water to be pumped out before the "mine" could be worked.

But the cost of living on the gold fields rose to spectacular heights. A freight of £120 per ton was charged on goods brought from Melbourne to Bendigo. Water was six shillings for a small barrel. Fruit and vegetables were almost unobtainable, and those who had horses had to walk them for miles after work to find pasture.

But men of all nations caught the gold fever. There were Poles, Swedes and Danes as well as Americans, French, Germans and New Zealanders. There were also Cornishmen who already lived in Australia or who had come specially from the mother country, to find in the deeper shafts something that reminded them of the tin mines they had left at home. And of course there were the Chinese, wearing, as ever, their blue padded jerkins, short wide trousers and cone-shaped hats, forming, as Dickens wrote in *Household Words* "long lines of those gentry marching to the gold fields—always in Indian file and each with his bamboo pole and evenly balanced panniers—the very men who, painted upon plates, had lurked under meat and lain in soup for generations".

On sites where every tree for miles had been levelled and the ground covered with yellow mullock (rejected soil, etc.) the Chinese would move in to work claims that had already been abandoned, examining even the tailings left by previous workings. They knew how to live on almost nothing.

Fortunes were certainly made. During the fifties, Australia produced four-tenths—nearly half—of the world's gold supplies. Bank deposits there multiplied nearly tenfold during the first two and a half years of the gold rush. Victoria's population increased from 77,000 in 1851 to more than seven times that figure in 1861. But although the number of diggers mounted steadily from 1852 the yield of gold began to decrease equally steadily from then onwards.

One reason was that once the "easy" gold had been taken, it became more and more necessary to provide machinery not only to pump the water out of the shafts but also to bring the ore to the surface for crushing so that the gold could be extracted.

Few of the diggers, even those who formed syndicates, had this kind of money, and the British capitalists were too preoccupied at the time with the Crimean war to think of extending Australia's railways as far as the goldfields.

Consequently the yield of gold per digger started to drop almost from the beginning. Naturally stories of good luck got the most publicity, and every time that someone wearing the typical digger's costume of a dark blue jersey, moleskin trousers, a fossicking (prospector's) knife and a cabbage-tree hat appeared in Melbourne, the word went round that another millionaire had come to town. Occasionally it was true, as when the artists of the Queen's Theatre, Melbourne were pelted during their act with gold nuggets.

But more often the money which the digger eventually received from the gold broker had already been spent in advance either on living in great discomfort at enormous cost or at some bush pub on the way to town.

And a cold dispassionate calculation made by dividing the estimated number of people on the gold fields into the value of the gold shipped, shows that in a good year, 1853, the average sum earned by each digger amounted to £3 6s. per week. Out of this had to come his own living expenses as well as the costs of mining and transporting the gold, and the fee charged by the gold broker in Melbourne.

It was against this background that the Australian digger, an independent cuss at the best of times, developed a strong spirit of resistance to the hand of authority. Not unnaturally the Authorities looked to the gold fields as a new source of revenue. If it had been otherwise they would hardly have rewarded Hargraves for his discovery and they soon came forward with regulations designed to protect the rights of the Crown as well as those of the miner, and to provide money for the extra policing and other services required for these remote areas.

The fee which the officials decided to charge for a licence was thirty shillings a month, to be paid by each and every miner whether his claim was producing or not. This added greatly to the expense of bringing in those mines where deep shafts had first to be sunk. The tax was bitterly resented by the diggers, who believed that the Government was trying to force them to leave the mines. The squatter, they noted, was charged nothing for developing *his* territory.

But the method of collecting the gold licence rankled even more than the hardship of paying it. In order to get his licence— or to renew it—the digger might have to walk several miles to the office of the nearest magistrate, a journey involving the loss of the best part of a day's work. Moreover the licensing system was enforced by raids at irregular intervals and the digger who did not have a licence, or who was not carrying it on him at the time, was forcibly marched then and there to the Gold Commissioner's office to make amends.

The miners were also angry about the difficulty which they found in getting permission to put up houses and other permanent buildings from the authorities, who no doubt considered that any such applications were just cover for an excessive mining claim.

Nor were the diggers able to air their grievances since they were not qualified to vote in the elections for the Victoria Legislative Council.

Feelings were especially strong against the local magistrate in Ballarat, following the murder there on the night of 6th October 1854 of James Scobie, a digger. His body was found near a drinking shanty patronized by diggers working the Eureka lead nearby and known in consequence as the Eureka Hotel. This establishment was kept by an ex-convict from Tasmania, James Bentley, whom the miners believed to be the guilty man. Bentley was tried and acquitted. But the verdict met with the disapproval of the miners who knew that Bentley was a friend of John D'Ewes, the Chairman of the Magistrate's Bench. The diggers held a public protest meeting attended by a mob of nearly ten thousand. Police endeavouring to keep order were overpowered. The "hotel" was rushed and burnt to the ground, and the crowd threatened to attack the Government's offices where Bentley was believed to have sought refuge.

Sir Charles Hotham, the recently appointed Governor of Victoria, took action. He marched up a posse of soldiers and arrested four of the ring-leaders of the riot. He also arranged for Bentley to be arrested and retried. But even Bentley's conviction which followed was not enough to restore peace. For the arrested ring-leaders were tried too and sentenced with a great deal of moralizing on the miner's riot by the judge.

On 11th November the Ballarat Reform League was founded to redress the miners' grievances. It was led by Peter Lalor, the son of a British Member of Parliament, a university graduate and civil engineer, who had formerly worked on the Melbourne to Geelong Railway.

On November 27th the League sent a deputation to Melbourne to the Governor over the heads of the magistrates and the local Gold Commissioner to ask for the release of the rioters. Hotham firmly rejected the appeal, and, two days later, the League held another protest meeting on Bakery Hill at which its leaders defied authorities by burning their miner's licences. They warned the other diggers that unless they joined within a fortnight, the League could not be responsible for their protection.

The Commissioner's reply was to send out the police the very next day to search for unlicensed miners. The "traps" as they were called, were met with showers of stones, and called in the military. There were casualties on both sides. The gloves were off. On 30th November members of the League swore oaths pledging themselves to defend their rights. Among them were a number of Americans from the goldfields of California.

The diggers next erected a stockade enclosing an area of nearly an acre. A German blacksmith fashioned pike-heads out of horse-shoes. Irishmen and Italians were to the fore as well. But with no political or military training and no maquis to fall back upon there could be no victory. Early on the morning of 3rd December when part of the garrison had left the stockade to look for stores and provisions, a mixed force of Government infantry, cavalry and mounted police staged a surprise attack, and after twenty-five minutes the revolutionary flag of the Republic of Victoria—a blue flag bearing the stars of the Southern Cross—was hauled down in token of surrender. Six of the Government forces were killed and nearly four times as many diggers. Peter Lalor, wounded in the arm, which he afterwards lost, was left unconscious in a shaft and had to be rescued later by friends and kept in hiding in the house of a Catholic priest, Father Smyth. A reward of £200, offered for his capture, was never claimed. Thirteen of the leaders were brought to trial accused of High Treason and were monotonously acquitted. But the authorities did score one triumph. Henry Seekamp, the editor of the *Ballarat Times*, was convicted of uttering a seditious libel and sentenced to six months imprisonment.

Karl Marx believed that the movement leading to the battle of Eureka Stockade was the "concrete manifestation of the general revolutionary movement in Victoria".

But closer examination suggests that the Victorian revolution was closer in style to that of the thirteen colonies, being a rising of small capitalists against meddlesome and maladroit administrators. In Victoria, however, the administration showed some adaptability. The miners were given the vote and their licence fee was reduced to £1 a year. The revenue was recovered by means of a tax on the value of gold exported. Lalor himself was finally pardoned and elected a year later to the Victoria Legislative Council as Member for Ballarat. Eventually he became the respected Speaker of the Legislative Assembly. Justice had been done.

But Australia could never be the same as in the days before gold was discovered. Within ten years she had exported metal worth £124 million and was able to finance her own industrial revolution with the proceeds.

During the same ten years the total population of the colony had trebled, and there were more people in Victoria alone than there had been in the whole of Australia in 1850. This statistically was the period when the convict strain in Australia was washed away decisively in a big flood of immigration.

White Australia, the policy of not admitting non-white immigrants, save in exceptional cases, was born at the same time, with the Chinese as the guinea-pig.

There were twenty-five thousand Chinese in 1857 (despite the fact that they had to pay a £10 poll tax) and that was quite enough. Already Australia preferred the Americans, whose light-weight carriages did so much better on the rough roads and whose light-weight tents were so much easier to manage than the old-fashioned English canvas models. There were nearly three thousand Americans in the colony at this time of whom nearly two-thirds were up in the gold fields.

But the immigrants, of whatever nation, were of a different type from those that had come to Australia "before the gold". The new men were non-agricultural and of a mechanical turn of mind. They were the future populators of Australia's cities and were prepared, nay determined to work there. They came from countries which had already begun to experience the industrial revolution and they imported it into their new home.

The Peninsular and Oriental Steamship Company had launched a regular fast service from England to Australia in 1852 and a year later the first telegraph was set up in Victoria. It was only a question of time before the railway system linked cities and even states, replacing the bullock-dray freight service which was tied to a speed limit of twelve miles a day. In areas where there was no railway the famous coaches of Cobb and Co. fetched and delivered. This service, which prospered right up to 1924, was founded in 1853 by an American, Freeman Cobb, and three other American partners. They arrived in Australia with a replica of a Wells Fargo coach and some Wells Fargo drivers. Cobb himself was bought out towards the end of the fifties and returned to the United States to become a Senator for Massachusetts. Three years later the firm transferred its headquarters from Bendigo to Bathurst, where that very same year one of their coaches, drawn by twelve greys, conveyed the English cricket team on its first Australian tour.

At the same time the revenue from gold made it possible for the public authorities to enlarge and improve the services which they offered. The police force was enlarged, the roads widened and inns that had offered accommodation only because it was one of the conditions of their drinking licence, made an effort to attract guests. Schools were improved and, with the opening of Sydney University in 1852 and of Melbourne two years later, the monopoly that England had once possessed in higher education was broken for good.

But perhaps the most significant changes brought about by the discovery of gold were political ones. The new immigrants with their mechanical skills stepped in to fill the gap between the big squatters and the agricultural labourers. They might, in a country such as Britain, with rigid social institutions, have headed a revolution. Australia, however, was several moves nearer to democracy. The landed gentry of Australia were not in the same unassailable position which the squires and other landowners enjoyed in Britain. For until shortly before the gold rush their tenure was uncertain and their livelihood, even afterwards, remained subject to interference from drought, flood and pestilence. In Australia there were no limits to reward which could be earned by effort. There was room for all to strike out for themselves. Moreover, once transportation had ceased (except in Western Australia) there was a shortage of labour. The artisan could normally demand reasonable working conditions without the need for the uprising Karl Marx might have expected. Moreover the changes that gold had brought proved to the authorities that society was not immutable and they in turn recognized that it might not be profitable to keep it so.

It was in these conditions that Australian democracy began.

The Home Government had realized as far back as 1840 that, once transportation had been abolished, it would be wise to grant representative government to the colonists. The British experience in America had been a clear warning of the kind of thing that happened when such precautions were neglected. At that time there was only New South Wales to worry about, for the other states had not yet achieved an independent existence.

Whitehall's first idea was to set up a Legislative Council, part elected and part nominated, by whom the laws of the colony should in future be fashioned. The Act was approved in London in 1842 and proclaimed in Australia the following year.

But it failed to satisfy the colonists. They found, for one thing, that they controlled only part of the revenue raised by taxation. An enormous sum, by their standards, had to be reserved for use by the Governor at his discretion largely for the upkeep of convict establishments set up under previous Governors.

The new Australian law-makers failed to see why they should be saddled with burdens incurred before they came to power. This arrangement also made it impossible for the legislators to bring pressure on the Governor by refusing to pass the finance bill. They were also disturbed to find in practice that, although they might make the laws, the Governor was still responsible for seeing that they were carried out and the legislators had no control either over appointments or the methods of enforcement. And even in law-making they were not really independent of the Governor, who could, for instance, withhold his consent to laws that they had passed.

But things could not stand still for long. Other colonies, Canada in particular, were moving on to new, more advanced systems of government.

In 1850 Whitehall acted. It promoted a Bill giving a new and important power to the Councils that already existed, namely that of framing their own constitutions.

The legislators of New South Wales were not slow to take advantage of the offer. They appointed Wentworth, the very same man who had pioneered the road across the Blue Mountains, as Chairman of a Select Committee formed to handle the matter of the new Constitution. Wentworth had been working out a new Constitution for New South Wales. He prized independence for its own sake but he dearly loved stability and believed that Australia should in many ways be modelled on the

England he himself knew. And the fact that he was both a traditionalist and a rebel made it possible for him to be the link between two groups of men who wanted the same thing—the squatters who wished to be free of the home government in order to profit from their land and the townsmen who had emigrated from Britain to avoid the kind of oppression they had suffered at home. In Wentworth's Constitution legislators of New South Wales were given power to control the money bags and even the Civil List of Crown expenditure. When Governor Fitzroy heard about this he panicked. He insisted that Wentworth's plans should be approved by the British Parliament, as well as locally. But Westminster raised no objection and the way was clear, not only for New South Wales, but for the other states in Australia to fashion their own constitutions.

In the end they were all much alike. Each State provided itself with an Upper and Lower House. In New South Wales the Upper House was nominated by the Governor and his Ministers for a five-year period (for Wentworth had a special respect for the kind of people who, in the House of Lords, helped to rule Britain not because they were elected but because being largely landowners they had the greatest stake in the country). In Victoria, South Australia and Tasmania both the Upper and the Lower Houses were elected.

The Members of both Houses had to satisfy a fairly stiff property qualification and, as they got no pay, only those with private means could afford to stand for election.

But you did not need to be a landowner to vote. In New South Wales anyone who earned £100 a year or more qualified. So did anyone who paid as much as £10 a year in rent (or £40 for their full board).

South Australia went further and gave the vote to anyone who had lived in the colony for six months.

The Act of 1850 made one other innovation. It enacted that, in view of the growth of population in and around Moreton Bay (to the north of New South Wales) any region of latitude 30° could be formed into a separate colony. Although this area had been opened to free settlers since 1842, it was more remote than Victoria and therefore less attractive and, in the early days had no gold to offer its settlers. Nevertheless by 1851 the population had climbed to 9,000, more than half of whom were free immigrants, and talk of separation began to be heard in Sydney.

There was opposition at first from the legislators of New South Wales, who feared that the big estate owners of the north wanted the Government to reintroduce convict labour to help them develop their land.

But Whitehall was able to reassure them on this point. And it also moved the proposed border further north so that the settlers on the Dumaresq and Clarence Rivers, which naturally communicate with the south, would remain linked with Sydney, while those on the Darling Downs would depend on Brisbane.

And so in 1859 a new State, Queensland appeared, the last but one to be born on the sub-continent.

9

Linking-up Time

In the 1860s, while Garibaldi was uniting Italy and Lincoln the
United States, Australia, too, was coalescing. Her settlers, still
clinging mostly to the fringes of the Continent, in pockets set
apart from each other, began to grope their way toward closer
acquaintanceship.

Count Paul Edmund de Strzelecki, the Polish explorer, had
helped to fill in that south-east corner of Australia known as
Gippsland in the 1840s, and, about the same time, John Eyre,
the son of a Yorkshire vicar, pushed northwards from Adelaide
up to the swampy territory south of Lake Eyre, in the hope of
reaching the centre of the Continent. Foiled there, he swung
south-west and struck along the south coast of Australia, across
1,500 miles of desert, to Albany, the main port on the south
coast of Western Australia. Governor Gawler of South Australia
had agreed to provide Eyre with an escort ship as far as Fowler
Bay, about 300 miles west of Adelaide, but no further, and so
the expedition had to be limited to five people—Eyre himself,
Baxter (a white overseer) and three aborigines. Most of the
food was eaten before the party had got half way and often their
only drink consisted of drops of dew collected by Eyre with a
sponge. As food ran short two of the natives shot Baxter and
ran off with as much as they could carry. Eyre and the third
native were left on their own. They were saved only by the

greatest good luck when they came upon a French whaler anchored in a remote bay and were given enough food and drink to finish the journey.

Their experience served as a warning not to follow the south coast but it encouraged other explorers, including Charles Sturt, to probe elsewhere. Sturt was still trying, about ten million years too late, to find the vast central sea lying in the centre of Australia to which he believed migrating birds would eventually lead him.

So in 1844 he started northwards along the western border of New South Wales and got to within one hundred and fifty miles of the centre of Australia through heat that shrivelled and scorched. That summer was so dry that the expedition was marooned for five months in a single creek which they did not dare to leave. "From the effects of the sun every screw in our boxes had been drawn, and the horn handles of our instruments as well as our combs were split into fine laminae," Sturt wrote. "The lead dropped out of our pencils, our hair, as well as the wool on the sheep, ceased to grow, and our nails became brittle as glass. . . . The bran in which our bacon had been packed was perfectly saturated, and weighed almost as heavy as the meat. We were even obliged to bury our wax candles; a bottle of citric acid in Mr. Browne's box became fluid, and escaping, burnt a quantity of his linen; and we found it difficult to write or draw, so rapidly did the fluid dry in our pens and brushes."

Then, on the way back, they were caught, while stopping in a creek, by the desert wind.

I sought shelter behind a large gum tree [Sturt wrote] but the blasts of heat were so terrific, that I wondered the very grass did not take fire. This really was nothing imaginary; everything, both animate and inanimate gave way before it; the horses stood with their backs to the wind, and their noses to the ground, without the muscular strength to raise their heads. The birds were mute, and the leaves of the tree, under which we were sitting fell like a snow shower around us. At noon I took a thermometer—graduated to 127 degrees—out of my box, and observed that the mercury was up to 125 degrees. Thinking that it had been unduly influenced, I put it in the fork of a tree close to me, sheltered alike from the wind and the sun. In this position I went to examine it about an hour

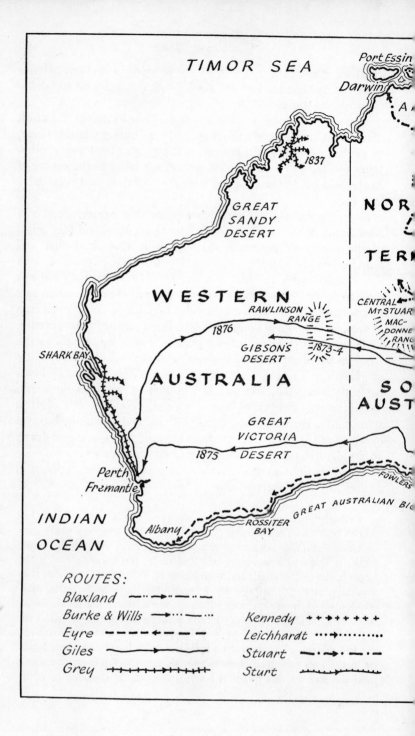

TIMOR SEA

Port Essin

Darwin

A

NOR

TER

GREAT
SANDY
DESERT

CENTRAL
Mt STUAR

WESTERN

RAWLINSON
RANGE

1876

GIBSON'S
DESERT

1873-4

MAC-
DONNE
RANGE

SHARKBAY

AUSTRALIA

S O
AUST

GREAT
VICTORIA
DESERT

1875

Perth
Fremantle

FOWLERS

INDIAN

OCEAN

Albany

ROSSITER
BAY

GREAT AUSTRALIAN BIG

ROUTES:
Blaxland   — · — · →
Burke & Wills   → · — · — ···
Eyre   — — ← — —
Giles   ————→
Grey   +++++++++

Kennedy   + + + + + + +
Leichhardt   ···→·············
Stuart   — · → · — · —
Sturt   ↝↝↝↝→↝↝↝↝

Cape York

SHELBURNE BAY

WEYMOUTH BAY

GULF OF
CARPENTARIA

CORAL
SEA

RN

ROCKINGHAM BAY

RY

prings

QUEENSLAND

1PSON
SERT

STURT
DESERT

L. EYRE

Depot

Creek

Cooper's

A

L.
TORRENS

M^T
HOPELESS

MORETON BAY
Brisbane

Darling R.

NEW SOUTH
WALES

Beltana

Menindee

BLUE
MTS

R GULF

Murrumbidgee R.

CENT GULF
LAKE A.

Sydney

delaide

Murray R.

Canberra

VIC TORIA

Melbourne

TASMAN SEA

0   250   500   750   1000

Miles

afterwards when I found that the mercury had risen to the top of the instrument and that its further expansion had burst the bulb, a circumstance that, I believe, no traveller has had to recount before.

Sturt's matches exploded when they touched the ground, his distress signal rockets too, and Punch, one of the horses, grew so thirsty that he tried to pull the bung out of the water cask with his teeth. Sturt of course never discovered that inland sea. But he did find and name something far more spectacular—the Desert Pea Plant, that waxy-looking scarlet flower with long cloak and black centre which never fails to startle those who see it for the first time.

Meanwhile, as Sturt probed the country from north to south, another explorer was hoping to travel across the centre of the continent from east to west.

Dr. Ludwig Leichhardt, who had run away from his native Brandenburg to avoid being conscripted into the Prussian army, and was educated in Paris, had made a name for himself in Sydney as a lecturer on botany, but he had explored parts of central Queensland, and the good people of eastern Australia, who did not want to be outdone by entrepreneurs from Adelaide were only too glad when he volunteered to head an east to west expedition across the continent. Leichhardt decided to travel light and for navigation he took with him only a sextant and artificial horizon, a chronometer, a hand-compass and Arrowsmith's "Map of the Continent of New Holland". His party consisted of only nine white men, an American negro and an Australian aborigine. The party left Brisbane at the end of September and set off across the Darling Downs, turning north-west to the Tropic of Capricorn and the Comet River, where they spent Christmas. Then they pressed on northwards, still relatively close to the coast. Half way up the Cape York peninsular Leichhardt struck west to the Gulf of Carpentaria and across Arnhem Land to Port Essington, the most northerly port then in use.

Leichhardt had no great talents as a writer, yet these words from his journal recall vividly how the explorers of Australia worked and played:

The routine of one of our days will serve as an example of all the rest. I usually rise when I hear the merry laugh of the laughing jackass—which, from its regularity has not been inaptly named the settler's clock; a loud cooee then rouses my companions; Brown to make the tea, Mr. Calvert to season the stew with salt and marjoram, and myself and the others to wash and to prepare our breakfast, which for the party consists of two pounds and a half of meat stewed overnight; and to each a quart pot of tea. Mr. Calvert then gives to each his portion, and by the time this important duty is performed, Charley generally arrives with the horses, which are then prepared for their day's duty. After breakfast Charley generally goes with John and Murphy to fetch the bullocks, which are generally brought in a little after seven o'clock a.m. The work of loading follows, but this requires very little time now, our stock being much reduced; and at about a quarter to eight o'clock, we move on, and continue travelling four hours, and, if possible, select a spot for our camp.

The camp fixed, and the horses and bullocks unloaded, we have all our allotted duties. To make the fire falls to my share; Brown's duty is to fetch water for tea; and Mr. Calvert weighs out a pound and a half of flour for a fat cake, which is enjoyed more than any other meal. The large tea-pot being empty, Mr. Calvert weighs out two pounds and a half of dry meat to be stewed for our late dinner; and during the afternoon every one follows his own pursuits, such as washing and mending clothes, repairing saddles, pack saddles and packs. My occupation is to write my log, and lay down my route, or make an excursion in the vicinity of the camp to botanize etc., or ride out reconnoitring. My companions also write down their remarks and wander about gathering seeds, or looking for curious pebbles.

Mr. Gilbert takes his gun to shoot birds. A loud cooee again unites us towards sunset round our table cloth; and while enjoying our meal, the subject of the day's journey, the past, the present and the future by turns engage our attention, and furnish matter for conversation and remark, according to the respective humour of the parties. Many circumstances have conspired to make me strangely taciturn, and I am now scarcely pleased even with the chattering humour of my youngest companion, whose spirits instead of flagging, have become more buoyant and lively than ever. I consider it, however, my invariable duty to give every information I can, whenever my companions inquire or show a desire to learn; and I am happy to find that they are desirous of making themselves familiar with the objects of nature by which they are surrounded and of understanding their mutual relations. Mr. Roper is of a

more silent disposition; Mr. Calvert likes to speak and has a good
stock of small talk, with which he often enlivens our dinners. He is
in that respect an excellent companion, being full of jokes and
stories, which, though old and sometimes quaint, are always pure,
and serve the more to exhilarate the party. Mr. Gilbert has
travelled much, and consequently has a rich store of *impressions de
voyage*, his conversation is generally very pleasing and instructive,
in describing the characters of countries he has known. He is well
informed in Australian ornithology. As night approaches, we
retire to our beds. The two blackfellows and myself spread out
each our own under the canopy of heaven, whilst Messrs. Roper,
Calvert, Gilbert, Murphy, and Phillips have their tents. Mr.
Calvert entertains Roper with his conversation; John amuses
Gilbert; Brown tunes up his corroborie songs, in which Charley,
until their late quarrel generally joined. Brown sings well, and his
melodious, plaintive voice, lulls me to sleep, when otherwise I am
not disposed. Mr. Phillips is rather singular in his habits, when he
erects his tent generally at a distance from the rest, under a shady
tree, or in a green bower of shrubs, where he makes himself as
comfortable as the place will allow, by spreading branches and
grass under his couch and covering his tent with them, to keep it
shady and cool, and even planting lilies in blossom—Crinum—
before his tent, to enjoy their sight during the short time of our
stay. As the night advances, the blackfellow's songs die away, the
chatting tongue of Murphy ceases, after having lulled Mr. Gilbert
to sleep, and at last even Mr. Calvert is silent, as Roper's short
answers become few and far between, the neighing of the tethered
horses, the distant tinkling of the bell, or the occasional cry of
night birds alone interrupt the silence of our camp. The fire which
was bright as long as the corrobories songster kept it stirred,
gradually gets dull and smoulders slowly under the large pot, in
which our meat is simmering; and the bright constellations of
heaven pass unheeded over the heads of the dreaming wanderers
of the wilderness, until the summons of the laughing jackass
recalls them to the business of the day.

During the leisure moments of the day, or at the recommence-
ment of night when seated by my fire, all my thoughts seemed
rivetted to the progress and success of my journey and to the new
objects we had met with during the day. I had then to compel
myself to think of absent friends and past times, and the thoughts
that they supposed me dead, or unsuccessful in my enterprise
brought me back immediately to my favourite object. Much, indeed,

the greater proportion of my journey had been occupied in long reconnoitring rides; and he who is thus occupied is in a continual state of excitement, now buoyant with hope, as he urges on his horse towards some distant range, or blue mountain, or as he follows the favourable bend of a river; now all despairing and miserable as he approaches the foot of the range without finding water from which he could again start with renewed strength; or, as the river turns in an unfavourable direction, and slips out of his course, evening approaches, the sun has sunk below the horizon for some time, but still he strains his eye through the gloom for the dark verdure of a creek or strives to follow the arrow flight of a pigeon, the flapping of whose wings had filled him with sudden hope, from which he relapses again into a still greater sadness; with a sickened heart he drops his head to a broken and interrupted rest whilst his horse is standing hobbled at his side, unwilling from excessive thirst to feed from the dry grass. How often have I found myself in these different states of the brightest hope and the deepest misery, riding along, thirsty, almost lifeless and ready to drop from my saddle with fatigue, the poor horse tired like his rider, footsore, stumbling over every stone, running heedlessly against the trees, and wounding my knees! But suddenly the note of Grallina Australis, the call of cockatoos, or the croaking of frogs is heard, and hopes are bright again; water is certainly at hand; the spur is applied to the flank of the tired beast, which already partakes in his riders anticipations, and quickens his pace, and a lagoon, a creek, or a river is before him. The horse is soon unsaddled, hobbled, and well washed; a fire is made, the teapot is put to the fire, the meat is dressed, the enjoyment of the poor reconnoitrer is perfect, and a prayer of thankfulness to the Almighty God, who protects the wanderer on his journey, bursts from his grateful lips.

A year later in 1847, Leichhardt prepared even more ambitious a journey from Brisbane to the Gulf of Carpentaria and from there south-west clear across the continent to Perth. He set out in March 1848 and expected that his trek would last more than two years, so it was not until the end of the year 1850 that serious anxiety began to be felt about his continued silence. Search parties were sent out and traced his route for more than five hundred miles inland from the Queensland coast. There the trail ended and no one succeeded in finding out whether Leichhardt's party had been murdered, as the natives maintained, or whether he and his party had perished in flood or fire, starvation or thirst.

Meanwhile Edward Kennedy, a young but experienced officer, had been given the task of exploring the York peninsula for the Government of New South Wales. The country proved so rough that the party had to leave behind their carts and most of their stores. One of the party wounded himself with his own gun and Kennedy himself was fatally speared by a native. His faithful native guide "Jacky-Jacky" escaped only by walking half a mile in a creek with only his head above water.

In 1855 a new name appears, Augustus Charles Gregory. He set out from the mouth of the Victoria River, on the shores of the Timor Sea, and penetrated about four hundred miles south before being turned back by the great Australian desert at the end of the rainy season. No doubt they would have gone further still but for a series of disasters. First the ship which was taking them to the starting point ran on to a reef and lay on her side for eight days, while the horses inside grew weaker and weaker as they plunged and strained. Later more horses died after eating a poisonous plant; others were attacked by alligators. Also the schooner carrying their stores up the river went aground on a mud bank and a large number of sheep, that had been unwisely kept aboard, perished.

Even so, Gregory succeeded in crossing back safely to Queensland and the interest of his fellow Australians in the north remained undiminished.

Two years later in 1858 Gregory pioneered a route between Brisbane and Adelaide. His technique, followed later by other explorers, was to travel light on horseback without a tent and to live off the country on "jerked" (sun-dried meat) and any game that could be shot. This cut costs and raised progress from about ten miles per day to twenty-five miles.

But so far no one had succeeded in crossing Australia from one coast to the other on a direct route through the centre. And now in the early sixties that, too, was to come.

John McDouall Stuart, who was to accomplish the feat, had learnt the technique of exploration from the great Sturt, and, in 1859 he had already been successful in finding a route northward across a well-watered district to the west of Lake Eyre. An offer of £2,000 by the South Australian Government inspired him to push north towards the Victoria River, down which Gregory had travelled on his journey southwards.

Stuart started out in 1860 with two companions only, and thirteen horses, and by June that year had already camped on Mount Stuart at the centre of Australia and on the Barkly Table-lands, about 250 miles from the nearest point on the Victoria River, and rather less from the Gulf of Carpentaria. But shortages of stores and attacks by the natives forced him to turn back while the party was still strong enough to make good its retreat. Stuart was suffering from sunblindness and double vision (for in those days explorers did not carry sunglasses), as well as from scurvy. However he got back to Adelaide in October and, by the end of the following month, had set off northward again, determined to break through to the coast. He spent most of that autumn at Chambers Creek in South Australia and by 15th April of the following year (1861) had pressed on to Attack Creek from which they had been compelled to turn back the previous year. A month later he had reached Newcastle Waters nearly 150 miles further north. But he found the path westwards to the Victoria River lay through tracts of dense mallee scrub (which tore the men's clothes from their bodies) and more or less waterless plains, and had to return to Adelaide.

In October 1861 Stuart set out again on what might well have been his last journey, for on the very day the expedition left Adelaide he was knocked down and almost killed by one of his own horses.

Soon afterwards, two of his men mutinied and left the convoy, and Woodforde, who had been with Stuart on previous expeditions, also deserted, taking with him one of the horses and some of the equipment.

It was the hottest season of the year, and, before it was over, they had lost several horses. While still short of their turning point of the previous year they were twice attacked by natives who had managed to get hold of rifles. Yet again they found that, while the countryside near the creeks was fine pasture land, near-desert soon began once they left the neighbourhood of the waters. In April Stuart even tried a course to the south-east (as though he were going back to Sydney) but found only dense scrub which tore even the horses' saddles to ribbons. At the beginning of May he started off again due north as if to reach Port Essington, and at last he found fine deep water, which he called Frew's Ponds after James Frew, a member of the expedition. Even so, there was not enough water there for them to make a permanent camp. So Stuart made one final attempt to go west to the Victoria River. For three days he travelled through dense scrub and forest, but saw hardly a sign of wild life and only one spring. And so the final push had to be northwards. They found a little water at King's Ponds and some more at McGorrerey's Ponds. Then came two days of drought and then a magnificent find—the Daly Waters, with fine gum trees and pelicans along its banks. Next came a splendidly grassed water meadow which they named Blue Grass Swamp. At last they were reaching better country. Further north there was lush grass around Purdie's ponds and the next day they struck a creek which ran northwards until it plunged through a gorge where they could no longer follow it.

Here they made a detour over the hills and met the river again at the northern edge of the gorge. Its waters were deep and clear and they were able to catch several fish, some like perch, and others like gold-fish. Gradually the river broadened out, and on the 25th June it joined up with the Roper River which Leichhardt's party had crossed seventeen years before. After getting across the Roper, Stuart and his men found grass from two to five feet high in some of the finest country any-where in Australia. The natives were friendly. On 9th July the party travelled across a sandy table-land, thick with pines, stringy barks and palm trees with leaves like a lady's fan. The next day they caught sight of the Adelaide River hustling away north-west to the sea. A week later they came to the river itself, eighty yards wide, its banks lined with stout bamboos and sur-rounded by palm groves and marshes in which strange lilies grew. One day Stuart decided to leave the river and its windings and made due north for the coast. "By this I hope to avoid the marsh," he wrote:

I did not inform any of the party except Thring and Auld, that I was so near to the sea, as I wished to give them a surprise on reaching it. Proceeded through a light soil, slightly elevated, with a little ironstone on the surface, the volcanic black rock cropping out occasionally also some flats of black alluvial soil. The timber much smaller and more like scrub showing that we are nearing the sea. At eight miles and a half, came upon a broad valley of black alluvial soil, covered with long grass; from this I can hear the wash of the sea.

On the other side of the valley, which is rather more than a quarter of a mile wide, is a line of thick heavy bushes, very dense, showing that to be the boundary of the beach. Crossed the valley and entered the srub, which was a complete network of vines. Stopped the horses to clear a way, while I advanced a few yards on to the beach, and was gratified and delighted to behld the waters of the Indian Ocean, in Van Diemen's Gulf, before the party with the horses knew anything of its proximity. Thring, who road in advance of me called out, "The Sea!" which took them all by surprise, and they were so astonished that he had to repeat his call before they full understood what was meant. Then, they immediately gave three long and hearty cheers. The beach is covered with a soft blue mud. It being ebb tide, I could see some distance; found it would be impossible to take the horses along it. I therefore kept them where I had halted them, and allowed half the party to come onto the beach and gratify themselves by a sight of the sea, while the other half remained to watch the horses until their return. I dipped my feet and washed my face and hands in the sea, as I promised the late Governor, Sir Richard McDonnell, I would do, if I reached it. The mud has nearly covered all the shells; we got a few, however. I could see no seaweed.

Stuart was thus the first man to travel right across Australia from coast to coast passing through the centre of the continent, but he nearly lost his life in doing so. Even before he reached the coast he was seized with violent pains and had to be lifted from the saddle. He was half blind and could not see the full moon when it rose, and had to be carried 600 miles of the way home on a stretcher. However he lived to receive the £2,000 reward so nearly snatched from him by other expeditions.

The most famous of these, and the best equipped, was the Burke and Wills cavalcade. It is sometimes assumed that this party was the first to make use of camels to overcome Australia's scarcity of water. This is not so. John Ainsworth Horrocks was using camels imported from Karachi as far back as 1840 and might well have discovered the way to the north if he had not accidentally shot himself when his camel lurched sideways.

Of course the camel had undeniable advantages. It could take in between thirty and forty gallons of water and if pressed could make this last the best part of a month, whereas the horse could not survive more than three days without water. The camel too was less particular about its food and was able to find green stuff on trees inaccessible to the largest horse. The camel could carry a standard load of at least 5 cwt. compared with a horse's 200 lb. and, although the horse could travel much faster, it needed frequent periods of rest. The camel, it is true, preferred soft ground for travelling and could not match a shod horse on the hard highway or across sharp rocks. But camels were less prone to fall and injure themselves and their burdens. They were cleverer at remembering any route that they had travelled before, and they could smell food and water from a greater distance than the most sensitive horse.

These arguments seemed unanswerable to Robert O'Hara, Burke and William Wills, who had been chosen by Melbourne's Royal Society, to which the city's most influential men belonged, to lead a new thrust across the centre of Australia from south to north, an exploration which, it was hoped, would not only consolidate what had been discovered before but uncover whatever mystery still surrounded the centre of the continent.

It was the expedition to end all expeditions. The Government of Victoria contributed £6,000. Camels were bought in large quantities—six from a local circus and two dozen others by an expedition specially sent to India almost directly after the Indian Mutiny. The Burke-Wills equipment included almost anything you might care to mention from fishing lines to sun-hats. They were provided with a special type of cart that could be floated across rivers, and the camels had swim-bladders as well as camel shoes. Food was bought on the assumption that the explorers would be away for a year or eighteen months. Indeed there was so much gear that some of it had to be sold off before the party could get under way.

Burke and Wills left Melbourne on 19th August 1860. By 6th September they had crossed the Murray River and the following month reached Menindee on the Darling River which was selected as a kind of base camp. Here Burke, who was under pressure to get results before he was beaten to it by some rival expedition, took the first of a series of disastrous decisions. He decided to push ahead to Coopers Creek with a light reconnaissance party of eight, leaving the main body of the expedition to follow with the heavier stores as soon as possible.

His impetuosity was undiminished when he arrived at Coopers Creek on 11th November and he then decided once more to split his party, leaving four men behind and taking three others, Wills, Gray and King with him to the north coast. His plan was to return in three months or less.

Before leaving, he gave orders that if the main body of his stores should arrive within the next few days then the four men, whom he had left behind in charge of William Brahe, should follow him. But if the stores did not arrive Brahe and his companions should remain at the depot on Coopers Creek for as long as possible. Burke and his party left the depot for the north on 16th December and on 11th February they successfully reached a tidal creek at the south-east corner of the Gulf of Carpentaria. But they were in a critical position. They had made the 700-mile journey at an average rate of nearly thirteen miles a day and it was not going to be easy to match this on the homeward path, especially as they had by now used up nearly two-thirds of their supplies. It was clear that even if they succeeded in returning to Coopers Creek at the same pace that they had hitherto kept up, they would have been away for four months rather than three.

Meanwhile the four-man rearguard in Coopers Creek continued to live in acute discomfort and even some danger from the natives, with no sign of the main body of stores arriving. Furthermore one of the group was seriously injured through a fall. Towards the end of April Brahe realized that if he stayed longer, he would be unable to leave enough rations behind for Burke and his men to use on the journey back from Coopers Creek to Menindee. He had already held out on Coopers Creek for four months—a month after Burke should have returned. He took the only possible decision and left.

Thus when Burke, Wills and King arrived back at Coopers Creek (minus Gray who had weakened and died during the return from the sea) they found the camp deserted and littered with empty cases and tins. On a tree nearby they read an ominous inscription reading "Dig 3 ft. N.W. Apr. 21 1861". When they dug they found with the rations a note which broke the news to them. They had missed salvation by nine hours and Brahe and his party were already on their way back to Menindee.

Neither Burke, Wills and King nor their camels were capable of the effort needed to overtake Brahe. But there was still a chance that they could make their way due south by another route to a police outpost near Mount Hopeless, towards Adelaide.

And so, in case a search party came back to the camp they left a note explaining that they were in poor shape but were pro- ceeding south along the creek. This they buried in a cache from which they had taken the rations. They then carefully covered the site once more with earth and camel dung to discourage the natives from digging there.

Then followed a series of tragic misunderstandings. Back at Menindee the main body of the expedition, entrusted with the heavier stores, had still not moved even as far as Coopers Creek. This was partly because of rumours that cheques drawn by Burke were not being honoured in Melbourne, and partly because the Committee in Melbourne failed to dispel these rumours by answering letters promptly.

But at last, on 26th January, after a special messenger had been sent down to Melbourne, Wright felt sufficiently reassured to leave his base. By mid-February when Burke had already reached the sea, Wright had progressed eighty miles away as far as Bulloo. Three of his men, softened perhaps by months of inaction, were already "passengers". Towards the end of April they met Brahe on his way back from Coopers Creek, and Brahe, now that he had more rations to draw on, felt that he should return once more to Coopers Creek and see whether in the meantime Burke had arrived there. Wright went with him.

They got to the camp on 8th May, fifteen days after Burke had left it. They noticed none of the traces left by Burke—a broken bottle, a displaced rake and a leather square missing from the door of the stockade. Or if they noticed any changes they attributed them to the natives. The letters which they had carved on the tree giving directions for digging were those that Brahe himself had left, and it therefore seemed pointless to dig up the cache to see whether Burke and Wills had been and gone taking the rations with them. Indeed they thought it might be dangerous to do so because the natives, seeing traces of fresh digging might think that something valuable had been buried there. Moreover it never occurred to them that if Burke and Wills had left Coopers Creek they might have done so by another route.

And so another chance of rescue was lost. For as it happened Burke and Wills, so far from reaching Mount Hopeless, had not even left Coopers Creek.

One of their camels had been lost in quicksand and the other wasted away. They had started out on foot for Mount Hopeless but after forty-five miles of plodding they found not a single waterhole and had to turn back. Their clothes were falling to pieces, and they thought it best to settle down in the creek feeding on seeds, and occasional fish and fresh-water mussels and waiting until someone happened to pass that way.

One day they thought that they had heard a shot fired and jumped to the conclusion that a rescue party had already arrived at Coopers Creek. They decided that one of them should return up the creek to the original stockade to get help. Wills was chosen, and by hard marching he got there in three days. He found no one and no signs, even in the cache, that Brahe and Wright had already been there. Wills left a second note in the cache. But again he left no outward sign that he had dug it up. On 30th May he went south again to rejoin Burke and King, now weaker than ever.

About this time the good people of Victoria, stirred by the fact that McDouall Stuart had returned safely from his expedition from one coast almost to the other, began pressing the Committee in Melbourne to look to the safety of Burke and Wills. Four rescue parties were despatched, and on 13th September one of them arrived at Coopers Creek. But again it never occurred to any of the searchers to dig up the cache and see whether the rations had been taken or messages left. Next day however natives directed the searchers to a white man living literally hand to mouth lower down the creek.

John King, an Irishman who had served seven years in the Indian Army and who had afterwards helped to look after the camels, was the only survivor of the Burke-Wills expedition.

Wills had died for lack of proper food towards the end of June and Burke about the same time. But their journey had not been in vain. For the rescuers had learnt more about Australia than the original explorers. And one of the parties led by John McKinlay, made a coast to coast crossing of Australia (though not across the centre) from Adelaide to the Gulf of Carpentaria, driving a flock of sheep.

But no amount of exploring could solve the land problem or provide any practical way of distributing sensibly and equitably the millions of unused acres still at the disposal of the Crown. In the days before the gold rushes the policy had been to settle small yeoman farmers in relatively fertile areas near the coast, while the squatters were permitted to roam far and wide over the less attractive areas, suitable for an occasional sheep nibble but not much more. The position of the squatters had been regularized in 1847 by an Order in Council which allowed them to take longer leases than before and gave them first refusal in case of a sale.

Runs began to be fenced and staffs of splitters, rouseabouts, station-hands, stock-hands and teamsters engaged. There were cow-houses, stable-yards, sheep-yards and slaughter-houses to look after.

But these treads were upset by the discovery of gold. Gold drew the population inland away from the coast and new farms were needed to feed them. Moreover the Gold Rush swelled the Australian countryside with disappointed prospectors for whom farming was often the only alternative. But how were the farms to be established in squatter territory?

New laws had to be introduced in New South Wales in order to bring about this highly desirable state of affairs. The laws allowed any would-be-farmer to select a piece of land of not less than 40 acres or more than 320 acres for a down payment of 5s. per acre and another 15s. per acre to be paid in instalments, provided that he lived on his selection for three years and spent £1 an acre on specified improvements. And as the law did not specify the age or sex of the would-be-farmer, a single family with a wife and several children could do very nicely thank you.

Moreover the land could be selected even from areas previously leased to squatters. In order to speed up action the leases granted to squatters were cut to one year in the not so remote areas and five years in the pioneer outback. At the end of the lease the squatters were given the chance of buying a twenty-fifth of their run for £1 an acre without competition. But for the rest of the land they were in competition with the new breed of farmers. And the latter by selecting and buying the best sections of land—particularly the areas surrounding the creeks and river beds—could freeze out the squatters or compel them to pay through the nose to recover the land they had formerly leased.

But the squatter could hit back too. He had the same right to select any piece of land and buy it for a down payment of 5s. per acre. And he had a better chance of being able to borrow money with which to buy more land. For a banker who had already lent money to a squatter naturally preferred to protect his investment by a further loan rather than finance an unknown newcomer.

Thus the sturdy yeoman farmer with his well-tilled and pastured holding failed to appear, not only in New South Wales, but also in Victoria and Queensland, where similar land laws were passed.

No doubt the wool men had influence in high places among bankers as well as in politics, but the twenty million sheep that Australia now had constituted a big investment and it is only fair to point out that the wide open spaces then being explored were not always the most suitable for close cultivation. Labour was far too expensive for small-scale production. Apart from which many new farmers had no idea of handling either crops or livestock. Indeed at one time it paid the Australians to import their wheat from South America, and by the time they began to grow wheat to feed their own population (which by the 1860s had spread over the million mark) the machine age had come to the farm, with several important inventions.

To begin with a machine first brought out by John Ridley in the 1840s stripped and threshed wheat. Then a kind of primitive bulldozer known as the Mullenizer was designed to clear anything smaller than a large tree, and even trees could be tackled mechanically. The "stump-jump" plough with shares that rose of their own accord to avoid obstructions came into its own in the seventies but was conceived many years before. All this needed capital.

Meanwhile the gradual spread of Australian railways and other forms of transport made new adventures unconnected with small holdings all the more attractive. Captain Towns, a Sydney merchant, invested in a cotton plantation on the coast of Queensland and imported natives from the Pacific islands to work it. The cotton market collapsed at the end of the United States Civil War, but sugar proved a good alternative crop.

In 1861 Thomas Mort established his freezing works at Lithgow, New South Wales, to prove that frozen meat could be exported to Britain.

In 1869 the Suez Canal was opened with the result that steamships could now reach Australia from London in four weeks or so. A new drive to the north followed.

By now some of the mystery had departed from Australia, the last of lands. Secrets concealed in the precincts of the sun for so many centuries were at last uncovered, and Australians had become familiar with creatures still strange to the outer world. They learnt to take for granted the whistling spider and the lungfish, sole survivor of a family that lived 200 million years ago, that can breath air directly into its air bladder. They knew about the stone fish, whose spines can kill a man through a leather shoe, had seen the rooster fish with its red comb and tail "feathers", and watched the dove-grey brolga crane that performs a stately rhythmic dance. They knew of the bower birds that build fences round their arbours and paint them with coloured dust, birds that can imitate almost anything from a crackling fire to a cat's "miaow". They had named a certain kind of parrot "twenty-eight" because of its call.

They had met with the "lawyer vines" that will not let go of anyone that falls into their clutches; they had met nettle trees that can sting a horse to death. They knew the yellow-spotted nyntucka, the world's second largest lizard.

The natives taught them to amputate a finger by tightening round it the thread of an Australian spider, and to stupefy and catch fish by scattering certain seeds in the water.

They learnt that sheep and horses did well on salt-bush, with its rubbery leaves coated with salt, that the soft shoots of the prickly spinifex could be eaten too, and the mulga tree, with its delicate grey leaves and twisting branches could be felled in times of drought to feed sheep. They had used the bloodwood for fence posts and the white stringybark for house frames.

These were now well-known friends (or enemies).

The Australians themselves put down roots of all kinds.

Australia was even beginning to develop a poetry school. In the forties Charles Harpur had tried, by using Australian slang, to describe the world of Windsor, N.S.W. William Anderson Forbes (younger brother of Archibald Forbes, the War Correspondent), who had been exiled to Australia in disgrace and had worked for settlers in Queensland, succeeded with a volume of poems *Voices from the Bush* in 1869.

Adam Lindsay Gordon, educated at Cheltenham College and the Royal Military Academy, Woolwich, and similarly exiled in 1853, worked as a mounted policeman and a horse-breaker, but also produced four books of verse including his most famous ballad "The Sick Stockrider" in 1868; and Henry Kendall, who lived out his life in poverty and comparative obscurity, was an outstanding native-born poet who tried with relative success to free himself from European tradition.

And so in the sixties came a cultural watershed and, once it was crossed, signs of a native Australian literature.

But links with Britain persisted. Marie Dolores Rosanna Gilbert, daughter of a British Army officer and better known as Lola Montez, mistress of the prodigal King Ludwig I of Bavaria, appeared with her troop of dancers at Ballarat in 1855 as well as at Sydney and Melbourne. In 1863 Charles Dickens was offered (and rejected) a fee of £10,000 for a lecture and reading tour of Australia by Spiers and Pond, the catering firm, which two years earlier had sponsored the first visit of an English cricket team. Two of Dickens' sons spent the greater

10

part of their lives down under. And it was often a case of "Behold the Milkman in his Cart! (First cousin to a Knight of Bart)", as the Australian poet Hugh McCrae put it.

But for the first time the native-born Australians were beginning to outnumber the immigrants.

10

Anthony Trollope Ignores Ned Kelly

Anthony Trollope, the novelist who had succeeded Thackeray as chief interpreter of the British upper class life, was fifty-six years old when he came in 1871 to visit his son in Australia.

Trollope's most famous offering, *Barchester Towers*, a cathedral city novel based on the diocese of Winchester, had appeared in 1857. He retired ten years later from an exalted position in the Inspectorate of Queen Victoria's Postal Service which had enabled him to travel and to hunt regularly both in Ireland and the English shires.

But he was quite ready to report on the social customs of the squatter and the jackeroo for the benefit of his English readers and to draw comparison between the "colonial" gold prospector eating a lump of beef out of a greasy frying pan with the aid of a pocket knife, and the English labourer. And the conclusions he drew were no doubt highly satisfying to those of his public who had decided not to take the boat to Sydney or any other port on the Australian Continent.

Whether his writings were helpful to good relations between Australia and the mother country is another matter.

Certainly Trollope brought with him behind that venerable beard some of the prejudices which have consistently failed to endear the average "fine old English Gentleman" to the average Aussie. But he was a trained reporter with an inspector's eye for detail and I have not hesitated to quote extensively from his observations, which might well have been those of any other Englishman of the same social standing.

> After a few days spent in Melbourne, the great metropolis of our Australian empire, I went direct to Queensland, in order that I might see and hear what was to be seen and heard in that semi-tropical colony before the great heat commenced. I arrived there on the 11th August 1871. The hot weather is supposed to begin in October and to last till the end of April. The subject of heat is one of extreme delicacy in Queensland, as indeed it is also in the other colonies. One does not allude to heat in a host's house any more than to a bad bottle of wine or an ill-cooked joint of meat. You may remark that it is very cool in your friend's verandah, your friend of the moment being present, and may hint that the whole of your absent friend's establishment is as hot as a furnace; but though you be constrained to keep your handkerchief to your brow, and hardly dare to walk to the garden gate, you must never complain of the heat then and there. You may call an inn hot, or a court-house, but not a gentleman's paddock or a lady's drawing-room. And you should never own to a musquito. I once unfortunately stated to a Queensland gentleman that my coat had been bitten by cockroaches at his brother's house, which I had just left. "You must have brought them with you then" was the fraternal defence immediately set up. I was compelled at once to antedate the cockroaches to my previous resting-place, owned by a friend, not by a brother. "It is possible," said the squatter, "but I think you must have had them with you longer than that." I acquiesced in silence, and said no more about my coat till I could get it mended elsewhere.

Trollope was not always so condescending. Indeed he was impressed by the standards of coach-driving:

> I had been very much advised against the coach. I was told that the road, and the vehicle, and the horses, and the driving were so rough as to be unfit for a man of my age and antecedents. One anxious friend implored me not to undertake it with an anxiety which could hardly have been stronger had I been his grandfather. I was, however, obstinate, and can now declare that I enjoyed the drive most thoroughly. It lasted three days, and took me through some magnificent scenery. Woodland country in Australia,—and it must be remembered that the lands occupied are mostly woodland, —is called either bush or scrub. Woods which are open, and

passable,—passable at any rate for men on horseback,—are called bush. When the undergrowth becomes thick and matted so as to be impregnable without an axe, it is scrub. In Queensland the scrubs are filled with tropical plants,—long vine tendrils, palms, and the parasite fig-tree,—and when a way has been cut through them the effect for a time is very lovely. The fault of all Australian scenery is its monotony. The eye after a while becomes fatigued with a landscape which at first charmed with its park-like aspect. One never gets out of the trees, and then it rarely happens that water lends its aid to improve the view. As a rule it must be acknowledged that a land of forests is not a land of beauty. Some experience in travelling is needed before this can be acknowledged, as every lover of nature is an admirer of trees. But unceasing trees, trees which continue around you from six in the morning till six at night, become a bore, and the traveller begins to remember with regret the open charms of some cultivated plain. I had to acknowledge this monotony before I reached Brisbane;—but I acknowledged also the great beauty of the scrubs and found some breaks in the mountains which were very grand.

But the wonder of the journey was in the badness of the roads and the goodness of the coachmanship. I have been called upon by the work of my life to see much coaching, having been concerned for more than thirty years with the expedition of mails,—and I remember well the good old patriotic John Bull conviction that go where one would round the world one could never find a man to drive like the English mail-coachman of the olden times. There was a fixed idea that coach-driving was a British accomplishment, and quite beyond the reach of any one out of Britain. Since then I have seen something of driving over the Alps and other European mountains; something also of driving in America; which lessened my belief in the "unapproachability" of the excellence of the Englishman. I have now travelled over the Gympie road, and I feel certain that not one of my old friends of the box,—and I had many such friends,—would, on being shown that road, have considered it possible that a vehicle with four horses should have been made to travel over it. There is often no road, and the coach is taken at random through the forest. Not unfrequently a fallen tree blocks up the track, and the coach is squeezed through some siding which makes it necessary for the leader to be going one way while the coach is going another. But the great miracle is in the sudden pitches, looking as though they were almost perpendicular, down which the coach is taken,—and then the equally sharp ascents,

—not straight, but at a sharp angle,—up and round which the coach is whirled. The art of driving on such roads depends very much on the foot. The vehicle is supplied with strong machinery for dragging the hind wheels, so as almost altogether to stop their rotation, and this the coachman manages with his right foot. I heard of various accidents to the coach, but of none to passengers.

A stranger cannot but remark, throughout the pastoral districts of Australia, how seldom he sees sheep as he travels along. As in this country they do not carry above one sheep to ten acres, and as the animals would hardly be observed if each sheep maintained solitary possession of his own ten-acred domain, the result is not wonderful. But the traveller expects to see sheep and is disappointed. It may be that he will also expect emus and kangaroos, and he will generally be disappointed also in regard to them. Kangaroos I certainly have seen in great numbers, though by no means so often as I expected. An emu running wild I never did see.

He saw fairly enough the advantages and drawbacks to life in the bush:

I don't know that there can be a much happier life than that of a squatter, if the man be fairly prosperous, and have natural aptitudes for country occupations. He should be able to ride and to shoot,—and to sit in a buggy all day without inconvenience. He should be social,—for he must entertain often and be entertained by other squatters; but he must be indifferent to society, for he will live away from towns and be often alone with his family. He must be able to command men, and must do so in a frank and easy fashion,—not arrogating to himself any great superiority, but with full power to let those around him know that he is master. He must prefer plenty to luxury, and be content to have things about him a little rough. He must be able to brave troubles,—for a squatter has many troubles. Sheep will go amiss. Lambs will die. Shearers will sometimes drink. And the bullocks with the most needed supplies will not always arrive as soon as they are expected. And, above all things, the squatter should like mutton. In squatters' houses plenty always prevails, but that plenty often depends upon the sheepfold. If a man have these gifts, and be young and energetic when he begins the work, he will not have chosen badly in becoming a squatter. The sense of ownership and mastery, the conviction that he is the head and chief of what is going on around; the absence of any necessity of asking leave or of submitting to others,—these things in themselves add a great charm to life. The squatter owes

obedience to none and allegiance only to the merchant;—who asks
no questions so long as the debt be reduced or not increased. He
gets up when he pleases and goes to bed when he likes. Though he
should not own an acre of the land around him, he may do what he
pleases with all that he sees. He may put up fences and knock them
down. He probably lives in the middle of a forest,—his life is
always called life in the bush,—and he may cut down any tree that
he fancies. He has always horses to ride, and a buggy to sit in, and
birds to shoot at, and kangaroos to ride after. He goes where he
likes and nobody questions him. There is probably no one so big
as himself within twenty miles of him, and he is proud with the
conviction that he knows how to wash sheep better than any
squatter in the colony. But the joy that mostly endears his life to
him is the joy that he need not dress for dinner. . . .

The squatter builds first a wooden hut which ultimately becomes
his kitchen, then a wooden sitting-room and bedroom near to it;
then a bigger sitting-room with two small bedrooms, still of wood,
—and so on. But when he has realised to himself the fact that he is a
rich man he rushes into brick and mortar or stone, and erects a
European country house,—with the addition of a wide verandah.
This has been done now very generally by the landowners of
Victoria. But still the place has rarely all the finished comfort, the
easy grace, coming from long habit, which belong to our country
seats at home. There is a roughness and a heaviness about it, a
want of completion about the gardens, of neatness about the paths,
and of close-shorn trimness about the plots and lawns, which
strikes the beholder at once, and declares that though the likeness
be there, it exists with a difference.

This difference is caused chiefly by the dearness of labour, a fact
which influences not only the outside of the Victorian gentleman's
house, but also every part of his establishment. Let his means be
what they may, he never has the retinue of servants which is to be
found in an ordinary English household. The high rate of wages
and the difficulty of getting persons to accept these high rates for
any considerable number of months together, cause even the
wealthy to dispense with much of that attendance which is often
considered indispensable at home even among families that are not
wealthy. On the other hand, certain luxuries are common among
Australian families, which few among us can enjoy without stint.
He who has a carriage and horses at home is supposed to be a rich
man. If a gentleman have daughters fond of riding he will perhaps
have one horse for two girls. Young men can hardly hunt unless

their fathers be wealthy. But horses on an Australian station are as
common as blackberries on English hedges, and the possession of a
carriage and pair of horses is as much a matter of course as the
possession of a pair of boots. But horses are cheap and servants are
dear in Victoria. . . .

But there was a rough side to the squatters' life and Trollope
saw this too:

I have said that squatters marry early. The reasons for doing so
are very strong; and those reasons for not doing so, which are
terribly familiar to us at home, hardly exist in the bush. The man
is alone, and can have at any rate no female companionship unless
he marry. In ordinary life, as we know it, the unmarried man enjoys
as many comforts,—unfortunately perhaps, more luxuries,—than
do they who take to themselves wives. But in the bush the unmarried man is very desolate, and will probably soon become forlorn
and wretched in his mode of life. He will hardly get a woman who
will cook for him decently, or who will sew a button on his shirt
when it is wanted. And he will soon care nothing how his dinner is
cooked, and whether his shirt be with or without a button. On the
other hand the cost of his household when he is married will hardly
be more than when he is single. If his wife know how to keep a bush
house, her presence will almost be a saving to him. At home, in
England, the young man when he marries has to migrate from his
lodgings to a house, he must make up an establishment, buy furni-
ture, hire servants, and enter altogether upon a new phase of life.
He must have ready money in his pocket to begin with, and a
future income probably very much in advance of that he has hitherto
been expected to expend. But on a station there is nothing of the
kind. There is the house, in which it may be necessary to put a few
additional comforts. There is the establishment,—already on so
large a scale in consequence of the necessity of supplying men with
rations that no recognised increase is created. When children come,
and education is needed, expenses of course will grow;—but at
first the thing is so easy that the young squatter simply goes out
in his buggy and brings home the daughter of some other squatter,
—after a little ceremony performed in the nearest church.

As a consequence of this, life in the bush is decent and moral.
The bulk of the labour is performed by a nomad tribe, who wander
in quest of their work, and are hired only for a time. This is of
course the case in regard to washing sheep and shearing them. It is
equally so when fences are to be made, or ground to be cleared, or

trees to be "rung". The ringing of trees consists of cutting the bark through all round, so that the tree cease to suck up the strength of the earth for its nutrition, and shall die. For all these operations temporary work is of course required, and the squatter seldom knows whether the men he employs be married or single. They come and go, and are known by queer nicknames or are known by no names at all. They probably have their wives elsewhere, and return to them for a season. They are rough to look at, dirty in appearance, shaggy, with long hair, men who, when they are in the bush, live in huts, and hardly know what a bed is. But they work hard, and are both honest and civil. Theft among them is almost unknown. Men are constantly hired without any character but that which they give themselves; and the squatters find from experience that the men are able to do that which they declare themselves capable of performing. There will be exceptions, but such is the rule. Their one great fault is drunkenness,—and yet they are sober to a marvel. As I have said before, they will work for months without touching spirits,—but their very abstinence creates a craving desire which, when it is satisfied, will satisfy itself with nothing short of brutal excess. Among the masters of these men,—among squatters with their superintendents and overseers,—drinking is not a common fault. I have seen a squatter drunk. I have seen a squatter very drunk. But he was a jovial exception.

Squatters, I think, do not as a rule go very frequently to church. Churches are not near to them, and as they are always either driving in buggies or riding on horseback in pursuance of their ordinary occupations, on Sundays they are not ready to add perhaps thirty miles, perhaps forty, to their week's work in quest of a sermon. I have spoken of stations which possessed churches of their own. When that is the case, the squatter is generally the parson for three Sundays,—being relieved by a real, but itinerant, clergyman on the fourth. I am, however, bound to acknowledge that Sabbath-day observances are laxly kept in the bush.

The resident squatter is generally a young man,—one at least not past the prime of life. For this state of things there are sundry causes. The squatter who succeeds in life, as he grows old does not cease to be a squatter. He sticks to his wool as closely as the lawyer does to his wig, or the banker to his ledger. He knows well every shilling that is spent and made. But he becomes an absentee squatter,—having a son, or a junior partner, or perhaps a manager, to manage the run and to send him the accounts. The money comes into his hand readily, as the produce of a sheep-station is never sold

on the spot. London is almost always the rich squatter's market.
Then again the work to be done is hardly fitted for an old man. All
that an old man can do, he can do away from the station. He has
become tired of buggies and bucking horses, perhaps tired of tea
and mutton; and he makes himself comfortable in a town.

And many no doubt are ruined before they grow to be old;—
for, to tell the truth of it, the growing of wool is at the best a
precarious trade. Thousands have made their fortunes at it,—but
thousands also with small capitals have gone to the wall in their
struggles, and have been no more heard of among the stations.
What becomes of them I cannot say. Who knows the fate of the
ruined man? The business is always on a large scale,—and being
large and also precarious cannot but be dangerous. With wool
ranging from 1s. to 2s. a pound, a squatter with 20,000 sheep, and
a small capital, may be made by high prices, or marred by low
prices, in one year. The year of favourable circumstances in regard
to weather and climate may put him at his ease for life,—and a
year's drought may beggar him. This also tends to weed out the
old men, and leave the young men in possession. At fifty the
squatter can afford either to live in town or in England,—or else
he can no longer afford to live on his station.

Later Trollope visited one other modest station:

When in New South Wales I spent a month at a small squatter's
station in the distant bush, and as the difference between bush life in
Australia and country life in England is more marked than I think
any other difference between the two countries, I propose to
describe the thing as I found it. I had already stayed at various
sheep-stations in Queensland, but only for a few days at each; and
these had been generally large places, where perhaps from one to
two hundred thousand sheep were shorn,—and into which consequently the comforts and luxuries of civilised life had been imported.
These were hardly typical bush residences. At that to which I now
went, a young squatter beginning life owned not much more than
ten thousand sheep, and was living quite "in the rough". The
number of sheep at these stations will generally indicate with fair
accuracy the mode of life at the head station. A hundred thousand
sheep and upwards require a professed man-cook and a butler to
look after them; forty thousand sheep cannot be shorn without a
piano; twenty thousand is the lowest number that renders napkins
at dinner imperative. Ten thousand require absolute plenty, meat
in plenty, tea in plenty, brandy and water and colonial wine in

plenty, but do not expect champagne, sherry, or made dishes, and
are supposed to be content with continued mutton or continued beef,
—as the squatter may at the time be in the way of killing sheep or
oxen. During this month we killed mutton. After six months I
returned to the same station, and beef was the provision of the day.
Wool had gone up, and sheep had become valuable, and the squatter
could not be persuaded to kill a sheep for love or money. He bought
cattle as he wanted them, and found that his beef cost him 1½d. a
pound.

The station I visited, and which I will call M——, was about
250 miles west of Sydney, and was decidedly in the bush. I have
already endeavoured to explain that nearly every place beyond the
influences of the big towns is called "bush",—even though there
should not be a tree to be seen around;—but in reaching this place
I journeyed for three days after leaving the railway through continuous woodland, doing about forty miles a day in a buggy. The
house stood on a small creek,—hardly to be called a rivulet, because
the water does not continually run, and in dry weather lies only in a
succession of water-holes,—and was surrounded by interminable
forest. Close around it was the home-paddock, railed in, and
containing about 50 acres. Such an enclosure about a gentleman's
house in England is an appendage of great value, and constitutes
with some who are ambitious almost a little park. In the bush it is
little more thought of than as so much waste ground round the
house. Two or three cows may run in it, or a horse or two for
immediate use. It is generally found convenient to have a horse
near the house for the sake of "running in" other horses. One horse
in the stable to catch two horses in the home-paddock wherewith
four horses when wanted may be run in from the horse-paddock,
make together a combination which in the bush is considered to be
economical and convenient. At M—— the home-paddock was partially cleared of timber, and was pretty enough. Outside it, meeting
the creek both before and behind, was the horse-paddock, containing
about 250 acres. This was supposed to be the domain appropriated
to the horses of the establishment needed for the working of it.
At that time there were about twenty, and I believe that there was
not one too many. My young friend also had his rams here during a
portion of the year, but hardly expected more from so small an
enclosure than food for the animals required for use. A public road,
such as bush roads are, ran through the horse-paddock,—very
inconvenient in that it caused the gates to be left open, and brought
travellers that way whose presence was hardly desirable, but not

without compensation, as a postman with the mails passed each way twice a week. The postman was a great blessing. If he wanted food for himself or his horse, he got it; and in return he complied with all requests made to him, conveying letters, telegrams, and messages with wondrous accuracy. A mailman coming by—they are mailmen and not postmen in the bush—is a great addition to the comforts of bush life. At the back of the horse-paddock was the wool-shed paddock, containing about 1,200 acres, with the wool-shed at one corner of it, distant about a mile from the house. For many reasons the wool-shed should not be close. The squatter does not want to have his shearers always in his kitchen, nor to hear their voices close to his verandah. But as it is well for his superintendent to be there constantly during the shearing, and for himself to be there often, any great distance is inconvenient. As my young friend sorted his own wool himself, he was generally in the wool-shed before the shearers, and did not leave it till long after they had "knocked off" work. The wool-shed was a wooden edifice, made of rough timber, roofed with bark, divided into pens, with room for eleven men to shear, and with outside pens for the shorn sheep as they leave the men's hands,—a pen for each shearer. It was constructed to hold about 300 sheep,—and that number would be put into it over-night, so that, even should rain come, there might be so many ready for the shearers in the morning,—for sheep cannot be shorn when wet. The form of the shed was that of the letter L, the base, however, being considerably larger than the upstroke. Along the base the shearers worked. At the corner were the sorting-table, and divided cribs for the different fleeces. In the upper part of the letter the wool was packed, and pressed, and stored, till the drays should come to take it away. My friend acknowledged that he did not think much of his own house, though he had built it himself,— but he was proud of his wool-shed, which was also the creation of his own ingenuity. About a quarter of a mile from the wool-shed was the shearers' hut, in which the men slept, and ate, and smoked their pipes. They had their own cook, who on this occasion was a Chinaman,—and, as is always the case with shearers, they gave their cook enough to do. He was generally to be seen outside the door of the hut chopping up onions. The cook had 25s. a week and his rations, —the shearers were earning on an average about 7s. 6d. a day, which was considered bad work. There was rain, and the weather was against the men. The shearers bought their own food from the head station, paying at the rate of 7s. 6d. a week each for it.

There were three other paddocks on the run,—one containing

12,000 acres, and the others 7,000 acres each. The greater part of the fencing necessary for these domains had been put up by my friend since his occupation at an average cost of £25 a mile. There were over forty miles of fencing on the run, made either with logs laid at length on short round blocks,—called in the bush chock and log,—or of bushes laid lengthways and staked down with forked timber. This fencing suffices for sheep, but would be of no use at all on a run intended for cattle. When a run is not fenced, each flock of sheep requires a shepherd, and the sheep are brought up at night to an enclosure close to the shepherd's hut. When a run is "paddocked", shepherds are not required;—but boundary-riders are employed, each of whom is supplied with two horses, and these men are responsible not only for the sheep but for the fences. They should see every portion of their fences at any rate three times a week, and repair the breaches. A bush fence is easily broken down, but is as easily put up again.

The natural grasses of the bush in the locality of which I am speaking would carry in ordinary weather a sheep to three acres. When the weather was damp and warm it would do much more; when there was either frost or drought, it would not do so much. At M—— there was back ground outside the paddocks as extensive as the fenced area, and it was computed that the run might carry safely about 16,000 sheep.

The house was built at right angles to the creek, to the edge of which the little garden ran. It was of course only of one storey. A squatter rarely builds a two-storied house till he be a very large squatter indeed, and then his habitation loses most of the characteristics of the bush. It was of one storey and contained but three rooms,—a sitting-room in the middle and a bedroom on each side; —but along the front there ran a verandah twelve feet wide, in which everybody lived,—using the sitting-room simply for meals. Life in the bush would be nothing without a verandah. The men of course spend their days mostly out of doors,—but in the evenings the verandahs are delightful. Here are congregated lounging chairs, generally very rough, but always comfortable,—with tables, sofas, and feminine nick-nacks, if there be ladies, till the place has the appearance of a room open to the heavens. A Verandah to be perfect should be curtained against the sun, and should be sheltered also from the heat by creepers. Behind the house, about thirty yards distant from it, was the kitchen, with a servant's room attached to it,—and behind that again another edifice, called the cottage, consisting of two rooms, in which slept the young men who were about the place;—for it must be remembered that there always are young men about a squatter's station. Then there were other buildings,—forming a quadrangle, which however was never as neat as such homestead quadrangle should be. There was a rough stable, and a rougher coach-house,—and that indispensable accessory the store-room. The place was altogether rough, and certainly not well kept; but it was comfortable and picturesque, and easily susceptible of improvement when increasing flocks and high prices for wool would justify the expenditure.

Almost all these pastoral homesteads are thus made up of various cottages,—till sometimes the place assumes the appearance of a village. When the station is large there will often be a church and a school,—and a separate house for strangers, and a shop for the stores, and an office. At M—— no such grandeur had as yet displayed itself. But there was a garden,—in which the opossums would eat the vegetables,—and an orchard had been commenced.

There was one house at a distance of only three miles which was a great drawback to my friend's happiness,—for it was inhabited by a free-selecter and a publican. I rather liked the publican, as he got up a kangaroo hunt for me,—but the vicinity of grog was looked upon as a serious evil by the squatter. And yet the men never drank when they were at work,—would work for weeks without anything stronger than tea. But if, on an occasion, any one of the station hands did take a drink, he would stay and drink till he was turned out of the house on the plea that he had consumed all his money. This public-house was a blistering thorn in the side of my friend. A gold-field town, whence the letters came, was twelve miles distant, but this was visited as rarely as possible, and was regarded as almost obtrusive in having caused itself to be built in a pastoral district. The nearest neighbour for any social purpose was another squatter, twenty-five miles off.

Of social gatherings, such as we know them, there are none in the bush. Squatters do not go out to dine, or ask each other to dinner. As a rule, I think, they rarely invite each other for country visiting. But they make the freest use of each other's houses,—so that society of a certain kind is created. They do not make visits exclusively of pleasure,—but when business calls them from home they make no scruple of riding up to each other's doors, and demanding hospitality. A bush house is never considered to be full. If there be not rooms apiece for the guests, the men are put together and the women together. If there be not bedsteads, beds are made up on the floors. If room be still lacking, the young men wrap themselves in blankets and stretch themselves in the verandah. It is a point of honour that the house shall never be full,—unless some one very odious comes the way. But even for those who are odious shelter and food are provided in some outside hut or barrack.

I was at M—— during washing and shearing. I speak of course of the washing of sheep. It was the busiest time of the year, and the squatter himself was always out soon after five, and rarely back at the house in time for dinner at eight. He had two assistants, one of whom was his permanent first lieutenant on the run, and the other was borrowed for the occasion. The three, who were all young, certainly worked much harder than any other men about the place, and seemed to have more on hand than a British prime minister in June. I rode about at my ease,—from the washpool to the wool-shed, and from the wool-shed to the kangaroos,—giving now and then a fantastic opinion as to the doing of the work, criticising the roughness of the mode in which the poor brutes were hauled into the water, or the cruelty with which they were wounded by the shearers. But my friends were terribly in earnest. Now and again a man would misbehave, and squatters' law had to be exercised with prompt decision. If a man would not work, or worked amiss, he was sent away with very curt warning,—for the deed of agreement which is always drawn up, gives the squatter the power of judging as to the man's deficiency, and of punishing him for being deficient. The sheep were always being washed, and always being shorn,—but if the rain should come between the two operations all would be spoilt. Rain did come,—but not thorough rain, and all was not spoilt. And then the "yarding" of sheep by hundreds at a time—getting them through one set of pens before washing, and through another set before shearing,—having them ready for the morning's work, and finished off before the dark night came,—weighing out tea and sugar and flour for the men, killing and preparing meat for them, sorting and packing the wool, pressing and labelling the bales,—all seemed to demand more than Herculean energy. At large stations all this is done easily, because the greater number admit of divided labour. It seemed to me that the care of ten thousand sheep was the most difficult task that a man could have imposed upon him.

Those rides through the forest either when I was alone, or when I could get my host to go with me,—which was rarely, unless on a Sunday afternoon,—were very pleasant. The melancholy note of the magpie was almost the only sound that was heard. Occasionally kangaroos would be seen,—two or three staring about them after a half-tame fashion, as though they had not as yet made up their mind whether it would be necessary for them to run. When approached they would move,—always in a line, and with apparent leisure till pursued. Then they would bound away, one here and one there, at a pace which made it impossible for a single horseman to get near them in a thickly timbered country. It was all wood. There arose at last a feeling that go where one might through the forest, one was never going anywhere. It was all picturesque,—for there was rocky ground here and there, and hills in the distance, and the trees were not too close for the making of pretty vistas through them;—but it was all the same. One might ride on, to the right or to the left, or might turn back, and there was ever the same view. And there were no objects to reach, unless it was the paddock fence. And when the paddock fence was jumped, then it was the same thing again. Looking around, one could tell by no outward sign whether one was inside or outside the boundary,—whether one was two miles or ten miles from the station.

Perhaps the most astonishing phenomenon on these runs is the apparent paucity of sheep. As a fact, there are thousands all around; —but unless looked for they are never seen; and even when looked for by experienced eyes are often missed. If the reader will bear in mind that an enclosure of 12,000 acres contains more than eighteen square miles, he will understand how unlike to anything in England must be even the enclosed country in Australia. One seems to ride for ever and to come to nothing, and to relinquish at last the very idea of an object. Nevertheless, it was very pleasant. Of all places that I was ever in this place seemed to be the fittest for contemplation. There was no record of the hours but by the light. When it was night work would be over. The men would cease as the sun was setting,—but the masters would continue till the darkness had come upon them.

There were four or five meals in the day. There was an early breakfast in the cottage for the young men,—there was another breakfast at nine for those who were idle,—for the ladies who were there and for myself. There was lunch at about two, to which one or two from the wool-shed might or might not rush in as things were going with them,—and there was dinner at about eight o'clock. My wife had brought a cook with her from England who was invaluable,—or would have been had she not found a husband for herself when she had been about a month in the bush. But in spite of her love, and her engagement to a man who was considerably above her in position, she was true to us while she remained at

Officers of the
Sydney Volunteer Corps

Native police

'Bailed Up', oil painting of a bushranger's hold-up in the 1860s, by Tom Roberts

M——, and did her best to make us all comfortable. She was a
good-looking strong woman, of excellent temper, who could do
anything she put her hand to, from hairdressing and confectionery
up to making butter and brewing beer. I saw her six months
afterwards,—"quite the lady", but ready for any kind of work that
might come in her way. When I think of her, I feel that no woman
of that kind ought, as regards herself, to stay in England if she can
take herself or get herself taken to the colonies. I mention our cook
because her assistance certainly tended very greatly to our increased
comfort. The viands provided were mutton, bread, vegetables, and
tea. Potatoes were purchased as an ordinary part of the station
stores, and the opossums had left us lettuce, tomatoes, and a few
cabbages. Dinner was always dignified with soup and salad,—which
must not, however, be regarded as being within the ordinary bush
dietary. In other respects the meals were all alike. There was
mutton in every shape, and there was always tea. Tea at a squatter's
table,—at the table of a squatter who has not yet advanced himself
to a man-cook or butler and a two-storied house,—is absolutely
indispensable. At this squatter's table there was colonial wine and
there was brandy,—produced chiefly to supply my wants; but there
was always tea. The young men when they came in, hot and fagged
with their day's work, would take a glass of brandy and water
standing, as a working man with us takes his glass of beer at a bar.
But when they sat down with their dinners before them, the tea-cup
did for them what the wine-glass does for us. The practice is so
invariable that any shepherd whose hut you may visit will show his
courtesy by asking you to take a pannikin of tea. In supplying
stores to men, tea and sugar, flour and meat are the four things
which are included as matters of course. The tea is always bought
by the chest, and was sold by the merchant at the rate of 1s. 6d.
a pound. There was but one class of tea at the station, which I
found to be preferable to very much that I am called upon to drink
in England.

The recreations of the evening consisted chiefly of tobacco in the
verandah. I did endeavour to institute a whist table, but I found that
my friends, who were wonderfully good in regard to the age and
points of a sheep, and who could tell to the fraction of a penny what
the wool of each was worth by the pound, never could be got to
remember the highest card of the suit. I should not have minded
that had they not so manifestly despised me for regarding such
knowledge as important. They were right, no doubt, as the points
of a sheep are of more importance than the pips of a card, and the

human mind will hardly admit of the two together. Whist is a jealous mistress;—and so is a sheep station.

Later he saw a very much bigger run:

The run which I visited bears about 120,000 sheep,—and they wander over about 1,200,000 acres. For all these sheep, and for all this extent of sheep-run, it is necessary to obtain water by means of wells, sunk to various depths from fifty to one hundred and twenty feet. The water can always be found,—not indeed always at the first attempt, but so surely that no land in that region need be deserted for want of it. The water when procured is invariably more or less brackish;—but the sheep thrive on it and like it. The wells are generally worked by men, sometimes by horses; but on large runs, where capital has been made available, the water is raised by wind-mills. Such was the case at the place I visited. The water is brought up into large tanks, holding from 30,000 to 60,000 gallons each, and from these tanks is distributed into troughs, made of stone and cement. These are carried out in different directions, perhaps two or three from each tank, and are so arranged that sheep can be watered from either side. If therefore there be three such troughs, the sheep in six different paddocks can be watered from one tank,—the well being so placed as to admit egress to it from various paddocks, all converging on the same centre. In this way 10,000 sheep will be watered at one well. As these paddocks contain perhaps 40 square miles each, or over 25,000 acres, the animals have some distance to travel before they can get a drink. In cold weather they do not require to drink above once in three days; in moderate weather once in two days;—in very hot weather they will lie near to the troughs and not trouble themselves to go afield in search of food. On the run which I visited there were twenty of these wells, which, with their appurtenances of tanks, and troughs, and wind-mills, had cost about £500 each;— and there had been about as many failures in the search of water, wells which had been dug but at which no water was found;—and these had not been sunk without considerable expenditure. It may therefore be understood that a man requires some capital before he can set himself up as a grower of wool on a large scale in South Australia.

He was impressed, too, by the standard of living of the average station hand:

Meat three times a day is the normal condition of the Queensland labourer. In the colony mutton may be worth three halfpence per pound, or perhaps twopence; but of the price the labourer takes no heed. He is provided as a matter of course with rations,—fourteen pounds of meat a week is the ordinary allowance for a labourer in Queensland,—and, as regards food for himself, he is called upon to take no thought of the morrow, any more than if he were a babe. Fourteen pounds of meat, eight pounds of flour, two pounds of sugar, and a quarter of a pound of tea are allotted to him weekly. This in England would cost, at the lowest price, something over 12s. a week,—more than the labourer can earn altogether,—and this the labourer in Queensland enjoys as a matter of course before he comes to the question of wages.

I may, however, as well declare at once that the all but divine happiness of such a state of existence,—as it will appear to the delver at home,—seems very soon to lose its brilliance in the eyes of the man when he is in Queensland. He has hardly eaten a few hundred pounds of colonial mutton, has not been on rations six months, before he has forgotten entirely that he was ever short of supply in the matter of animal food. The Irishman who has come from the unchanging perpetuity of potatoes to a plethora of meat, teaches himself to believe within twelve months that he never sat down to dinner at home without a beefsteak or a roast fowl. I came to a little dispute once with a working man at Rockhampton. "If you knew what it was," he said, "to have to eat mutton three times a day, day after day, week after week, month after month, you would not come here and tell us that we ought to be contented with our condition." Looking at the matter in his light, I see that he has some justice on his side. I told him, jeering at him ill-naturedly, that if he would give up one meal a day, he would lessen his sorrow by at least a third;—but I saw that I was not regarded as having the best of the argument. I would wish therefore that the would-be emigrating English labourer should understand that when he gets his meat in plenty it will not be to him a blessing so unalloyed as he now thinks it. Alas, is it not the same with all blessings? What is there for which we toil and sigh, which when gained does not become to us like mutton served thrice daily? The seat in parliament, the beautiful young wife, even accumulated wealth, all pall upon us; and we exclaim, as did my labouring friend at Rockhampton,—"If you too had to eat this mutton three times a day you would not think your condition so blessed."

But he demolished part of the Australian legend and classified the swagman as a mixture of super-tramp and blackmailer:

The nomad tribe of pastoral labourers,—of men who profess to be shepherds, boundary-riders, sheep-washers, shearers, and the like,—form altogether one of the strangest institutions ever known in a land, and one which to my eyes is more degrading and more injurious even than that other institution of sheep-stealing. It is common to all the Australian colonies, and has arisen from the general feeling of hospitality which is always engendered in a new country by the lack of sufficient accommodation for travellers. In the pastoral districts it is understood that when hospitality is demanded from a squatter it shall be given. At small stations there are two classes of welcome. The labouring man, with his "swag" over his back,—the "swag" being his luggage, comprising probably all the property he has in the world,—is sent to the "hut". There is a hut at every station, fitted up with bunks, in which the workmen sleep. Here the wanderer is allowed to stretch his blanket for the night,—and on all such occasions two meals are allowed to him. He has meat and flour in the morning, and meat and flour in the evening. Then he passes on his way. If the traveller be of another description,—a squatter himself, an overseer journeying from one station to another, a man who on any pretence claims to be akin to gentlehood,—he is taken into the squatter's house, and sits at the squatter's table, and has tea as well as bread and meat,—and brandy and water, if brandy and water be the family beverage. On large stations, at which the overseer has a separate residence, travellers of this superior class are relegated to his house, and the great squatter hears nothing about it,—except that he defrays the cost of the entertainment. In this way a wide hospitality is exercised, which has become proverbial; which, when thus described, has an Arcadian charm about it which is quite refreshing to the imagination:—but which has led to a terrible evil under which the squatter groans with all but acknowledged impotence.

This evil concerns only the first-named class of wanderer. I have heard no squatter complain of the burden of entertaining men who are travelling from one part of the colonies to another on legitimate business. A certain allowance is made for the expense, and the practice is recognised as being convenient to all parties. But it has come to be very far from convenient as regards the so-called workman with his "swag". By many men it has been found to be a way of living which enables them to spend in rapid debauch the money earned by the labour of a few months, and to exist in idleness during the remainder of the year. By many others it has been adopted as the practice of the entire twelvemonth. The expense thus entailed upon stations has become incredibly great. One gentleman told me that such men cost him £300 a-year. I heard of a squatter's establishment in Victoria at which £1,000 a-year was expended in this involuntary entertainment of vagabond strangers. And the evil by no means ends here. A mode of life is afforded to recusant labourers which enables men to refuse work at fair terms, and to rebel against their masters when their work or their wages are not to their liking. They know that the squatters of the colonies do not dare to refuse them food and shelter.

Such men, when they appear, generally ask for work. They not unfrequently come on horseback, and always bring their luggage,— a blanket, a tin pot, and some small personalities wrapped up in the blanket. The squatter,—or more probably the overseer,—knows very well from the man's aspect that he does not mean to work. Sometimes he is asked to chop wood before he has his supper, but as a rule it is understood that such demand will not be efficacious for any good purpose. It is better to let him have his lump of meat and his flour, with use of a bunk,—and then pass on to the next squatter. But the lump of meat, and the flour, and the use of the bunk he must have.

But why must he have them? The overseer could refuse the accustomed liberality, and the man with some growling would pass on and "camp out" with an empty stomach under some log. Or why, at any rate, should not the food be refused till it have been first earned by sufficient work? "There be the logs, my friend. Reduce them to convenient firewood,—as may be done by three hours' work,—and you shall be fed. Dark is it? Then you should come earlier and earn your victuals. But victuals without earning you shall not have." The squatter who did so would be at once known; his sheep would be slaughtered; his fences would be burned; and his horses would be houghed. The vagabond wayfarers are too numerous and too strong, and are able to obtain by terrorism that which hospitality no longer bestows. A squatter with his fences burned would be a ruined man.

Trollope is as prosaic as one might expect him to be about the pleasures of camping under the stars:

I travelled to Perth with a friend, having made a bargain with the mail contractor to take us,—not with the mail, which goes through without stopping in seventy hours,—but by a separate conveyance in four days, so that we might sleep during the nights. This we did, taking our own provisions with us, and camping out in the bush under blankets. The camping out was, I think, rather pride on our part, to show the Australians that we Englishmen,—my friend, indeed, was a Scotchman—could sleep on the ground, sub dio, and do without washing, and eat nastiness out of a box, as well as they could. There were police barracks in which we might have got accommodation. At any rate, going and coming we had our way. We lit fires for ourselves, and boiled our tea in billies; and then regaled ourselves with bad brandy and water out of pannikins, cooked bacon and potatoes in a frying-pan, and pretended to think that it was very jolly. My Scotch friend was a young man, and was, perhaps, in earnest. For myself, I must acknowledge that when I got up about five o'clock on a dark wet morning, very damp, with the clothes and boots on which I was destined to wear for the day, with the necessity before me of packing up my wet blankets, and endeavoured, for some minutes in vain, to wake the snoring driver, who had been crouched but a few feet from me, I did not feel any ardent desire to throw off for ever the soft luxuries of an effeminate civilisation, in order that I might permanently enjoy the freedom of the bush. But I did it, and it is well to be able to do it.

No man perhaps ever travelled two hundred and sixty miles with less to see. The road goes eternally through wood,—which in Australia is always called bush; and, possibly, sandy desert might be more tedious. But the bush in these parts never develops itself into scenery, never for a moment becomes interesting. There are no mountains, no hills that affect the eye, no vistas through the trees tempting the foot to wander. Once on the journey up, and once on the return, we saw kangaroos, but we saw no other animal; now and again a magpie was heard in the woods, but very rarely. The commonest noise is that of the bull-frog, which is very loud, and altogether unlike the sound of frogs in Europe. It is said that the Dutch under Peter Nuyt, when landing somewhere on these coasts,—probably near Albany,—were so frightened by the frogs that they ran away. I can believe it, for I have heard frogs at Albany roaring in such a fashion as to make a stranger think that the hills were infested with legions of lions, tigers, bears, and rhinoceroses, and that every lion, tiger, bear, and rhinoceros in the country was just about to spring at him. I knew they were only frogs, and yet I did not like it. The bush in Australia generally is singularly destitute of life. One hears much of the snakes, because the snakes are specially deadly; but one sees them seldom, and no precaution in regard to them is taken. Of all animals, the opossum is the commonest. He may be easily taken as his habits are known,

but he never shows himself. In perfect silence the journey through
the bush is made,—fifteen miles to some water-hole, where breakfast is eaten; fifteen on to another water-hole, where brandy and
water is consumed; fifteen again to more water, and dinner; and
then again fifteen, till the place is reached at which the night-fire
is made and the blankets are stretched upon the ground. In such a
journey, everything depends on one's companion, and in this I was
more than ordinarily fortunate. As we were taken by the mail
contractor, we had relays of horses along the road.

He is at his best—as one might expect the author of *Hunting
Sketches* to be—when he describes an Australian race-meeting
and a drag hunt:

The English passion for the amusements which are technically
called "Sports", is as strong in these colonies as it is at home.
Why the taste should have transported itself to Australia and not
to the United States I am not prepared to explain,—but I think
any one who has observed the two countries will acknowledge that
it is so. Trotting matches and yacht-racing are no doubt in vogue
in the States, and there are men, few in number, who take kindly to
shooting,—especially they who live near the Chesapeake and have
canvas-back ducks within their reach. There is a set of betting-men
at New York, who probably are beaten by none in the ferocity of
their gambling. But "sport" is not a national necessity with the
Americans, whereas with the Australians it is almost as much so
as at home. Cricket, athletics, rowing matches, shooting, hunting,
flat-racing, and steeplechasing are dear to them. There is hardly a
town to be called a town which has not its racecourse, and there are
many racecourses where there are no towns. As I was never either a
cricketer nor an athlete, and know nothing of shooting or of racing,
I am not qualified to describe the fashion in which our Australian
cousins fulfil their ambition in these respects; but I can say that
they are ambitious and are successful. In Queensland I saw kangaroos, wallybies and iguanas shot down with precision. In Gipp's
Land I was witness to a great slaughter of wild ducks and black
swans. At Hobart Town, in Tasmania, there came off while I was
in the neighbourhood a regatta, for not being present at which I
was much abused. And I know that I was wrong, for the scene must
have been very lovely. No spot could be better arranged for boat-
racing than the mouth of the Derwent, with the open public park
rising high and close above the water. I was inspecting a lunatic
asylum at the time, and think that the regatta would have been

more amusing. Horse-racing I hate. As the horses run, I never can distinguish the colours; I generally lose sundry small bets; and I don't like champagne. But I did go to the Launceston races in Tasmania, in reference to which I can only remark that the number of betting-men who came over from Melbourne to make money out of the small performances on that occasion surprised me very much. When the meeting was over I went back to Melbourne with a ship-load of them, and was lost in speculation how so many carrion birds could live on so small an amount of prey. As to the professional activity of the confraternity, the diligence with which they worked at their trade, the unremitting attention which they paid to the smallest chances, I had no doubt. They all looked as though they would eat each other on board the boat, and I thought that some such unsatisfactory meals were made. Though the night was very cold I slept upon the deck, as the banquet was going on below. The songs of triumph and the wailings of despair at such festivals do not make pleasant music for an outsider.

I went also to see some hurdle-racing and steeple-chasing at the Melbourne racecourse,—partly because I had been told that the course itself was especially worth seeing, and partly as having been invited to join a pleasant party. It had been impressed upon me as a duty that I should see at least one day's racing at Melbourne, in order that I might report on the aspect of the racecourse, the skill of the riders, and especially on the manners of the people. The course itself is something under two miles round. The courses run can, here as elsewhere, be arranged to any distance. The races I saw were described as being about three and two miles, and were all leap-races. I can only say of the fences prepared that I never before saw any which appeared to me so dangerous. They consisted chiefly of timber built up so stiffly that no horse and rider could break them, and were about four feet eight inches high. There was also a wall or two in the distant part of the course;—but I regard walls as very much less dangerous to men and horses than timber. The riding appeared to me bold to a fault, men being utterly reckless in riding beaten horses at barriers of built-up timber. The fashion and traditions of the place require that men shall so ride, and they certainly keep up the fashion and traditions. Consequently, on the occasion to which I allude there were almost innumerable falls. I think seven men and horses were down in one race, and four in another. I heard afterwards that the sports of the day were considered to have gone off with very harmless success. One jockey was a good deal crushed, and another had his collar-bone broken. Why half-a-dozen were not killed I cannot explain. Some of the horses jumped with admirable precision, taking just all the labour that was necessary and no more; but, as I afterwards learned, these horses will jump almost any amount of timber, but know nothing of fences, which are less dangerous, but more complicated and requiring greater skill. From the stewards' stand, and from the top of the great stand,— and indeed from the seats below,—every part of the course can be seen, so that with a good field-glass the working of any horse or any jockey may be watched throughout the whole race.

But perhaps the most remarkable feature of the performance was the demeanour of the people. From the beginning to the end of the day, I saw no one drunk; I heard no word that could shock any lady; I found no one rough, uncourteous, or displeasing. There was no thimble-rigging and no throwing of sticks. All the world was decent and decently dressed. Within a certain enclosure,—if it was enclosed,—ladies walked about with gentlemen; and outside of it, the world amused itself with orderly propriety. The meeting was not by any means the largest of the year, but I was assured by those who were qualified to give an opinion,—among others by the Governor of the Colony,—that the conduct of the crowd was the same even when the crowd was the greatest. It should be understood at home that the people of these colonies are almost invariably decent in their dress, and decent in their language. There certainly was no reason why ladies should not be present at the races I saw,— unless ladies dislike to see jockeys falling over high railings.

There was indeed a betting-ring, in which the usual applications were being made to some outside and invisible world to accept lavish offers of complicated bets. Men were walking about making unintelligible appeals apparently to each other,—which nobody ever seemed to accept. I am bound to say that the Melbourne ring looked to be as villainous as any other ring that I ever saw. The men wore the same objectionable clothing, were conspicuous in the same manner for indescribably abominable hats, and talked in that tone which to ordinary ears seems to be in itself evidence of rascality sufficient to hang a man. There were present, perhaps, two or three dozen of them ready to pick out any man's eyes; but I could not discern the prey. There is prey no doubt, as the profession thrives and wears jewellery. But the betting-ring on the Melbourne racecourse will hurt no one who does not expressly seek its precincts.

On the following day there was a great hunt breakfast,—or luncheon,—and the opening meet of the season with the Melbourne staghounds. Of other sports I practically know nothing.

In regard to hunting I have for many years been striving to do something. So much was known of me by certain kind friends, and I was therefore invited to the entertainment and provided with a horse,—as to which I was assured that though he was small he was up to any weight, could go for ever and jump anything. The country would be very rough;—so much was acknowledged,—and the fences very big; but it was suggested to me that if I would only drink enough sherry I might see a good deal of the run. I thought of my weight,—which is considerable, of my eyesight,—which is imperfect, of my inexperience in regard to timber fences four feet six inches high—which up to that moment was complete; I thought also that my informant in respect to the little horse, though indubitably veracious in intention, might probably be mistaken in his information, never having ridden the horse himself. Wishing to return once more to England so that I might publish my book, I resolved that discretion would be on this occasion the better part of valour, and that I would save my neck at the expense of the ill-opinion of the Melbourne hunting-field.

Such a hunt-banquet I never saw before. The spot was some eight or ten miles from Melbourne, close upon the sea-shore, and with a railway-station within a quarter of a mile. It was a magnificent day for a picnic, with a bright sun and a cool air, so that the temptations to come, over and beyond that of hunting, were great. About two hundred men were assembled in a tent pitched behind the house of the master of the festival, of whom perhaps a quarter were dressed in scarlet. Nothing could have been done better, or in better taste. There was no speaking, no drinking,—so to be called, but a violent clatter of knives and forks for about half-an-hour. At about two we were out on a common smoking our cigars in front of the house, and remained there talking to the ladies in carriages till nearly three, when we started. I found the horse provided for me to be a stout, easily-ridden, well-bitted cob; but when I remembered what posts and rails were in this country, I certainly thought that he was very small. No doubt discretion would be the better part of valour! With such a crowd of horses as I saw around me, there would probably be many discreet besides myself, so that I might attain decent obscurity amidst a multitude. I had not bedizened myself in a scarlet coat.

We were upon a heath, and I calculated that there were present about two hundred and fifty horsemen. There was a fair sprinkling of ladies, and I was requested to observe one or two of them, as they would assuredly ride well. There is often a little mystery about

hunting,—especially in the early part of the day,—as all men know
who ride to hounds at home. It is not good that everybody should
be told what covert is to be drawn first; and even with staghounds
the officials of the pack will not always answer with full veracity
every question put to them by every stranger. On this occasion there
seemed to be considerable mystery. No one seemed to know where
we were going to begin, and there was a doubt as to the quarry to
be chased. I had been told that we were to hunt a dingo,—or wild
dog; and there was evidently a general opinion that turning down a
dingo,—shaking him I suppose out of a bag,—was good and genuine sport. We do not like bagged foxes at home,—but I fancy that
they are unpopular chiefly because they will never run. If a dingo
will run, I do not see why he should not be turned down as well as a
deer out of a cart. But on this occasion I heard whispers about,—a
drag. The asseverations about the dingo were, however, louder
than the whispers about a drag, and I went on, believing that the
hounds would be put upon the trail of the animal. We rode for some
three or four miles over heath-land, nobody around me seeming to
be in the least aware when the thing would commence. The hunts-
man was crabbed and uncommunicative. The master was soft as
satin, but as impregnable as plate armour. I asked no questions
myself, knowing that time will unravel most things; but I heard
questions asked, the answers to which gave no information whatever. At last the hounds began to stir among the high heather, and
were hunting something. I cared little what it was, if only there
might be no posts and rails in that country. I like to go, but I don't
like to break my neck; and between the two I was uncomfortable.
The last fences I had seen were all wire, and I was sure that a drag
would not be laid among them. But we had got clear of wire fences,
—wire all through from top to bottom,—before we began. We
seemed to be on an open heath, riding round a swamp, without an
obstacle in sight. As long as that lasted I could go as well as the
best.

But it did not last. In some three minutes, having ridden about
half a mile, I found myself approaching such an obstacle as in England would stop a whole field. It was not only the height but the
obduracy of the wooden barrier,—which seemed as though it were
built against every-rushing herds of wild bulls. At home we are not
used to such fences, and therefore they are terrible to us. At a four
foot and a half wall, a man with a good heart and a good horse will
ride; and the animal, if he knows what he is about, will strike it,
sometimes with fore as well as hind feet, and come down without

any great exertion. But the post and rail in Australia should be taken with a clear flying leap. There are two alternatives if this be not done. If the horse and man be heavy enough and the pace good enough, the top bar may be broken. It is generally about eight inches deep and four thick, is quite rough, and apparently new,— but, as on this occasion I saw repeatedly, it may be broken; and when broken the horse and rider go through unscathed,—carried by their own impetus, as a candle may be fired through a deal board. The other chance is to fall,—which event seemed to occur more often even than the smashing of the rail. Now I was especially warned that if I rode slowly at these fences, and fell, my horse would certainly fall atop of me; whereas if I went fast I should assuredly be launched so far ahead that there would be room for my horse between me and the fence which had upset me. It was not a nice prospect for a man riding something over sixteen stone!

But now had come the moment in which I must make up my mind. Half-a-dozen baulked it. Two fell, escaping their own horses by judicious impetus. One gentleman got his horse half over, the fore quarters being on one side, and the hind on the other, so that the animal was hung up. A lady rode at it with spirit, but checked her horse with the curb, and he, rearing back, fell on her. Another lady took it in gallant style. Of those before me no one seemed to flinch it. For a moment it seemed as though the honour of all the hunting fields in England were entrusted to my keeping, and I determined to dare greatly, let the penalty be what it might. With firm hands and legs, but with heart very low down, I crammed the little brute at the mountain of woodwork. As I did so I knew that he could not carry me over. Luckily he knew as much about it as I did, and made not the slightest attempt to rise with me. I don't know that I ever felt so fond of a horse before.

At that moment, an interesting individual coming like a cannon ball, crashed the top bar beside me, and I, finding that the lady was comfortably arranging her back hair with plenty of assistance, rode gallantly over the second bar. For the next half-hour I took care always to go over second bars, waiting patiently till a top bar was broken. I had found my level, and had resolved to keep it. On one occasion I thought that a top bar never would be broken,—and the cessation was unpleasant, as successful horsemen disappeared one after another. But I perceived that there was a regular company of second-bar men, so that as long as I could get over a rail three feet high I need not fear that I should be left alone. And hitherto the pace had not been quick enough to throw the second-bar men out of the hunt. But soon there came a real misfortune. There was a fence with only one bar,—with only one apparent obstacle. I am blind as well as heavy, and I did not see the treacherous wire beneath. A heavy philanthropist, just before me, smashed the one, and I rode on at what I thought to be a free course. My little horse, seeing no more than I did, rushed upon the wire, and the two of us were rolled over in ignominious dismay. The horse was quicker on his feet than I was, and liking the sport, joined it at once single-handed; while I was left alone and disconsolate. Men and horses,—even the sound of men and horses,—disappeared from me, and I found myself in solitude in a forest of gum trees.

I was certain that we had been running a drag all the morning. As I wandered about I felt the ignominy of the whole thing. If a man does ride to a drag he should at any rate ride well, and not lose his horse and be alone after the first half hour. And in that wild country I might be wandering about for a week without seeing anything but a cockatoo or an Australian magpie. There does, however, always come some relief in these miseries. I first encountered another horseless man, then a second companion in misery,—and at last a groom with my own little nag. As for the run, that, as regarded me, was of course over; but I had legs besides my own to take me back twelve miles to the place at which I was stopping.

Trollope, of course, never met the Australian son, also alive in the seventies, whose name has undoubtedly outshone that of the author—namely Ned Kelly the famous bushranger.

Bushrangers had existed in Australia ever since John "Black" Caesar escaped from Sydney jail in June 1789.

They learnt to live in the bush, in the confines of Tasmania as well as on the mainland. And in the days when most of the population were ex-prisoners the bushrangers were heroes at war with a hated police force. Well-spoken Matthew Brady achieved fame in 1824 when he held up the township of Sorrell, Tasmania, locked the soldiers and police in the town jail and freed the prisoners.

Jack Donahue who was transported from Dublin after being found guilty of intending to commit a crime drew the sympathy of every Irishman when he escaped from Sydney jail. He enjoyed three years of freedom and engineered many successful hold-ups before being shot in 1830 in a battle with the police. Pipe bowls were modelled from his death mask and the ballad of Bold Jack

Donahue became so popular that it was at one time banned in public houses.

Martin Cash, the gentleman bushranger, who made two escapes from the notorious Port Arthur jail in Tasmania, also came from Ireland, and was equally popular. He eventually became caretaker at Hobart Botanical Gardens.

Ben Hall, the son of a selector who ranged over the Weddin Mountains of New South Wales, was said to have turned bush-ranger after an ex-trooper had run off with his wife. Like many other bushrangers he was betrayed by a "friend".

The gold rushes of the fifties encouraged the idea that wealth could be easily got, and opened a new field of activity to the bushranger, who could hold up the coach which was transporting nuggets from the mine to the big city.

Frank Gardiner, an ex-horse thief, held up the gold escort coach at Eugowra Rocks in June 1862 for £12,000. He was pardoned and later kept a saloon in San Francisco.

As squatters pioneered further and further into the interior, there were new prizes to be won. Giant squatter estates offered giant temptations to cattle thieves who were good bushmen and knew how and where they could alter the brand marks and sell the stock. Some cattle thieves, known as poddy-dodgers, specialized in unbranded calves (clean skins). Harry Redford in 1870 "lifted" 1,000 head of cattle and drove them from the Bowen Downs Station near Roma in Queensland across 600 miles of uncharted wilderness and sold them at the Blanchewater Cattle Station for £5,000.

Sometimes wild cattle were rounded up by using a tame mob as a decoy. Confederates used smoke signals as a warning when troopers or boundary riders were in the offing. But much of the work was done by night.

But of all bushrangers, Ned Kelly stands alone in fame. He personified the Australian's desire for freedom in a land that was still untamed. He represented the Australian's contempt for the city-bred officials and for the city police armed with numbers rather than courage.

He was the national Robin Hood who burned the mortgage deeds held by the banks on the cattle of the small farmer, the friend of the people, the enemy of the rich squatters, a man whose courage gave rise to the phrase "Game as Ned Kelly".

Born in 1854 Ned Kelly learnt to ride amid the maze of ridges, gullies and scattered clearings of the foothills of the Australian Alps in the eastern part of Victoria. By the time he was sixteen he was already in trouble with the police for suspected horse-stealing and assault. At seventeen he was given a prison sentence of three years for resisting arrest. Freed six months early, he took a job in a sawmill but after three years he was back on the Oxley plains, at war with the squatters who, he claimed, were wrongfully seizing stray cattle belonging to the smaller farmers. A formidable outbreak of horse-stealing followed and, in a single year, Kelly's gang stole, rebranded, and sold more than two hundred horses. The police were so ineffective that the squatters themselves formed the "North Eastern Stock Protection Society".

In 1878 a warrant was issued for the arrest of Ned's brother, Dan Kelly, but when the police arrived at the Kelly home at Eleven Mile Creek, near Benalla, they met with a spirited resistance. Dan shot his way out and joined Ned. Mrs. Kelly, however, was found guilty of striking a policeman and given a three years' sentence.

Ned Kelly, now virtually an outlaw, set himself up with Dan on a small estate in the backwoods of Victoria, the very existence of which was unknown to the police, and it was about this time that two other famous members of the gang, Joe Byrne and Steve Hart, joined the two brothers.

Four policemen, disguised as prospectors, were sent to search for the outlaws, but the gang surprised and shot three of them.

Next, in December 1878, Kelly and his mates held up the bank at Euroa and carted the bank manager and his family into the country without anyone being the wiser. A reward of £1,000 was put on his head.

The Government was attacked for its incompetence and the newspapers profited from the best story for years. Banks in outlying districts demanded and were given guards; police began arresting anyone suspected of having helped the Kelly's by warning them of police movements, but the authorities had to release most of their captives for lack of evidence.

The gang's next *coup* was even bolder. In February 1879 they seized the police station at Jerilderie in New South Wales on the Murray River, put on police uniforms, and robbed the bank there, clearing some £2,000. They stayed overnight, using the Royal Mail Hotel as a lock-up for anyone who might have given the alarm, and left the same evening after cutting the telegraph wires.

The reward for the capture of the gang was raised to £8,000. Black trackers were sent south from Queensland, but after nearly a year and a half the police withdrew their search parties, and the gang were ready for one more strike. This time they attacked a police informer at a house near Beechworth, in Victoria not far from the New South Wales border, knowing that the police there would send for help to their headquarters at Benalla, forty miles to the south-west. They planned to stop the train at Glenrowan by pulling up the tracks; they could then capture the police force and drive the train back to Benalla to rob the bank there. They duly took over the village of Glenrowan. But one of the prisoners, a schoolmaster, escaped in time to wave his wife's red muffler and warned the driver of the train before it reached the break in the line. The Kelly gang, although wearing armour made from ploughshares, lost an unequal two-day battle with a force of fifty police who had no compunction about shooting indiscriminately into the mixed crowd of prisoners and civilians trapped in the burning hotel.

Kelly, who said that he could have escaped if he had been prepared to desert his mates, was tried and condemned in Melbourne with as much speed as possible, so that the case could be over before the races. He was said to have been unconcerned at the death sentence and sang bush songs in the death cell.

That is the foundation of the Kelly legend with the "sheriff" on the wrong side among the "baddies" and the hero a good deal less scrupulous than Robin Hood.

Perhaps less than a century ago it could only have happened in Australia—or possibly Ireland from where so many Australians had sprung.

It was the telegraph service coupled with the cheque system of banking which put an end to bushranging, just as it put an end to Australia's isolation from the rest of the world.

Charles Todd, a bushy bearded, quietly spoken Londoner,

Sheep-shearing in Australia in the 1860s

A miner's hut in New South Wales

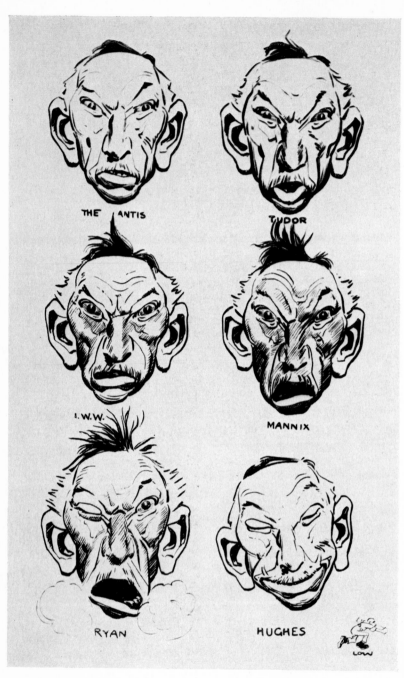

William Morris Hughes 'The Complete War Winner': cartoon by
Low from the *Bulletin*, 13th December 1917

was the man who linked Australia with the cable-head to the outer world by carrying the first telegraph line across the centre of Australia. He had worked at Greenwich Observatory and as assistant astronomer at Cambridge University. When Todd arrived, aged twenty-eight, in South Australia in 1855 as Government Astronomer and Superintendent of Telegraphy, news from Britain, even of events such as the Crimean War, still took three months to reach Australia, and when foreign mail arrived in Sydney the post office used to signal the event by displaying a blue flag on its flagstaff.

This was a severe handicap to the Colony, for other parts of the world had already been linked to one another by submarine cable for years past. Morse code signals were being sent beneath the English Channel in 1851. The bed of the Irish Sea was successfully crossed two years later and in 1858 messages sped underneath the Atlantic by a line between Britain and Newfoundland.

The opening of the Suez Canal in 1869 had speeded traffic between Britain and the Far East and made it all the more necessary for Australia to be tied into the new network of commerce and trade.

But to which point on the Australian mainland should the cable head be brought? The big centres of population, where most of the messages would be received, and sent, were in the south of the continent. But sea-cable, which had to be protected from chafe, and other perils of the ocean was expensive to manufacture and costly to lay.

It was therefore more practical to take the submarine cable to Australia by the shortest sea crossing and bring it ashore somewhere on Australia's north coast. Messages could then be relayed to the south by land-line.

But the question of exactly where to establish the cable head was undecided. Western Australia naturally favoured the north-west cape and argued that this was the nearest point to Ceylon. The Queensland Government urged that the cable head should be brought further east into the Gulf of Carpentaria which was relatively close to Brisbane and the east coast.

But South Australia, which had recently been entrusted with the administration of the mostly unexplored Northern Territory

12

including the central section of the north coast, had other ideas.

And it was Todd who promoted the idea of a land-line running from south to north right across the continent.

It was with his encouragement that the South Australian Government offered to build a land-line from Port Augusta on the south coast of South Australia to Port Darwin, the Northern Territory's most promising haven, provided that the British Australian Telegraph Company, who were financing the submarine cable, would guarantee to bring it to Port Darwin. This arrangement would certainly prevent Queensland or Western Australia from securing the cable head.

But in return the South Australian Government had to promise to fulfil a very important condition. They had to undertake to see that this land-line would be complete and open to business by 1st January 1872, i.e. in about eighteen months. And this line had to be built across 1,200 miles of territory unsettled as yet by white men.

Some idea of the problems which faced the telegraph pioneers can be gathered from the experiences of those who had tried in earlier years to colonize "the Territory".

The first settlement made in 1824 at the suggestion of Sir Stamford Raffles had to be withdrawn four years later, because the pioneers considered themselves as military garrisons to be supported from outside rather than a self-supporting community.

A second expedition made in 1838 soon encountered hurricanes, outbreaks of fever, and rivalry from the financiers of the south, who urged London to invest money in Melbourne, Sydney and Adelaide rather than in the north where, they pointed out, rivers could rise ninety feet during "the wet" or rainy season.

The second expedition, like the first, was a military rather than a civilian enterprise. The settlers brought no fencing materials with them. Their sheep were lost in the long tropical grass or drowned, their ploughs could not cut their way through the herbage. In 1848 they were evacuated. In 1864 another attempt was made to establish an Acting Government Resident in Port Darwin, which was to be the capital of the area. But his

report of the surrounding countryside was so discouraging that
the official post was withdrawn in 1866. In 1870 Darwin
remained a trading port of only fifty whites dependent entirely
on sea traffic. The only available descriptions of the terrain were
to be found in the journals of Stuart and Leichhardt who had
himself perished somewhere in the area. There was not a single
metalled road over the total span from south to north of the
1,780 miles over which the telegraph line would pass.

However, once committed to the project the South Australian
Government lost no time in idle talk. The necessary legislation
was drafted and rushed through Parliament in a week. In the
next seven days the route was planned in three sections, and the
north and south sections (500 miles) put out to tender. The
Government made itself responsible for the centre link of 621
miles.

No one appeared to worry about food supplies for the teams
who were to set up the poles, or about fodder for the bullock
teams which were to pull the wagons. But at least the Government could buy in quantity. Contracts were placed without
delay for 2,000 miles of galvanized iron wire gauge 8, and
36,000 insulators and wrought iron supports—enough to cover
1,800 miles at ten posts to the mile. The poles had to be 20 feet
long, 9 to 10 inches in diameter at the foot and 5 to 6 inches at
the top. They had to be planted vertically and in line 4 feet deep
and the ground cleared for 15 feet round each pole.

The southern section from Port Augusta to latitude 27
degrees, being the easiest, was contracted for at £41 per mile.

The northern section from Port Darwin to the Roper River
was reckoned more difficult and the Government accepted a bid
of £60 per mile. From the Roper River southwards to a latitude
of 18°, through unknown territory, the contractors were to set
for £89 per mile.

Despite these signs of activity the Cable Company were
anxious to secure a guarantee that the operation of the cable
would not be held up by unforeseen delays. They insisted that
the South Australian Government should guarantee to pay the
sum of £70 for every day the overland line was delayed beyond
December 1871—and they insisted that this meant 1st December, not the end of the month. And if the delay was longer than

twenty-five days, the Cable Company reserved the right to cancel the contract and take their line elsewhere—perhaps through Queensland.

So what should have been an orderly operation turned out to be a "cliff-hanger" effort to beat the clock.

The northern teams, starting from Port Darwin in September, made good progress during the dry season and had completed just under ninety miles in less than eight weeks. But when the rains came in December the contractors found difficulties in getting supplies and forage for the horses up the boggy, flooded tracks. The men's food went mouldy, the flour was full of weevils, and at times the rum ran short, a serious matter. In March when the sugar ran out some of the men went on strike.

The Government Inspector thereupon cancelled the contract and said that South Australia herself would complete the work. It was almost the end of the wet season but because of the Inspector's action in cancelling the contract almost no progress was made even when the better weather came. Nothing more was done until the beginning of next "wet" with its promise of a further 60 inches of rain. And on 1st January 1872, the deadline for the contract, 394 miles of telegraph line had still to be laid in the north, although the central and southern sections had by a magnificent effort been completed to time. By June a gap of 262 miles still existed, and they had laid on a "pony express" to ferry messages across the gap. It was not until 22nd August that the line was completed.

The finances of the South Australian Government were safeguarded only by the fact that the submarine cable from Port Darwin under the Timor Sea to Banjoewanji had gone dead on 24th June. This not only absolved the South Australian Government from paying £70 a day, but also made it unlikely that the Cable Company would be able to spare the engineers and capital to lay another line to Australia other than the one that was already laid through Port Darwin to Port Augusta. On 21st October the submarine cable was once more in working order and South Australia was making £70 a day instead of having to spend it. And later Australia made far more when a £1 cable warned Australian farmers of a disastrous wheat harvest in

Europe in time for them to profit by the news to the extent of
£1 million or so.

New names had appeared on the map: Alice Springs named
after Charles Todd's wife; Dalhousie Springs named after Lady
Edith Ferguson, daughter of Marquis of Dalhousie, who gave
each of the telegraph parties a pack saddle full of books; Warlock Swamps named after Warlock, a horse with water-divining
capabilities; and Lake Woods named after Woods whose party
camped in sight of it for three days without realizing it was not a
mirage.

It was about a century since the world discovered Australia,
and now Australia had discovered the world.

11

Australia Looks Out

On 13th October 1887 Melba made her début as Gilda in
Verdi's *Rigoletto* at the Théâtre de la Monnaie in Brussels.

She was, of course, an Australian whose accent persisted so
strongly that it deterred her backers from letting her sing
anything in English.

She was so thoroughly Australian that when she retired she
built herself a house on the fringe of the bush within sight of the
hills that she had loved as a child. She chose her strange name
because it reminded her of home.

Helen Porter Mitchell, the daughter of a successful brick
manufacturer, was born on 19th May 1861 in a common-
place suburb of Melbourne, and was brought up near the
small bush township of Lilydale about forty-five miles from
Melbourne.

Her father was a strict Presbyterian who had an organ built
into the wall of his sitting-room to provide music for the private
services conducted, in this remote area, by a travelling priest.
Even as a girl Nellie loved to sing. Predictably Mr. Mitchell
discouraged her from giving concerts even at home and was
strongly opposed to her being trained as a singer. He was
delighted when, on a trip to Queensland following the death of
her mother, she fell in love and married Charles Armstrong,
younger son of the late Sir Andrew Armstrong, baronet, of

Gallen Priory, King's County, Ireland, the manager of a sugar plantation near Port Mackay.

But the rain, the boredom and the isolation soon proved too much for her and two months after the birth of her child, George, she left her husband for good, and returned to Melbourne, taking her baby with her. She hoped once more to make a career as a singer. Her father still refused to pay for any lessons, but, as Mrs. Armstrong, Nellie was soon giving successful concerts in Melbourne and was saving up to go to England for expert training.

In 1886, however, her problem solved itself. Mr. Mitchell was appointed to be Commissioner for the State of Victoria at the Indian and Colonial Exhibition to be held that year in London, and he decided to take his daughter and her small son along. The party landed at Tilbury in May 1886 and with London looking its fairest, settled down in a house in Sloane Street.

Then came the big disillusionment. Despite letters of introduction Nellie found that it was a handicap to be an Australian. Sir Arthur Sullivan, of Gilbert and Sullivan fame, thought that she would need a year's training before she could get even a small part in the *Mikado*, and the audience at a small concert she gave at the Prince's Hall in London was no more enthusiastic.

Nellie, however, had one more introduction given her by Mrs. Elise Wiedermann-Pinschoff, wife of the Austro-Hungarian Consul in Melbourne. It was to Madame Mathilde Marchesi, one of the world's great singing teachers, who lived in Paris. Mr. Mitchell reluctantly gave Nellie a modest sum for the trip and allowed her to go, on the clear understanding that if Madame Marchesi did not consider her voice worth training, she would come back to Australia and forget all about the idea of a singing career.

Nellie packed a couple of suitcases and set off for Paris, taking George, then four, with her. In two hours she had found a cheap hotel and was on her way to Madame Marchesi's house in the Rue Jouffroy not far from the Etoile. Nervously she rang the bell and handed in her letter of introduction. Yes, Madame Marchesi would see her at ten o'clock the following morning.

After a night of suspense Mrs. Armstrong presented herself to Madame Marchesi, a small, somewhat formidable, stiffly

erect grey-haired figure, dressed in black. Madame Marchesi
asked her questions about her background and her previous
experience, told her to step up on to a small platform in front
of her other students and asked her what she would like to sing.
Nellie chose "Sempre Libera" from *La Traviata*. Few of the
whispering students could have realized that they were witness-
ing an historic event in the world of music. Least of all Nellie
herself, for half-way through the song Madame Marchesi broke
off and asked her to stop screeching the top notes and sing them
"piano". However, before long the recital was over and Madame
Marchesi agreed to train her. Nellie settled down in two poorly
furnished rooms in Montmartre. She found that her savings and
the money that her father had given her were barely enough to
rent and feed and clothe herself and her son. The thick blue and
white striped serge dress that she had to wear day after day so
infuriated Madame Marchesi that she threatened to break off
the lessons. Nevertheless at the end of nine months Madame
Marchesi gave a special salon party (with electric light especially installed for the occasion) to introduce Nellie to Paris.

One day two directors of the Brussels Théâtre de la Monnaie
called at Madame Marchesi's house to hear the pupils sing. One
hopeful after another tried but the directors were unimpressed.
Then Melba sang—the Mad Scene from Ambroise Thomas's
opera *Hamlet*. The effect was immediate. The two men looked
at each other and, without saying another word, took Madame
Marchesi into another room. After a few moments she came
back and said to Melba, "My dear, these gentlemen want to
engage you to sing in Brussels at La Théâtre de la Monnaie."
A few minutes later Melba had signed a contract giving her
three thousand francs a month with all costumes found.

Melba's first appearance in Brussels must have been an un-
usually trying ordeal because Gilda is not on stage at all in the
first act of *Rigoletto*, and Melba had to keep up her courage
during a long wait. But, of course, she enjoyed tumultuous
success and when she next got back to Australia she was able
to ask £2,350 for a single appearance in Sydney.

It was enough to encourage every other Australian artist
lurking in the wings—and they were beginning to appear in
more than one field.

Australian sport had become "international" too. Cricket came to Australia with the military, who first played a straight bat—without pads or gloves—on a dirt patch close to the present site of Sydney Town Hall. In 1840 a cricket pitch was set up in Hyde Park where the race track formerly stood. But the first Test Match between England and Australia was played in Melbourne in 1877; it was won by Australia by forty-five runs. In 1882, after Australia had won a second Test victory by seven runs, this time in England, the famous "Ashes" trophy was presented: "In affectionate remembrance of English cricket which died at the Oval 29th August 1882, lamented by a large circle of sorrowing friends and acquaintances. R.I.P. (N.B. The body will be cremated and the ashes taken to Australia.)" Britain and Australia have been struggling ever since for the custody of the body.

Meanwhile in Australia in the eighties it was not "Go west, young man", but "Go north".

In 1883 various members of the Durack family drove cattle in mobs of 1,500, 2,000 and 2,500 from Coopers Creek north to the Ord River, which they reached after two and half years of travel across unmapped country.

And so the big cattle stations took root: the Alexandra station in the Barkly Tablelands which stretched for 11,000 square miles and the Victoria River Downs station, once 14,000 miles in extent—bigger than Belgium.

There, the jackeroo would have to be able to find cattle grazing somewhere in a 5,000 acre paddock; he would have to see if any were missing or if any strays had joined the mob from another herd. He would be looking for any gaps in the fencing made by kangaroos or by falling trees. He would know how to repair the boundary with wire stretched tight with a strainer and made fast by twisting the end with a key. Or, perhaps, he might have an unfenced territory, and be on permanent watch over a herd—except on every other Saturday when he would collect his rations of tea, flour, baking powder, sugar, salt, tobacco, soap powder and shot. He would be given clothes, boots, a mount and saddle—and thirty shillings a week. He would kill his own meat.

In the northern territory six men looked after as many as

100,000 head of cattle ranging over thousands of miles of steep ranges.

Calves for the market would normally be weaned at six to nine months and then yarded every night for some weeks to accustom them to being handled. After three years they would normally be ready for sale, the stockman having taken care meanwhile to see that during this period they were not allowed to run wild. In order to find their market they had to be driven to the rail head or to one of the big centres on the sea coast.

Gradually the well-worn tracks were established—the Murranji track from the Victoria River clear across Australia to Queensland; the Canning stock route from Hall's Creek diagonally across Western Australia; the Birdsville track sweeping down the east of the newly established telegraph line; and the "Great North Road" leading south through Alice Springs. Each year for nearly eighty years between 50,000 and 100,000 cattle were to pass along these precarious pathways.

Droving became a skilled calling, staffed by specialists who defied drought and flood alike to bring the cattle home, losing perhaps no more than one in two hundred during a journey lasting months if not years.

Once the route had been selected and the contract signed, the boss drover would attend the station accompanied by a tallykeeper.

The stockmen would then open the gate of the mustering yard and the cattle would be counted with the tallykeeper tying a knot in his stock-whip after each hundred. Four hundred was an average size mob.

A droving team would probably include the boss drover, a cook and several "ringers" or riders who would travel with the mob by day and "ring" it by riding round it when it was time to settle in for the night. Sometimes the ringers were white, but in time the black boys showed remarkable talent for the job.

Eight to ten miles a day was normal progress in easy country. The day would start with tea and a hunk of bread eaten standing. Then the boss and one black boy would move the cattle off the camp where they had spent the night, while one of the ringers and another black boy packed up the camp, loaded the pack-horses or dray, if there was one, and caught up as soon as possible. Lunch was eaten in the saddle with water from the water bag.

Meanwhile the boss would ride on ahead to select the night's camp and watering spot for the cattle—for in those days there were no government bore holes. This accomplished, the boss returned to the mob on a fresh horse and sent the cook ahead to cook supper and the next day's meal. But, even after riding all day, one could not depend on a care-free evening. Bad "black" country with sandhills or concealed gullies, or rocky surfaces covered with loose clattering stones made the cattle wild and unwilling to settle. If something disturbed them at rest they might set off in a wild stampede or "rush".

Sometimes when a river was running a banker the cattle had to swim for their lives. Sometimes, in the dry season, the cattle might have had to move eighty or even a hundred miles without water and in this case, at the end of the day, it could be vital for the drover to approach the water hole down wind to prevent the cattle from smelling it in advance and making a mad rush to get there. As soon as they got the chance, they would wade in to the water up to their bellies. Some might be too thirsty even to feed.

Meanwhile the horses must be hobbled and belled and the packs unloaded and piled to form a shelter from the wind. The cook shouts "Right-o" for dinner—corned beef, stewed or curried, to be followed by prunes and rice. And then, at last, sleep comes, on canvas ground sheets spread on a mattress of Mitchell grass under a mosquito net . . . except for the night watch which each man has to take in turn.

The eighties were good to Australia, as James Anthony Froude, the English historian, who was among the visitors to Australia in the 1880s, found on his first trip on an Australian railway train, from Melbourne to Ballarat. "Mr. Gillies was waiting for us at the station with Chief Justice Way," Froude wrote. "We were conducted to a superlative carriage, lined with blue satin, with the softest sofas, cushions, armchairs, tables to be raised or.let down at pleasure. A butler was in attendance in a separate compartment, with provision—baskets, wine, fruit, iced water, and all other luxuries and conveniences."

The year 1886 saw the start of the big gold rush in Western

Australia, a bonanza which allowed that province to catch up, in
a few years, with the other more prosperous Australian states.

The first rushes started in the extreme north of the state, in
the Kimberley area, but the difficulties of getting machinery and
supplies there blighted the chances of development. The next
year, however, there was a sensational find at Mallina, a small
town east of Roebourne, the port which lies about one third of
the way down the coast of Western Australia. A boy named
Jimmy Withnall picked up a stone to throw at a crow and
noticed a small speck of gold in it. In a matter of weeks the
whole area was being prospected. Rich alluvial deposits were
found at Pilbara Creek. Prospectors were lucky, too, in the area
to the east of Perth in the southern part of the state, in the
Yilgarn and Southern Cross areas, and in 1891 in the Murchison
area, 350 miles to the north. The following year Arthur Bayley
and John Ford, who had prospected successfully in the Murchison field, pushed out eastwards from Southern Cross and reached
a place known to the aborigines as Coolgardie. Finding there
was good pasture there, they let the horses graze while they
looked around for an hour or two. Here Ford picked up a quarter
ounce nugget and by lunch-time they had got twenty ounces.

They named the site "Fly Flat" and decided to stay there
until their provisions ran out. They made one short dash back
to their base at Southern Cross and said nothing about their
strike. On the first Sunday after their return they struck the
main reef, broke off the cap of the reef with a tomahawk and
crushed about five hundred ounces by hand. Next morning they
pegged out their claim. Two other prospectors, Foster and
Baker, who had smelt treasure and had tracked them from
Southern Cross, staked a claim next door and got two hundred
ounces of gold from it in only three days. Then the rush was
on, although there was no water for anything except drinking
and although food supplies were undependable.

The following year two prospectors, Hannah and Flanagan,
who were on their way to investigate a reported discovery at
Mount Youle, ran short of water and camped at Mount Charlotte for a couple of days while their teams went back to
Southern Cross for fresh supplies. Flanagan, while looking for
his horses, picked up a couple of nuggets. In a few days the

two men collected more than a hundred ounces. In June 1893 Hannah returned to Southern Cross and registered the claim, for his site afterwards known as Kalgoorlie.

1894 saw the discovery of the Londonderry Mine by a party of six on their way back to Coolgardie from a profitless expedition. In four days they had taken between 4,000 and 5,000 ounces of gold hidden behind a mossy outcrop of rock. One nugget, christened Big Ben, contained gold worth £3,500. The same year J. G. Dunn found the reef, afterwards christened the Wealth of Nations Mine, which yielded £20,000 of gold in a few days. The mine was afterwards sold for £147,000.

Of course these mines were not easily worked. Lack of water meant that the gold particles had to be separated from the lighter dust by "dry blowing" as was already the practice in some Mexican mines. In places where it was hard to find timber, valuable carts had to be broken up to make gold separating equipment.

In the northern fields some men had had to walk seven miles a day to get water, and often only salt water was to be had, which meant that the prospector had to set up a condenser and chop wood to heat it in order to quench his thirst.

Thus Australia, too, had its wild west.

And all was not gold that glittered. On 9th September 1883 Charlie Rasp, a boundary rider on the Mount Gipps station, pegged out a claim, having discovered, as he thought, a tin deposit.

With six friends he formed a syndicate to work the lode. Other partners bought themselves in later. George McCullock won a fourteenth share from his winnings at Euchre. Bowes Kelly paid £150 for his title.

The Broken Hill Mine that Charlie Rasp had found turned out to be a mountain of almost pure silver lead ore, together with zinc, which proved easily recoverable by a process imported from the United States by Herbert Hoover. It has already yielded £350 million worth of metal and is good for at least another fifty years.

But almost as soon as Australia discovered herself and her wealth, she was drawn into world politics.

There was, to begin with the Chinese "invasion". Chinese

labourers had found their way to the goldfields as early as 1853 and by 1860 there were more than 50,000 of them there. Some came on their own account as free lances; others were sent to Australia to work under supervision for their masters. They formed there a separate community. Their girls wore tunics and trousers. They celebrated the Chinese New Year with a "dragon" stretching for a furlong and powered by two hundred human legs. When they found gold they sent it out home and so drained the wealth out of the country. They spent almost nothing in Australia. They provoked riots and from time to time were driven away from the goldfields. They provoked more trouble when they returned to the ports and offered to work ships at lower wages than Australian seamen would accept.

In 1855 the Victorian Government restricted Chinese immigration by decreeing that no ship should carry more than one Chinaman for every ton of cargo and that there should be a poll tax of £10 on each Chinese head entering the state. South Australia, New South Wales and Queensland eventually followed suit.

But despite all obstacles the Chinese landings continued. By 1861 more than one adult male out of ten in the state of Victoria was Chinese. In the Northern Territory Chinese at one time actually outnumbered the white population. There were fears that Australia would go Chinese peacefully or perhaps through a massacre.

In 1880 all the Australian States, with the exception of Western Australia where cheap labour was still desperately needed, met and decided on a common defence policy against Chinese immigration. Poll taxes were reimposed or increased, and the White Australia policy—a selective form of preventive apartheid—was born.

Not long after this battle the Japanese (who were about to seize Formosa and the Pescadores from China) became the bogeymen. Some Australian states refused to recognize the Anglo-Japanese Commercial agreement of 1894.

But Asiatics were not the only cause for anxiety in Australia. Europeans, too, were invading the Far East and the Pacific. The French had set themselves up in New Caledonia, 1,500 miles east of Queensland, soon after the middle of the century

and in 1882 annexed Raiatea, near Tahiti. The German Southern Trading Company of Hamburg had established itself at
Mioko (Duke of York Island) in 1871, and there were other
tempting prizes to the north-east and east of New Guinea. For
instance the Marshall Islands, and the Gilbert and Ellice
Islands, all on the trade routes to Australia's east coasts. The
United States and Germany had special trading privileges in
Samoa. Germany, Italy and even Russia were under pressure to
annex New Guinea.

In 1883 Queensland offered to pay all expenses of a British
expedition to get in there first. Whitehall was uninterested.
But Queensland's Prime Minister McIlwraith, worried by
rumours that a German company was being formed with
Government support to exploit the island, stepped in and
annexed the south-east part of New Guinea around Port
Moresby. Mr. Gladstone, who had in fact been secretly discussing the disposal of New Guinea with Germany's Chancellor
Bismarck, tried to disavow the act, but pressure in Australia
grew so strong that Britain was compelled to take over her new
possession first as a protectorate and later as a Crown Colony.

Two years later Australians went further afield than New
Guinea when New South Wales' government sent a contingent
of troops to fight alongside the British in the Sudan campaign of
1885. It was a pattern to be followed by Australia for half a
century to come.

12

The Gay and Not-So-Gay Nineties

Many historians regard the nineties as a decisive turning point in the story of Australia.

The gold strikes of Western Australia and Queensland had convinced the world that Australia was one big treasury of undiscovered wealth from which pleasurable surprises could be expected almost every season. The newly established Trans-Australian telegraph line was bringing more and more business south of the equator. The Australian railroad lines had stretched from a modest 3,830 miles at the beginning of the eighties to 9,500 miles in 1891. The sheep population had risen over the same period from 65 million to 105 million and humans from a little over two million to more than three million. In another ten years the figure would have risen to nearly four million. You could hardly go wrong if you bought land, people told one another, and they were willing to pledge their souls in order to get it. Farmers in Australia mortgaged their holdings, their crop and finally their stock in order to expand. They bought new acres without considering what the land might be expected to produce and how, once produced, the yield could be sold, and they invested in development schemes which could have yielded dividends only at the end of years rather than of months. They were expensive schemes too, since in those prosperous days there was a shortage of labour. The Australian bankers, some of whom were no more than jumped up money lenders, found themselves having to borrow cash at high rates of interest from abroad. Then came the dawn, when, towards the end of the eighties, the price of wool, which was still Australia's main export, kept falling. The farmers failed to repay the money they had borrowed from the banks.

Then, after a slump in the Argentine, Britain began to cut down her overseas investments. This made it difficult for the Australian banks to borrow from Britain. In Australia the State governments found a sharp drop in their own tax revenues and were forced to abandon some of the expensive public works projects which they had undertaken when times were better. Unemployment soared. New South Wales, which had been financing the budget by selling Crown lands, found that no one wanted to buy. The Victorian Government, which had balanced its books by charging duties on imports, suddenly found that the importers had disappeared. Squatters dismissed their station hands and builders their labourers. Melbourne's largest building society failed and thirteen out of twenty-five banks closed their doors. It was a classic slump, made worse by labour troubles.

In some ways the Australian worker had been slow to organize himself. He was too much of an individualist to welcome the idea of a Trade Union. But his hand had been forced by the employers.

In 1834 Britain had set the example by deporting the Dorchester labourers or Tolpuddle Martyrs as they came to be called, for having tried to form a farm labourers union in which oaths were administered. Here was a warning that was not lost on the Australians. They had agricultural labourers too. But the earliest Australian Trade Union was a city affair, the Australian Society of Compositors. It was not organized until 1840. The Journeymen Tailors of Sydney, the Carpenters and Joiners of Melbourne and the Operative Stonemasons' Society were not far behind. But it was only after the first gold rushes when labour became scarce that the Trades Unions felt strong enough to press for better conditions.

In 1855 the coalminers employed by the Australian Agricultural Company at Newcastle struck for higher wages. The

13

following year the stonemasons came out. In 1858 the compositors took the field again. Other sporadic call-outs included the ironworkers of Sydney and the cabmen. The bush unions came last because they were hardest to recruit. But William Guthrie Spence, who had already succeeded in forming the Amalgamated Miners' Association of Victoria in June 1886, established the Amalgamated Shearers' Union covering New South Wales, Victoria and South Australia. This was an organizational triumph in as much as the places of work were remote and scattered and the workers irregular and unpredictable in their movements. But it was this Union which first applied the term "scab" (reminiscent of the revolting scab disease from which sheep suffer) to non-union labour employed during the shearing season. The "scabs" if found were often given the treatment prescribed for suffering sheep; they were thrown into the nearest dip.

Sixteen thousand shearers who were paid at rates often arbitrarily fixed by the station foreman according to his estimate of the quality of the work and who had to buy their food from the station at equally arbitrary prices were involved in the mammoth strike of 1890 which started with a walk-out by the Marine Officers' Association and was joined by the Amalgamated Miners' Association. With wool and coal both declared to be "black", Australian commerce was almost at a standstill. The railways were short of fuel and exports dropped away. The dockers and the carters also joined the strike.

The strike lasted for three months—and involved fifty thousand workers. Attorneys and clubmen, dressed in top hats and lemon-coloured gloves, tried to break the strike by loading wool. In Brisbane an Anglican bishop worked on the wharf. In city and country the strike breakers had to be escorted by armed guards. The authorities had to read the Riot Act on Circular Quay, Sydney, as a formal warning of the strike-breaking measures they intended to take.

In the end the trade unionists got little benefit from the fight, for a slump is the wrong time for a strike. But "mateship", the responsibility that an Australian feels for his comrades, showed itself in the form of labour solidarity, and was never afterwards lost sight of.

One way to avoid the depression, of course, was to emigrate and that is what one of the Australian Labour Leaders did.

William Lane, a compositor and journalist, son of a Bristol nurseryman, had come to Australia in 1885 at the age of twenty-four. In a few years he had risen to the forefront of the Labour Movement and had established the Australian Labour Federation. He was the chief organizer in the big strikes of 1890 and, when these failed, he decided that Australia could never become the communist paradise for which he longed. With three friends he sailed for South America to found a new settlement in which all goods and even children, would be shared in common. The Argentine Government, to whom Lane first suggested the idea, showed no enthusiasm, but Paraguay, anxious for new blood, promised a grant of 450,000 acres, political freedom and duty-free imports for ten years in return for an undertaking that eight hundred families should be established in the new colony within four years. Lane jumped at the offer and was soon back in Australia drumming up recruits. He addressed meetings of shearers, small farmers, skilled men and clerks. They listened but remained, for the most part, unconvinced. For was not this Lane the same man who had said only five years earlier, "Behind us lies the past with its crashing Empires, its falling thrones, its dotard races; before us lies the future into which Australia is plunging, this Australia of ours which burns with the fervent energy of youth"?

Lane succeeded, however, in signing up 240 kindred spirits, prepared like himself to forswear religious fanaticism and strong drink. The pilgrims chartered a small ship, the *Royal Tar*, manned it themselves, and set off on 17th July 1893 for the promised land. It took them three months to reach the River Plate and there was still another 1,200 miles to go upstream before they would arrive at the settlement. Not surprisingly it turned out that Lane, in order to give the project any chance of success, had to behave like a dictator. Not three months after the colonists arrived some of them broke out of the settlement and went on the spree at a nearby village. Lane wanted to expel them from the community but there were riots when he tried to do so and he had to call on Paraguayan soldiers to restore order. In March 1894 a new batch of settlers arrived under the leadership of Gilbert Casey. But Lane quarrelled with him too and petitioned the Paraguay Government to allow him to make yet a new settlement which he christened Cosme, further out in the wilderness. The Paraguayan Government agreed provided that it contained at least seventy-two families. So Lane decided to look for recruits in England. When he got back to Paraguay with some converts he found Cosme almost deserted. Most of the pioneers had defected and made their way to the British Consul at Montevideo who agreed reluctantly to repatriate them. Lane himself, realizing that his cause was lost, went home in 1900, but eventually settled in New Zealand where he found work on a Conservative newspaper.

Meanwhile things in Australia went from bad to worse. Plague broke out in Sydney and a large part of the dock area had to be sealed off in quarantine, and its residents given an unemployment subsidy of six shillings a day. (Needless to say when the area became so overcrowded with "new residents" the authorities were only too glad to end the restrictions.)

The countryside, too, had its plague—rabbits. Rabbits came to Australia with the First Fleet, and before long there was scarcely a settlement where they were not kept for food. But comparatively few got away until 1859 when whole families were intentionally liberated in Geelong by Thomas Austin. From that time on they lolloped across Australia on a front that advanced about seventy miles every year. They were seen in South Australia in 1891, and in the south of Western Australia only three years later. The first rabbit fence was built in 1880, eleven years too late to have prevented the spread of rabbits from Victoria westwards. New South Wales waited another six years to put up a fence high enough to keep out not only rabbits but dingoes, emus and kangaroos. Soon after the turn of the century the Western Australian Government alone put up more than two thousand miles of fence, which needed a rider for every 300 miles and £40 a mile a year for maintenance. But by then the rabbit was already almost half way up the west coast.

Rabbits ate Australia's best grass. They ringed the bark off the young trees and devoured the young mulga more quickly than it could replenish itself. During the drought the rabbits killed off even the cane grass and the spinifex. Seven rabbits eat as much as one sheep. It was the rabbits that forced the sheep to eat the saltbush and that, too, failed to renew itself. Each rabbit colony became a miniature dustbowl producing clouds of grit which scoured away the vegetation wherever the wind blew. Sandstorms not only whipped away the fodder but also filled up the water holes. Rabbits' burrows were traps that cost the legs and perhaps lives of cattle, horses and even men.

Yet nothing could stop the rabbit population from growing. In the 1930s it was reckoned that Australia supported some 750,000,000 and that without them could have supported 100 million more sheep. Even myxomatosis, the artificially introduced virus which probably killed 300 million rabbits in two years, has not proved the final solution to the problem, and farmers have had to return to the old-fashioned methods of poisoning rabbits or gassing them or ripping out their warrens.

The rabbit plague in the nineties was all the more serious because it came during a long series of droughts . . . droughts which hardly worried Australia's native animals such as the frogs, which can sink themselves beneath the mud with a year's supply of water, but which were lethal for flocks and herds.

It was perhaps natural for the Australian sheep farmer to keep his stock as high as possible, for the profit margin often depended on those last few sheep. But this policy, which might have worked well enough in a European climate, was fatal in a country where the reserve areas of pasture might turn overnight into near desert and where the secrets of modern discoveries were unknown. No one had yet told the Australians that the Ninety Mile Desert could be renamed the Coonalpyn Downs by adding traces of copper sulphate and zinc to the soil . . . that botanists could produce a subterranean clover whose flowers would penetrate into the ground, planting seeds underground clear from the killing rays of the sun. Veldt grass had not been imported from South Africa.

Some progress in the science of dry farming can of course be traced back to the nineties and even earlier. Chief among these was the discovery of new strains of wheat, resistant not only to drought but to the rust that so often followed a wet, warm Australian spring. After more than twelve years of research,

William Farrer, experimental botanist in the New South Wales
Department of Agriculture, produced a short-stemmed metallic-
looking wheat, and farmers in South Australia soon learnt that
it was possible to raise crops beyond the so-called Goyder Line
that marked the boundary of the areas receiving an average of
fourteen inches of rainfall.

One of the more profitable if not the most picturesque occupations disappeared about this time from the Australian
economy—whaling. There had been whalers in Australia ever
since 1790 when five whaling vessels arrived with the Third
Fleet, and in Governor King's days whale oil threatened to rival
wool as Australia's most profitable export. From the beginning
of the nineteenth century whalers used Tasmania and the islands
of the Bass strait for bases and frequently one could see fifty
to sixty whales being cut up at the same time in the estuary
of the Derwent River. In the early days of the trade one ship
alone was able to bring in 66,000 seal-skins into Hobart Town.
A flourishing ship-repairing industry soon grew up. Whaling
being neither a clean nor a pleasant occupation; whalers were
a rough and ready lot and those who lived on the islands in the
Bass Strait thought nothing of acquiring four or five native
wives. Indeed a well-built native wife could be a great asset,
for it was the practice of seal-hunters to get native women to
swim out quietly, naked among the seals, who apparently took
them for their own kind. When close enough to the animals the
women would spring up and start clubbing their prey. Whaling,
however, finally became so profitable that American whalers
began to join in the hunt. Moreover in those days there were
no restrictions on the numbers of whales or seals that might be
taken, and already before the middle of the century the seals had
disappeared.

Furthermore the East India Company, which, for many years,
had had a monopoly of Far East Trade, placed as many obstacles
as possible in the way of those who wished to sell seal skins and
other products in the Far East. And so in 1896 the last of the
whaling crews was paid off in Hobart Town. It was half a
century before new scientific methods allowed the whaling
industry to revive once more, and in the meantime Australian
butter had become much more important than whale blubber.

In at least one other way the nineties marked a water shed for Australia. These were the years in which, despite the strikes, the droughts and the slump, the prosperity of the country reached the point where it was possible for the Australian artist to make a living without degrading himself by giving lessons to Philistines or painting portraits of the daughters of upstart merchants, as he had to do in the early years of the century, when, as Lord Rosebery put it, wealthy Australians sat on thirty-guinea ottomans looking at 30s. oleographs. Instead the artist moved out in mid-century into the open air, and some of the canvases painted by S. T. Gill of the gold rushes of the fifties, by Tom Roberts of the open road, by George Lambert and Frank Mahony of the scenes on sheep runs and cattle stations, and later by Julian Ashton of Australian travel scenes, are of historic if not artistic importance.

A third period in Australian art began, however, towards the end of the sixties, when Abram Louis Buvelot, a Swiss, born at Morges on the lake of Geneva, began to paint and inspired other artists on the banks of Melbourne's Yarra River.

Around Buvelot in tents above the Yarra, there gathered artists who could interpret the golden distances and blue horizons of Australia in an idiom that Australians knew as their own. Buvelot's "Summer Evening at Temple Stowe" and "Waterpool at Coleraine" helped to found a school of Australian painting, a novelty which had never previously existed. Arthur Streeton's "Golden Summer" and "Australia Felix" may have dated titles but the artist's work lives on. Rupert Bunny, Streeton's contemporary, studied in London and Paris with such success that the French Government bought two of his paintings for the Luxembourg collection. Charles Conder and Streeton were in the vanguard of Australia's impressionists.

These men exploited the violets, the chocolates and the turquoise blues of the Australian scene; Elioth Gruner in New South Wales, found the misty mauves and greys of the Australian dawn, and in South Australia Hans Heysen fixed for ever the olive and sea greens of the gum tree against the blinding heat haze of lilac and salmon-coloured rocks.

At first one does not, perhaps, see Australians as men of letters. But, by the nineties, Australians had already established themselves in three particular aspects of literature. There were, first of all, the novels that recorded so much of early Australian life. There was Henry Kingsley's *Geoffrey Hamlyn*, a tale of upper-class life written on a station in the Western District of Victoria in those days "before the gold". There was Marcus Clarke's *For the Term of his Natural Life*, a powerful, vivid story of the convict system and a man wrongly subjected to it. There was Thomas Browne, who spent thirty years in the bush first as a squatter and later as a magistrate and warden in the goldfields in New South Wales, and who, as Rolf Boldrewood, wrote in an easy conversational style such Australian classics as *Robbery Under Arms 1888* (on bushranging), *The Miner's Right* and *The Squatter's Dream*. Henry Handel Richardson (her real name was Ethel Florence Richardson) won fame with a trilogy of novels *The Fortunes of Richard Mahoney*, though they were written outside Australia. There were other women novelists such as Mrs. Cross, wife of the Rev. George Cross, who wrote nineteen middle-class love novels in an Australian setting under the name of Ada Cambridge. Mrs. Campbell Praed, who also wrote about Australia from a safe distance, produced more than forty readable novels.

Then there were the Australian-born poets—Charles Harpur (1813–68), who settled down in 1843 at the age of thirty to farm in the Hunter River Valley in New South Wales and wrote on themes such as "The Creek of the Four Graves", "Midsummer Noon in the Australian Forest" and was for a quarter of a century, almost unrecognized. Henry Kendall (1839–82), who came almost a generation later was more successful with his "Leaves from Australian Forests" and "Songs from the Mountains", and has been included in some British anthologies.

Then in a third class came those rivals of the poets, the Australian bush balladists, greatly encouraged by the Sydney *Bulletin*, which paid for and published many of their efforts. Bush ballads were the kind of verse that could be sung in the outback either with or without the primitive accompaniment of a banjo. Sometimes perhaps drovers used bush ballads to sing the cattle to sleep. Or perhaps they kept people awake in the evenings at parties during the gold rushes, or in the wool shed when the shearing was over. In town, bush balladists persuaded the metropolitan sparrow that he was akin to those splendid fellows in the bush.

The bush ballad made no great literary pretensions but it was packed with action, humour and sympathy. There was the one about the "Sailor Who Rode the Brumby" ("brumby" is Australian for a wild horse). There was another about "Mad Jack's Cockatoo", who pulled all the bungs out of the barrels at the "Swagman's Rest" and drowned himself and his master. And there was the "Flash Stockman" who boasted: "So in everything I do, you could cut me fair in two, for I'm much too bloody good to be in one."

Adam Lindsay Gordon, who, as noted, arrived in Australia in 1853 under a cloud and became, in turn, a mounted policeman, a horse-breaker and a Member of Parliament, set the pace for the Australian ballad, although he wrote more about horses in general than about Australia. His verse was poetry to the extent that it expressed many thoughts in few words; it was often powered by a tale of action written in language which every horseman recognized as genuine, but with the deep melancholy that sometimes come to us all.

In 1870, on the day that his fourth book of poems was to be published, he went out into the bush and shot himself. He is commemorated by a plaque in Westminster Abbey.

Henry Lawson (1867–1922) was another of the great melancholics—and had reason to be. The son of an unsuccessful Norwegian miner, Peter Larsen, he was born in a tent on the Grenfell gold fields in New South Wales, amid a landscape of mullock and rusty cans, and was brought up on a barren bush farm near Mudgee. His teacher in the bush school was an Irishman with no love for the English. Lawson became partly deaf at the age of nine and never fully recovered his hearing. It took an alarm clock placed on a sheet of tin to wake him in the mornings. Most of his adult life was spent in Sydney, though he tried his luck in Western Australia, in New Zealand and even in Britain. He was often out of a job and was reduced at times to getting up at 4 a.m. so that he could go down to the *Herald* office and read the situations vacant column on the board outside with the help of a match.

Lawson's first published writings were in verse, and their

unaffected style and sense of disillusionment caught the mood
of the moment. "Tired of all," he wrote, "is the spirit that sings
of the days when the world was wide."

Lawson had the sentimentality of Dickens and the direct
appeal of Burns. Some of the resentment, too, of Burns and
some of the same weakness. For Lawson was an alcoholic whose
friends could not save him. He separated from his wife, and
drank all the more because of this.

> What's the good of keeping sober?
> Fellers rise and fellers fall;
> What I might have been and wasn't,
> Doesn't trouble me at all.

He had a wonderful memory for words and phrases, and could
develop complete poems in his head before having to write
down a single word. It was no effort for him to use the words of
the men and women he had known as a child—the shearers and
the drovers, the timber splitters, the diggers and the shanty-
keepers, and the other inhabitants of the bush. Misfortunes of all
kinds rained down upon the farmers, drovers, selectors and
rouseabouts in Lawson's verses. They never seemed to have a
good season. In their experience there was either a drought or
the rivers ran "bankers" in a flood. Failing which there was a
fire or a run-away horse.

Lawson was a republican who warned his countrymen against
"the good old English gentleman over them; the good old
English squire over them, the good old English lord over them,
the good old English aristocracy rolling around them in
cushioned carriages scarcely deigning to rest their eyes on the
common people, who toil, starve and rot for them; and the good
old English throne over them all."

And when the Duke of York, heir to the throne, visited
Australia in 1901 for the inauguration of the Commonwealth,
Lawson was one of the first to point out that, although the royal
visitors would meet "the men who own Australia but who never
knew the bush and who could not point their runs out on the
map", together with the "Awful Lady of the latest Birthday
Knight—(She is trying to be English, don't-cher-know?)", the
men who made Australia would not be asked to the celebrations.

Call across the blazing sand wastes of the Never-Never Land!
There are some who will not answer yet awhile,
Some whose bones rot in the mulga or lie bleaching on the sand,
Died of thirst to win the land another mile.
Thrown from horses, ripped by cattle, lost on deserts and the
    weak,
Mad through loneliness or drink (no matter which),
Drowned in floods or dead of fever by the sluggish slimy creek—
These are men who died to make the Wool-Kings rich.

Lawson preached the message that many a failure redeemed
himself by kindness to his "mate":

He shall live to the end of this mad old world as he lived since
    the world began
He never has done any good for himself, but was good to every
    man.
He never has done any good for himself, and I'm sure that he
    never will;
He drinks, and he swears, and he fights at times, and his name
    is mostly Bill.

Or again:

No church-bell rings them from the Track,
No pulpit lights their blindness—
'Tis hardship, drought, and homelessness
That teach those Bushmen kindness:
The mateship born, in barren lands,
Of toil and thirst and danger,
The camp-fire for the wanderer set,
The first place to the stranger.

Lawson would never have been a politician or an agitator for
long. You have only to read "The Sliprails and the Spur", by
far the best of his sentimental verses, to see this.

Lawson wrote short stories too and many prefer these to his
verse, for one can still read with pleasure such tales as "The
Loaded Dog", "His Colonial Oath" and "The Drover's Wife".

But eventually the time came when he had lived too long in
the city to write about the world outside it. And in Australia's
new century the world soon got tired of failures however gallant
they might be. Lawson died in Sydney in 1922, poverty-
stricken, lonely and uncared for.

Happiest of the bush balladists—and perhaps the most immortal was A.B. (Banjo) Paterson (1864–1941) who thought well of anyone who did not live in a city.

One of his best-known pieces "The Man from the Snowy River" tells how

> There was movement at the station, for the word had passed
> around
> That the colt from old *Regret* had got away,
> And had joined the wild bush horses—he was worth a thousand
> pound,
> So all the cracks had gathered for the fray.

In the end, it was the man from the Snowy River on a small and weedy but courageous pony who followed the mob, rode after them to the top of a mountain range and down the other side and made them wheel completely exhausted and turn for home. But who does not still enjoy "The Man from Ironbark", "It's Grand to be a Squatter", "A Bushman's Song" and of course "Waltzing Matilda" ("Matilda" is the bushman's swag or bundle of possessions, and "Waltzing Matilda" means stepping out carrying one's swag).

But there *was* one other respect in which the nineties was indisputably a turning point for Australia. For it was during these ten years that the decision was taken to convert the continent from a necklace of colonies stretching for thousands of miles into a single nation.

Only those who have watched the same process—still incomplete in the United States—can understand the magnitude of the achievement in a land unaided by any declaration of independence.

It is true that the United States had, like Australia, to overcome the barrier of poor communications between States. Federation was accomplished in the United States in the days before railways existed and when the United States Constitution allowed for the fact that it might take a newly elected President some two months to find his way from his log cabin to the White House. Australia of course had railways, but the distances between the states which had to federate were much greater than in the United States and the inducements for politicians to devote themselves to federal politics correspondingly less. You could send a telegram, but the nearest telegraph office might be two hundred miles away, and at a remote station stores for delivery in April goods had to be ordered in the previous October.

In Australia, the constituent states had been set up at different times and for different reasons, and they were at different stages of development. New South Wales and Queensland, where gold too had now been discovered at Mount Morgan, had been penal settlements. Western Australia, the largest state in the world, had been a commercial venture, and South Australia a political experiment which was to include, until 1911, a northern tropical wilderness ten times the size of England. And they were not even based on a common seaboard.

Nevertheless the arguments in favour of federation in Australia were unanswerable. For example the New Guinea crisis and the unrest in the Pacific had shown the Australians how important it was for the states to have a common policy on foreign affairs. It was equally important for them to have a united front on the White Australia issue, for how could Whitehall flout great powers like Japan and China when theAustralians themselves were divided on whether to admit Asiatics to their territory? And it was doubly hard for any given state to keep out the Chinese if a neighbouring state was admitting them without restriction.

But it was not only external politics that inclined the Australians towards federation. It was clear to those who lived in Australia that the land could be developed only as one whole. Roads for instance and also postal services and the cable across the Pacific to Canada had to be planned according to the needs of Australia as a continent and not primarily for the convenience of any single state. Moreover communications and many other projects were long-term ones which could not be expected to return any dividends for years to come, and which would therefore not attract private capital. The money would have to come from a government with resources provided by all states acting together.

Then there was the question of tariffs. A united front was needed on this issue too. Victoria favoured a policy of protection.

New South Wales favoured free trade. As long as this contradiction existed Victoria was under pressure to operate a frontier customs inspection service to prevent goods being imported duty free from Sydney. And the internal borders between the states of Australia were not the easiest to police. Eventually Victoria had to accept a relatively small payment of £60,000 per annum from New South Wales in full satisfaction for the duties.

The irrigation and water storage systems of individual states planned largely by experts from India and Canada would clearly in the end have to be co-ordinated between dependent communities on the same water supplies. And there would be no point in one state boring holes to bring up water from an Artesian water table far below to serve a cattle route in which a neighbouring state might profess disinterest.

In the political field, the Labour movement was another powerful influence in favour of federation. Trade Unionists to whom unity was strength saw that small individual unions with limited membership must be absorbed into wider brotherhood.

Back in Whitehall the Imperial Government views on Federation were predictable. Would it save expense? Particularly the expense of defending distant colonies that might be able to foot the bill themselves? (And would it save the trouble of having to negotiate each problem with six states which were inhabited by the same type of people and which, from the vantage point of London, looked as alike as any six English counties.)

Mr. Gladstone had addressed himself to the problem of colonial defence as far back as 1860 by the time-honoured practice of establishing a Royal Commission, and ten years later the British forces were withdrawn from Australia and replaced by militia, which it was soon clear would have to be merged into a single defence force capable of moving without a by-your-leave across the frontiers between the Australian states. Queen Victoria's Golden Jubilee celebrations in 1887 were deemed a suitable opportunity for discussing the future naval defence of the colony. It was decided that seven warships should be added, at Australian expense, to the regular British squadron.

For these reasons, therefore, Her Majesty's Ministers were in favour of the big take-over in Australia. Earl Grey had suggested in 1850 that Australia should have a General

Assembly, presided over by a governor-general, to which each
of the colonies should send representatives. In 1870 Charles
Duffy, the Victoria statesman, staged a Commission to discuss
Federal Union. Ten years later, Sir Henry Parkes in New South
Wales succeeded in launching a Council to promote the idea of
federation. It was Parkes who in 1889 in an after-dinner speech
flattering to Australian maturity, urged that a Convention be
set up to devise a government for the whole of Australia.

A conference of Prime Ministers met in Melbourne in 1890
but again produced nothing but recommendations. Eventually
after a good deal of delay it was decided, at a conference held in
Hobart in 1895, that Federation had become "the great and
pressing need of Australian politics" and that delegates to a
Convention should be elected to prepare a Federal Constitution
which could be placed before the people in a referendum. Only
Queensland held back.

By the middle of 1898 the draft constitution was ready to be
put to a referendum. Victoria, South Australia and Tasmania
approved. But New South Wales showed less than the required
majority, and amendments had to be made before the Constitution was accepted there too. Queensland by this time had joined
in the plan and Western Australia soon followed. Whitehall was
a little alarmed by the shape of the new political monster that
had now materialized, but the House of Commons was undaunted and agreed to the Australian constitution with only
small alterations. Queen Victoria gave her assent on 9th July
1900.

Under it the new Commonwealth was given power over
defence, external affairs, immigration, customs and excise, posts
and telegraphs, banking and currency, foreign and inter-state
trade, and inter-state taxation. The individual states were left to
manage their own lands, railways, education, police and direct
taxes. Parliament was to consist of two Houses, the Senate with
six representatives elected for six years from each State and the
House of Representatives with members elected for three years,
roughly in proportion to the population of each state.

Like most of their kind, the makers of the Australian Constitution thought that theirs was the perfect product, and took
elaborate precautions to make it almost unalterable.

Any amendment to the Constitution had to be passed by an absolute majority of both Houses, or by one House twice. In either case the bill must afterwards be submitted to a referendum within a period of not less than two months or more than six months, and must then be approved by a total majority of votes and by a majority in each separate state.

And so on 1st January 1901, the first day of the new century, the Earl of Hopetoun was sworn in, in Sydney, as Australia's first Governor-General.

The Commonwealth had been officially born.

13

From Hughes to Gallipoli

In some ways it was easier to form a Federation than to find a capital for it. It had been agreed that the capital city should be set up in New South Wales, not less than a hundred miles from Sydney (for fear that it should be dominated by that city), on a territory of not less than a hundred square miles.

But there were almost too many suitable sites, and the Royal Commission which had to choose one had inspected more than forty before the first Federal Parliament had even assembled in Melbourne, where it was to meet for nearly twenty-five years. After two years these were whittled down to eight, after which the Bill for an Act to Determine the Seat of Government was drafted, and, as a non-party measure, introduced first in the Senate.

The Senate came down heavily in favour of Bombala in the south-east corner of the State near the Victorian border. The House of Representatives, however, favoured Tumut about one hundred miles further north. A compromise was made on Dalgety, a location situated about half-way between the two. But difficulties about buying the land then arose as the area was on the border of Victoria and therefore not wholly within the State of New South Wales. So the whole matter of a capital was dropped for five years. In 1908 the question was revived and a Parliamentary Commission left their comfortable homes to tour the countryside and inspect four sites at Albury, Tumut, Bombala and Dalgety for themselves. It meant travel by train and horse-coach and nights of revelry and song in bush hotels but still no decision. Dalgety was in the Snowy River country and was voted too cold. Albury was rejected as being too close to Melbourne; Tumut and Bombala were almost as cold as Dalgety. When the House voted, Dalgety led in the first seven ballots but not with a large enough majority to clinch the matter. So a new district, the Yass area, which had previously been almost overlooked, came to the fore in a last minute sprint and was eventually adopted with a majority of eight votes. In February 1909 the surveyors reported that Canberra was the most suitable site for the capital in the Yass area, since it was accessible, with a pleasant climate, good water supply, fertile soil and plenty of building material nearby.

On 1st January 1911, after the land had been duly transferred, the Commonwealth entered into possession of its Federal Territory.

Thus ten years sped past. But that was only the start of the matter. An international competition was next held to design the capital. Designs were received from 137 architects in many different countries. The prize of £10,000 went to a team headed by Walter Burley Griffin, a thirty-five-year-old Chicago architect, who had worked in the office of Frank Lloyd Wright and had since come to practise in Australia. He was strongly influenced by Daniel Burnham's "City Beautiful" shown at the Chicago Fair of 1903, and produced a design consisting of circular avenues and interlocking vistas radiating from a central axis and landscaped with lakes and shady trees, attractive on paper and even on canvas but not too easy for a stranger who has to go shopping or visiting. Perhaps this is why the critics still describe Canberra as a "bush capital" consisting of seven suburbs in search of a city. The building of Canberra had to be halted during World War I and it was not until 1927 that Parliament finally met there.

For almost a quarter of a century after Federation, Labour dominated Australian politics, and one man, a wiry, quick-tempered, short-statured Welshman dominated Labour.

William Morris Hughes was born in the village of

Llansantffraid, Montgomeryshire in 1864, and emigrated to Queensland at the age of twenty, convinced that he was about to enter the promised land. He was something of a scholar, having learnt Latin at Llandudno Grammar School before he could speak English, and his volume of Shakespeare's works was presented to him by Matthew Arnold. But when he landed at Brisbane during a severe drought Hughes found that there was no demand for scholars. He looked for jobs inland at Mitchell, Roma, Wambulalla, Charleville and Adavale and was permitted to break ballast and sink boundary posts and engage in other occupations suitable for a newcomer. After enduring this life for a few months Hughes walked most of the five hundred miles back to Brisbane, having become a true colonial swagman, able to patch his own boots, cook his own meals and sometimes go for a day without food. From Brisbane he pushed north with a friend towards the goldfields at Gympie, convinced, once more, that fortune was round the corner. The two of them got lost in the bush without blankets, fire or food and had to live for four days on two pounds of flour and half a pound of sugar.

Another season of discontent followed, during which Hughes worked as a seaman, a ship's cook, corn-stook gatherer, a grape picker, and a blacksmith, even occasionally driving a mail-van. For fifteen months he was a drover taking sheep from Queensland to New South Wales on distances of up to 1,500 miles. For a full year he never slept in bed. At Orange, where he had been promised a job on a farm, he dossed down one night near the railway line with some trucked sheep on a cold night and got a chill which left him partially deaf for life.

In 1886 he decided to come to Sydney and lived for a while in a cave in the public park or Domain as it was called.

Then he took a job in a bookshop, and as a sideline repaired locks and umbrellas. He watched the birth of the Trades Union movement. His bookshop in Balmain was used as a rendezvous during the great maritime strike of 1890 and Hughes himself began to learn to speak, first in private debating clubs, and then in public at speaker's corner in the Domain.

Though he was little over five foot tall he could hold his audiences. There was something arresting in that large leathery face with its high cheekbones and Roman nose, jug-ears and slanting eyes a-glitter with the political evangelism of a tiger. His style was jerky and nervous, his voice high pitched and penetrating, and his speeches were punctuated with eye-catching movements, of long thin hands at the end of a pair of thin spidery arms. He seemed to stop from time to time to search for the right word but the phrase when it came was apt and telling and at times corrosive. He had the advantage over his opponents in eating and drinking little. He was a lettuce and cheese man.

Hughes was one of the first to realize that strikes alone would not accomplish the programme of the Trade Unionists for better working conditions, and that they must work through a political party represented in Parliament. After the failure of the strike the Union leaders were quickly converted to his views. They made him secretary of the Wharf Labourers' Union.

The election of June 1891 was the first to be held in New South Wales since Members of Parliament had been awarded a subsistence allowance. Labour's programme was for an eight-hour day, free education, National Federation and Military Service for volunteers only. Labour fielded forty-five candidates and Hughes was one of those who helped in the campaign, speaking from carts and other improvised platforms which cost less than halls. He was not himself a candidate but shared in the joy throughout the Labour movement when the results of the elections were announced. For thirty-six Labour candidates were elected out of a total house of 144.

In the next poll, taken three years later, Hughes himself was elected for the Lang division of Sydney, despite the fact that he had spent much of the campaign up country campaigning on foot, horse and bicycle.

In Parliament he found all the cut and thrust he could wish for, particularly from William Crick, a successful police court lawyer who in reply to a Labour member's complaint that "they" (the politicians of earlier times) had stolen all our public lands, retorted, "If they stole the hon. member's public lands, they must have made a searching investigation under his finger nails!" Even the Prime Minister, Sir George Reid, was not immune from attack and was heard to say in Parliament as he wiped himself clean: "That egg, my friends, is as rotten as the b—— that threw it!"

From 1894, because of divided counsels, the New South Wales Government was dependent on the Labour vote for its majority, and to some extent the same held good after Federation in the Federal Parliament where opinions were sharply divided on the issue of free trade versus protection.

Between 1901 and 1914 there were nine different governments. Of these the first two were entirely dependent on Labour co-operation. In 1904 the first Labour Government led by John Watson, ex-compositor, came to power with Hughes, who in the meantime had qualified as a barrister, as Minister for External Affairs, and the real political force within the Cabinet. After four months, however, the Labour Government was defeated over a Bill designed to protect Trade Unionists in industrial disputes. Two more governments manned by Conservatives or near-Conservatives, followed, but they continued to be dependent on Labour support, and in 1908, Andrew Fisher, leader of the Australian Labour Party, by then the strongest in Parliament, was himself asked to form a new government. This, too, fell when two of the Conservative leaders forgot their differences and formed a coalition.

In April 1910 Fisher got back to power and stayed in office for just over three years. He was defeated in the following general elections and the Conservatives returned, with a very narrow majority. An election campaign to increase this majority was being held at the very time World War I broke out.

It all happened so suddenly. In June 1914 the Archduke Francis Ferdinand of Austria and his wife the Duchess of Hohenberg, who had been visiting Bosnia as guests of the Serbian Government to watch military manœuvres, were assassinated. Austria demanded reparations from Serbia. Germany sided with Austria. Russia, in support of Serbia, mobilized her troops. France and Britain were allied with Russia, so they were involved too. They were also committed to protecting Belgium, which constituted France's northern flank.

Australia was shocked by the speed with which the crisis had developed. Through a technical hitch, neither the Prime Minister nor the Defence Minister were able to decipher the vital messages announcing that war was about to be declared, and learnt of it first through their own navy. But the country was solidly behind Britain, and the Labour party in Australia, though still in opposition, pledged its support for the Government. The party was even ready to consider postponing the election. Hughes, speaking in Sydney, said that this indeed was the occasion when "none is for a party but all are for the State", and Andrew Fisher in a speech at Colac, Victoria, on 31st July proclaimed that "should the worst happen, we will stand behind the Mother Country to help and defend her to the last man and the last shilling!"

This speech alone was probably enough to win the election for the Australian Labour party, and it ensured that Australia fought the war under Labour leadership, first with Andrew Fisher as premier and then, after his resignation in October 1915, with Hughes at the helm. He was showing more and more clearly that within his puny frame there beat the heart of a lion.

Once the die had been cast Australia was quick off the mark. She already had an independent Navy which included a battle cruiser, two cruisers and three destroyers. She had her own Sandhurst, the Royal Military College at Duntroon, and she was making her own small arms. In addition the Government offered to equip a division of 20,000 Australians and have them ready for sailing within six weeks. Long before the first soldier stepped aboard the Australians were in action. The German merchant vessel *Pfalz*, which was lying in Port Phillip on 4th August, received her clearance papers only ten minutes before Britain's declaration of war became effective, and had not cleared the three-mile limit before the deadline. She was stopped with a shot across her bows and captured.

The German possessions in the Pacific were soon occupied and the cruiser *Emden*, which had threatened convoys crossing the Indian Ocean, was sunk by Australian light cruiser *Sydney*. These victories, near home, were encouraging. Australia's losses (60,000 killed in action or died of wounds with 320,000 casualties) were however suffered later and farther west, in the Old World of Europe and the Near East. It was the Gallipoli campaign which first won the Australians their immortal reputation for valour.

The idea of a naval attack on Istanbul, then called Constantinople, the capital of the Ottoman Empire had many attractions for the strategists. A military stalemate seemed to have been reached on the Western front where the two sides were occupying fixed positions in trenches from which it seemed almost impossible to dislodge them. Consequently there were demands for a show of force to be made elsewhere. Russia had also appealed for some diversionary move to be made to draw off the Turkish offensive in the Caucasus. It might be possible to knock Turkey out of the war and at the same time set the Russian wheat flowing westwards again.

The allied plan was for the British navy to force a passage through the narrows of the Dardanelles into the sea of Marmora at the eastern end of which the city lay. The waters of the Dardanelles were protected by mines laid in its waters and by forts placed along the peninsula of Gallipoli which ran along the north side of the narrows but it was assumed that these defences could soon be pounded into rubble by powerful naval guns allowing the minesweepers to clear a channel for the rest of the fleet.

The Royal Navy steamed into action on 18th March 1915 and planned to open the attack with a long-range bombardment to be followed by one at medium range and finally by a point-blank finale. But the naval commanders soon found that a long-range bombardment from moving ships was inaccurate and ineffective. To get hits, the vessels had to approach much closer than they had intended and were then within range not only of the land batteries but of mobile guns and howitzers which the Turks were able to conceal in the scrub. This was risky even for the armour-plated cruisers with their seasoned Royal Navy crews. But it was still more chancy for the soft-shelled mine-sweepers which were operated by trawlermen only recently recruited from Britain's fishing ports. These men had not expected that they would be called on to sweep mines under fire without adequate protection from other warships. They were not safe even at night, for the minesweepers could be picked out by enemy searchlights which defied all efforts of the navy to destroy them by gun fire. The result was that the work of clearing the mines was frequently held up, and the Turks were able to re-mine one area which had supposedly been swept. Several naval vessels were lost in consequence.

The decision to bring in the army to follow up the naval operation was taken only a few days in advance of the first bombardment and, when it became clear that the navy by itself would have difficulty in silencing the batteries, a plan was made for capturing and occupying the whole of the Gallipoli peninsula. But this involved elaborate preparations, and delays by the War Office in releasing the necessary men and equipment gave the Turks extra time to prepare their defences. The Army's attack in Gallipoli, launched in April, was delivered with the greatest bravery and almost equally great lack of co-ordination. Maps were sketchy; navigation too, and Australians and New Zealanders who were expecting to land from the boats on flat beaches were carried away by the strong currents and found themselves having to scale cliffs surrounding the famous Anzac (Australian and New Zealand Army Corps) Cove at the narrowest part of the peninsula.

The military commanders on their floating headquarters were not in close touch with the various attacking parties, who in turn were out of touch with each other. The signalling system was ineffective and erratic.

But at first the War Office in London was blissfully unaware of the possibility of a conspicuous and costly failure. To them the shortage of shells on the Western Front was a far more disturbing issue.

Then gradually the casualty figures leaked out. Twenty-seven thousand Australian troops whose training had been finished in Egypt had been landed in Gallipoli between the 25th April and 1st May. Of these, nine thousand—one in three—became casualties. Two thousand were killed.

As in France, the two sides then settled down to trenches from which it was impossible to evict them without alarming casualties. One single all-out attack on 5th July cost the Turkish forces 16,000 casualties without any ground being gained and an allied attack a week later, on a one-mile front, gained only 400 yards at a cost of 4,000 allied casualties and 10,000 Turkish.

That summer in their beachheads the allies had to face new discomforts and dangers. The soil, which had been soft and sticky during the winter, began to harden and crumble. A permanent cloud of dust hung over the battlefield. Swarms of flies harassed the men and contaminated their food. There were mass outbreaks of dysentery. Water was short and supplies had to be brought seven hundred miles from Egypt. A German U-boat appeared on the scene and the *Queen Elizabeth*, the pride of the fleet, had to be withdrawn from the Dardanelles area into safer waters. Two other British battleships were torpedoed.

In June, however, the War Council in London decided to mount a really massive attack on the peninsula. Thirteen divisions equivalent to 120,000 effective fighting men were now allotted to the Gallipoli front, and ammunition was held back from France in order to supply it. The plan was to make a new assault during the first week of August further up the peninsula in Suvla Bay, cutting off the Turks in the tip of the peninsula from their line of communication from the east. Other attacks, some feints, others in earnest, were to be made at other points in order to confuse the defenders. But once again the initial attacks petered out. The officers proved ineffective, the signals and co-ordination faulty, and the supply system inadequate. So a second wave of attacks had to be made. They were carried out with great gallantry. Seven Victoria Crosses were awarded to Australians within a few days, and the story of their sortie made from a tunnel dug secretly in front of their lines at Lone Pine, above Anzac Cove, still makes the heart beat faster. Even this second assault failed to win the day. The guides who were supposed to shepherd the advance lost their way. The British Commanders were old and incompetent and failed to press home their advantage even in areas from which the Turks had fled, and in one case a successful attack was halted by shelling from the Royal Navy. Forty-five thousand allied soldiers fell in a few days. The Turks and Germans, though taken by surprise, were more ruthless towards their commanders than the allies. Those who failed were dismissed and replaced at once with better material. And in a three-day battle ending on 10th August the Turks threw the British troops off the vital heights of Sari Bair. The following month the Bulgarian Army mobilized and it became necessary for the Allies to send troops to attack it through Greece. That was the end of the Gallipoli campaign— except for the brilliant evacuation of the troops carried out without the enemy's suspicions being aroused and almost without casualty.

In those few months, 7,600 Australians had been killed and 19,000 wounded. Already their courage had become a legend. But it appeared that they had not done enough. More of them were needed on the Western Front. And this led to one of Australia's greatest political crises over conscription, with Hughes, who had replaced Andrew Fisher in October, in the thick of it.

Hughes was not a man to let the war effort flag for a single moment. He organized the war-time sale of Australia's wheat and wool. He re-organized the Australian metal market, which had previously been dominated by German holding companies. Hughes did an unheard of thing at a time of shipping scarcity. He bought up a fleet of vessels to move a bumper Australian wheat harvest.

Early in 1916 he set off for England where his undoubted energy and drive earned him immediate popularity. He visited his old school in Rochester Street, Westminster. He returned to the land of his fathers and was made a freeman of Cardiff. He made wake-up speeches of Imperial solidarity which warmed hearts of the British at a time when many were growing impatient with our failure to win the war. He told the workers that the war meant Life or Death to the Labour movement. He attended Cabinet meetings and electrified them by pounding on the table. Afterwards Lloyd George, that other Welshman, asked him what he thought of the meeting and was told, "It is not for me to revile my creator. . . . As I sat there, I looked round the table and I thought the members all looked very clever men. That is your trouble. You have got too many clever men. It would be better if you had fewer clever men and more ordinary ones. You would get more done." Lloyd George agreed that twenty-three clever men could not run anything.

Hughes visited the Australian troops in France and they broke ranks to carry him shoulder high. He was invited to stay with the King and Queen at Windsor. He was pressed to remain in London for the duration, and when the news came that he had decided to return to Australia the *Morning Post* under a headline "Well Done, Hughes", said that he had made friends not by the score but by the million.

When he got back in the summer of 1916 Hughes found himself as popular there as he had been in Britain. But everyone knew that the intake of volunteers had fallen off in Australia at a very serious period of the war and that something would soon have to be done to sustain the Australian forces overseas with reinforcements. Casualties in France were almost as spectacular as those in Gallipoli had been. The first Anzac Corps, for example, had lost 23,000 officers and men in France during a period of seven weeks. The Army Council had asked for a special draft of 20,000 men from Australia with reinforcements of 16,500 men a month to follow. The idea that Australians should be compelled to serve in the militia at home in time of war had been adopted back in 1903. Six years later training in peace-time had been introduced. Hughes was already calling up "Hughes-eliers" for home service. But now the idea of conscription of forced service overseas began to be discussed.

There is no doubt that Hughes, if he had wished, could have decreed conscription by executive order with a stroke of the pen. But he knew that there would be opposition to it in the Trade Unions and in the Senate and that the Labour Party and Cabinet were split on the issue. Some politicians believed sincerely that it was wrong for the State to take people's lives, and impossible for it to enforce military service from those who were unwilling to give it. Farmers feared that conscription would leave them no one to work the land. Workers resented the contrast between their army pay and the big profits which they believed were being made by the people who stayed behind. Women resented being asked to decide a question which, for many of them, was far too personal. Even fighting men did not want to trust their lives to reinforcements made up of unwilling recruits.

Certainly this was the view of Frank Tudor the Minister for Trade and Customs, who resigned his post on 14th September. Dr. Mannix the Roman Catholic Coadjutor Archbishop of Melbourne also entered the campaign on the side of the anti-conscriptionists. Born in County Cork, Mannix had come to Australia with all the prejudices of the Irishman against British supremacy. He was a militant speaker as fiery in his Irish style as Hughes was when words poured from his lips in a Welsh torrent. Mannix had a ready made audience among the Irish in his home state of Victoria—Irishmen whose feelings against Britain had only recently been stirred up once more by the failure and repression of the Easter Rebellion in Dublin. Australian Trade Unionists warned that a call-up would mean that cheap coloured labour would be imported again to cut the sugar crop and that women would have to do the harvesting.

Perhaps it was asking too much of a nation that it should decide for itself on such a question.

Hughes, however, pressed forward his campaign with as much vigour as ever. "The great offensive, in which our troops have covered themselves with glory, has cost a fearful price," he said; "yet it is being, and must be, pressed forward with implacable resolution. To falter now is to make the great sacrifice of lives of no avail. . . . The sure road, the speedy road, the only road to victory is to press on. . . . Now is the psychological moment when every ounce of effort is called for. . . . The country must not fail. It dare not; its honour and its safety are alike at stake. . . ."

But when the country spoke on 28th October 1916 the verdict was unfavourable: 1,160,033 "Noes" to 1,087,557 "Yeses". A "No" majority of 72,476. No doubt many had concealed their intention to vote "No". New South Wales, Queensland and South Australia were all against it; and so were a sizable minority of the soldiers who voted.

Two of Hughes' Ministers resigned, and Mr. W. F. Finlayson, a member for Brisbane, who had played a leading part in the anti-conscription campaign, proposed at a meeting of the Labour party's Caucus or policy-making body that a vote of no confidence should be recorded against Hughes. Hughes, disdaining efforts which were still being made to heal the split, interrupted one of his attackers at the Caucus meeting in mid-speech, picked up his papers, and called on all those who were willing to see the war through to the end to follow him out of the room. Twenty-three of the sixty-five members present at the gathering rose and followed Hughes to the Senate Club room where they formed a new party, the National Labour Party.

Hughes eventually formed a new National Coalition Government in partnership with the Liberals, against his former Labour colleagues, and won a bitterly fought election on a "Win the War" platform. But a second referendum on conscription, held after heavy Australian losses on the Western front, ran into the same difficulties as the first, despite the fact that the new proposals provided only for a call-up of 7,000 men per month, chosen by lot from single men including widowers and divorced men without children, and excluded families with relatives already serving. Nor did the fact that conscription had been introduced in Britain, the United States, Canada and New Zealand have any decisive effect.

Mannix revived his campaign, attacking Hughes for sponsoring what he called a "Lottery of Death" and a "Blood Vote" and declared that it was not his duty to advise any man to go to war.

There was a battle royal when a Government censor tried to suppress an anti-conscription speech by T. J. Ryan, the Prime Minister of Queensland, and Hughes was pelted with eggs (one of which hit his hat) and became involved in a scuffle when he tried to address a meeting in the railway station of Warwick, Queensland. And this time Victoria, as well as New South Wales, Queensland and South Australia, voted "No".

Hughes had declared before the referendum that he would resign if the Government were not given compulsory call-up powers, but there was no one who could replace him, and conscription or no, there was nothing to touch the bravery and daring of the Australian troops.

By April 1916 the Australians withdrawn from Gallipoli to Egypt had reached France. In April they defended Armentieres. In July they were ordered to the Somme, where they lost 21,000 men in a nine-weeks battle for Pozieres. That autumn, amid the early snowfalls, the Australians attacked once more on the Somme and took the Butte de Warlecourt. The new year of 1917 saw the fighting grow more furious still. During 1917 Australian troops drove the Germans from Bullecourt, Messines Ridge, Hill 60, Polygon Wood, Zonnebecke. They took part in the ghastly Passchendaele offensive which cost nearly half a million casualties. The Australians alone lost 30,000 men, a

fact which led Hughes to attack the British generals for persist-
ing in the methods of an age that had passed.

But there could be no slackening. The revolution had put
Russia out of the war and the Italians were near to collapse. The
Germans in the early days of 1918 were able to concentrate
their troops on the Western Front for a last effort. In March the
Australians had to be rushed into the line to help defend
Amiens, only forty miles from the English Channel. Then the
Germans actually broke through the allied lines at Villers-
Bretonneux a few miles east of Amiens and were cut off and
killed almost to a man after an extremely daring and well-
matched pincer movement by British and Australian troops.
Finally in July, Hughes, who had been invited to attend the
supreme War Council of the Allies, heard of the victory which
the Australians won at Hamel. It was a small action and at first
few recognized how significant. But the Australians had found
a new commander of outstanding talent in General Monash,
who had discovered how to feed his troops on victories over a
series of limited objectives. That summer King George himself
knighted Monash on the battlefield.

Clemenceau the French leader hurried over to offer his
congratulations in English to the Australians, who, he said, had
astonished the whole continent with their valour. Ludendorff
afterwards admitted that the Hamel engagement, which some
Americans unofficially joined in because it was 4th July, was his
black day, the beginning of the end. Soon after, Australians and
Canadians, helped by British armour, broke through the German
line and advanced for eight miles. Hughes had insisted that the
Australian troops should be rested after their continuous battles.
He had threatened to withdraw the whole Australian force if
they were not given leave before the great push that everyone
was expecting. But in August, before the Australians were out
of the front line, the great push started.

By the 16th August the Australian Army Corps, which
included not only five Australian divisions, but a British division
and a special force containing an Australian brigade and two
American regiments, had taken nearly 9,000 prisoners and
200 guns.

The allied leaders, Clemenceau, Lloyd George, Hughes and

even the men in the field sensed that victory, perhaps before Christmas, was in the air. On 6th October the British High Command agreed at last to rest the Australians. The following day the Germans made their first definite offer of peace. The Aussies had fought through almost to the end. But not only in Gallipoli and the Western Front. They had fought in Palestine and Syria where their horsemanship and the resourcefulness of the bushman was of special value.

There were Australians in Mesopotamia (now Iraq) and in Persia. Australian nurses served in Salonica and India.

When peace came Australia had indeed earned her place at the conference table. And Billy Hughes was ready and waiting to fill it.

14

The Great Depression

At the end of World War I Australia found herself, in practice if not in theory, a world power . . . and in opposition to President Wilson of the United States. The President held strongly that the victors should not be allowed to annex territories they had conquered. Hughes felt equally strongly that the Solomon Islands and New Guinea should be Australian Territory. And there were sustained clashes between the two leaders at the Peace Conference Table. After one such passage of arms President Wilson is reported to have asked Hughes, "Mr. Prime Minister of Australia, do I understand your attitude aright? If I do, it is this: that the opinion of the whole civilized world is to be set at nought. This Conference, fraught with such infinite consequences to mankind for good or evil, is to break up with results which may well be disastrous to the future happiness of eighteen hundred millions of the human race, in order to satisfy the whim of five million people in the remote southern continent whom you claim to represent."

Hughes, after listening carefully, with his hearing aid moved close up to the President, answered, "Very well put, Mr. President. You have guessed it. That's just so." He said the words so calmly that they got a laugh from all except the President himself. But the battle went to Hughes in the end and New

Guinea became a "C" class mandate to be administered under Australian law for the benefit of the inhabitants.

Hughes claimed that at one point the President, who was deeply interested in freedom of religious opinion, asked him whether the natives in the proposed mandate would have unrestricted access to missionaries of any denomination. "By all means, Mr. President," said Hughes with but a momentary hesitation. "I understand that these poor people often go for months together without half enough to eat."

Hughes had an equally difficult fight over reparations, over which the allies were divided. Some held that the Germans should be called on to make good only the material damage that they had inflicted during the war, but others, including Hughes, demanded that Germany should pay for the whole costs of the war including war pensions, for otherwise Australia, whose territory had not been fought over, would be left out in the cold. Here Hughes was not so successful. At the time of the signing of the Armistice he had given no pledge to the Germans not to include the total cost of the war as reparations. But the allies had done so and there was no going back.

Australia, however, was invited to take part in the Disarmament Conference as a power in her own right with the same standing as Britain herself. It was now only a few steps away from the Balfour Declaration of 1926 which proclaimed that the British Dominions were "autonomous communities within the British Empire, equal in status, in no way subordinate one to another in any aspect of their domestic or external affairs, though united by a common allegiance to the Crown, and freely associated as members of the British Commonwealth of Nations."

By this time, however, the long reign of Hughes had ended and a new era of Australian politics had opened.

It was perhaps inevitable that the little Welshman who had had to carry out many so unpopular and autocratic measures in war-time, should have been considered a liability now that peace had broken out. His opponents claimed that he was too much of a dictator. In the 1922 elections the Country Party, which had been formed at the end of the war to safeguard the interests of the Australian farmers, wool-growers and other agriculturalists,

15

won fourteen seats in the House of Representatives, which gave it the balance of power there, and Dr. Earle Page, leader of the Country Party, refused to support the Nationalists if Hughes was their leader.

Hughes, therefore, had to step down, and was replaced by a comparative newcomer to politics, Stanley Melbourne Bruce; Bruce and Page then formed a coalition which lasted till after the start of the next major event in Australia's history—the Great Depression.

The slump was the same blight that was highlighted in the United States by the stockmarket crash of 29th October 1929 when sixteen million shares were unloaded in a single day. In America production had risen far more quickly than the real wages needed to buy the goods produced. Dealers found that, to stay in business they had to sell on hire purchase terms to householders and others, who bought far more than they could hope to pay for. Yet, as if in ignorance of all this, stock exchange prices continued to rise so steeply that John Raskob of General Motors was quoted as saying that any man who could invest fifteen dollars per week could amass 80,000 dollars in cash and an income of 400 dollars a year within twenty years.

There had, however, been storm warnings of a depression ever since 1926 when the world-demand for raw materials began to fall away. But the true slump did not begin in the U.S. until the flood of manufactured goods rose beyond the level of what people could afford. Then buyers vanished. Unemployment rose. People sold their savings, including shares, in order to eat, and got almost nothing for them. Even three years later prices on the New York stock exchange were still down 83 per cent and wages down 60 per cent.

Australia, as a raw material producing country, was one of the first to suffer from the fall in the price of wheat and wool. In May 1929 Bruce as Prime Minister declared, "The situation that confronts us today cannot fail to cause anxiety to every thinking citizen. Australia has in the past experienced periods of temporary depression, which have been due in the main to adverse seasonal influences. Our present position is, however, due I suggest to causes that are more deeply seated, and good seasons alone will not restore prosperity. . . . We must take up immediately the task of setting our house in order by reducing costs of production to an economic level."

Australia, like the United States, had had its own boom helped by John Miles' discovery in 1923 of the rich Mount Isa silver-lead lode. And the Australian State Governments had been borrowing money just as rashly as the hire purchasers in the U.S.

But when Bruce tried to reduce the costs of production by reforming the wage arbitration procedure he was defeated and swept out of office by Labour, who were then forced to deal with the crisis by the kind of orthodox finance that they had always attacked in the past.

Their first move was to put up tariffs against foreign goods and cut down on immigration of foreign labourers in the hope of providing work for the unemployed. But these measures were not drastic enough and Australia earned so little abroad that in December 1929 she had to abandon the gold standard, even though this weakened her credit and made it harder to get new loans. The Loan Council, a body set up in 1923 to take over and manage the chaotic borrowing programmes of the Australian States, decided at their meeting in June 1930 to cut down their programme drastically to half what it had been during the previous two years. But the State Prime Ministers did not begin to trim their budgets until August when they held a meeting attended "by invitation" by Sir Otto Niemeyer of the Bank of England. Things were now so serious that Australia needed help to meet her short-term debts. Revenue continued to fall. Budgets were unbalanced. The trade balance was unfavourable and likely to become still more so, for the Australian standard of living had raised production costs above world levels. There was no money even for those loans which the Government had already promised to make. Sir Otto, who appeared on the Australian scene in the guise of a bailiff, said that Australia's problems could easily be solved once they were faced, and the Prime Ministers at this Melbourne Conference, as it came to be called, were sure that they could count on the co-operation of all classes of the community to help restore stability.

But the Australian Labour party as a whole would have none of this and said so clearly in October when they elected as

Premier of New South Wales the famous J. T. Lang, who cam-
paigned on the slogan "For brighter times change the Government", and was committed to repudiating Australia's liabilities.

Lang was a brother-in-law by marriage of Henry Lawson and
was as belligerent and bellicose in Parliament as Henry had
been on paper. And he was a great deal more ruthless and
domineering towards his fellow beings. He was a large man
with a large head, a large mouth and large teeth. He embodied
all the fears and resentment of the working class and argued that
Niemeyer's plan to restore the economy by cutting down public
and private spending was in the interests not of Australia but
of the London bond holders. He claimed that Australia's difficulties were due to debts which Australians had accrued on
Britain's behalf during the war.

In October the Labour Party Caucus, whose members were
no more friendly to the bond holders than Lang, voted to compel
bond holders of a £27 million Government loan, who were
to have been repaid in December, to leave their money
unclaimed.

In February 1931 at a Premier's conference at Canberra, Lang
tabled a motion to pay no further interest to British bond holders
until Britain had "dealt with the Australia overseas debts in the
same way as she settled her own foreign debt with America".
He also moved to cut the interest on public debt in Australia to
3 per cent and to establish a new currency based on Australia's
own wealth rather than on gold. Here he clashed with Mr.
E. G. Theodore, the Commonwealth Treasurer, who hoped to
solve the problem in another way by granting extra loans to
private enterprise and cutting down State expenditure. But
neither the Commonwealth Bank nor the Australian Senate were
willing to give the green light for anything except a drastic
"squeeze". In April the Senate also refused to allow Australia
to balance her books by exporting more gold. Theodore's reply
was to attack the banks for trying to force the Government to
reduce wages and pensions which he said played into the hands
of the political agitators. In March the Commonwealth Bank
warned the Australian Federal Treasury that a situation "might
arise in London in the near future which the bank would be
powerless to meet".

The same month Lang passed a Bill through the Lower House forcibly cutting the rates of interest on money already lent to the New South Wales Government. His Legislative Council compelled him to put off the measure for six months but they could not prevent him from defaulting on the interest on the overseas loans due in April, and the Commonwealth Government, in order to fulfil its obligations under the Finance Agreement of 1927, had to pay up instead. In order to recover the money, amounting to roughly half a million sterling, the Commonwealth and the remaining states then sued the state of New South Wales. In a panic investors rushed their money from New South Wales into other states. The State Savings Bank of New South Wales had to close its doors, freezing more than £55 million of deposits. A run on the Commonwealth Bank itself was only headed off by a Government radio broadcast.

By this time the Australian Labour party had split into two wings, with the Lang group on one side, and the more moderates on the other, under Mr. Scullin, the Federal Prime Minister.

The Loan Council, with the aid of four economists and five under-treasurers, had been preparing a special report, afterwards known as the Prime Ministers' Plan, on who to balance the Government's finances. They decided to cut Government expenditure by 20 per cent. Salaries and pensions too. They suggested increased sales and import taxes. They proposed a campaign asking all who had lent money to the Government to accept a lower rate of interest (a reduction of $22\frac{1}{2}$ per cent was finally chosen). Bank interest rates and mortgage rates would be similarly reduced. Capitalists were warned that it might be wiser for them to accept a drop in interest rates rather than still more taxation or, worse still, Government default.

R. G. Menzies, then still a private citizen, attacked the Bill as being the Lang plan plus hypocrisy, but it was generally realized that Labour would never co-operate unless the bond holders shared in the sacrifices which others were being called on to make. Lang, indeed, said that he would oppose the proposals until he had actually seen the bond holders demonstrate their willingness to co-operate. But in the end all but 3 per cent of them did so. Dissenters were subjected to semi-official threats that the names of those who did not exchange their bonds for certificates carrying lower rates of interest would have their names published in the papers.

In spite of this success, however, Mr. Lang made very little effort to carry out the Prime Ministers' Plan, and such laws as he did introduce had a class warfare flavour. His first move after the Prime Ministers Conference was to introduce a Bill cutting the salaries and wages of all Members of Parliament, judges and civil servants to £500 per annum, on the principle, as he said, of cutting off the heads of the tallest poppies. His own Upper House would not agree to this, and he had to introduce a second bill with graduated cuts, instead of a flat slash.

Lang's next move was to approach the Loan Council with the news that the Prime Ministers' Conference had calculated wrongly so far as New South Wales was concerned and that the New South Wales budget deficit would be greater than they had foreseen. Lang, therefore, asked for permission to raise money from the banks by issuing extra Treasury Bills. The Loan Council gave Lang a very firm "No". Lang's reply was to default again in February 1932 on the interest of overseas loans. The Commonwealth Government, in order perhaps not to appear too eager, did not this time step in at once, but waited for ten days before agreeing to make good the default. Then, after paying it, the Government slapped on a new suit against Mr. Lang, for breaking the Financial Agreement. They also decided to seize money collected as income tax by the New South Wales Government. Lang then called on the High Court to declare that the Commonwealth was not entitled to seize the State revenues, and, in order to make sure that the central Government did not put him completely out of action by raiding the State bank deposits, Lang withdrew more than a million pounds from the banks and deposited them in the State treasury which he fortified with barricades. He also gave orders that all other revenue collected in future should be paid not into a bank account but directly to the State Treasury. This in fact was illegal, for under the Finance Act all revenue had to be paid first into a bank. But it allowed Lang to continue to pay his Government employees. He began, however, to default on some pensions and on part of the unemployment relief to which the state was already committed.

On 23rd April the High Court ruled by four votes to two that the Commonwealth was empowered to seize the New South Wales revenues, and the Central Government followed this up with an order calling on income tax payers to pay their instalments to the Commonwealth Bank, instead of to Mr. Lang's officials. Lang then put a freeze on all New South Wales income tax collection by sending away on leave the officers who prepared the taxation assessments. This at least prevented the Government from getting any money even if Lang himself received none. At the same time Lang asked, without success, for permission to appeal to the Privy Council in London.

Meanwhile business in New South Wales was at a standstill. No one knew what to expect. The New Guard, a semi-fascist organization with a private army, was formed to "suppress disloyal or immoral elements" and particularly to "stamp out the bush fire of Langism". (The New Guard, incidentally, deprived Mrs. Lang of the credit of opening Sydney's famous bridge in 1932 by sending one of their own men to cut the tape prematurely.)

It was easy for Lang to blame the authorities and the banks for the fact that New South Wales was now bankrupt, but his protests were no consolation to those who had been deprived of their money.

On 4th May Lang had to default on a further £2 million due as interest on previous loans, and the Commonwealth Government, which had previously interested itself only in the collection of income tax, now announced that it would insist on Lang handing over not only what he collected in income tax from the inhabitants of New South Wales but also death duties, Crown land rents, stamp and liquor duties and motor licences. New South Wales officials were given orders to hand over any money they collected or received in this way to the Commonwealth Bank. Lang issued a defiant circular to the Heads of Departments in the New South Wales Civil Service, calling on them to continue handing the money they received to the New South Wales local treasury.

This was definitely breaking the law and Sir Philip Game, the Governor of New South Wales, after warning Lang of the consequences of his acts, felt compelled to dismiss him from office and to ask the opposition to form a Government.

Lang's last piece of legislation—introduced shortly before the General Elections of 1931—was to impose a tax of 10 per cent on the value of all mortgages. It was a disguised capital levy designed to appeal to the Labour vote. But when the New South Wales poll was counted Lang's supporters got only 531,442 votes compared with 1,322,513 for the opposition. The mortgage levy law was repealed.

Australia had come to her senses.

15

MacArthur Was Here

Australia, like Britain, slumbered through the "thirties", although there had been signs of trouble in Europe ever since 1924 when Hitler wrote *Mein Kampf*.

Hitler came to power nine years later and one of his first decisions was to withdraw from the League of Nations over the issue of disarmament. Austria's Chancellor Dollfuss, who had discovered a Nazi plot to take over the country, was murdered. In 1935 Mussolini, who had much the same ideas about democracy as Hitler, invaded and conquered Ethiopia. The two men fought as allies in the Spanish Civil War. In 1936 Hitler marched his troops into the "demilitarized" area of the Rhineland. In 1938 German troops seized not only the whole of Austria but, with British consent, the most valuable part of Czechoslovakia. But since Mr. Chamberlain, who had been face to face with Hitler, believed that the Munich agreement would bring "peace in our time", it was not surprising that Australians who had perhaps never interested themselves greatly in the whereabouts of the Sudetenland or even the Alcazar of Toledo, should have succumbed to complacency.

However, once Britain had declared war, even though it was for the defence of Poland, the Australian Government led by Mr. Robert Menzies once again followed her example and received a pledge of support from Mr. Curtin the Opposition Labour leader.

It was a brave decision from a country that had only 2,800 professional soldiers and whose Department for External Affairs had been in the business for little over three years.

For Australia was now far more isolated than she had been in World War I. At that time Japan had been among the allies, but in 1939 she was morally in alliance with the German-Italian axis. Furthermore Russia, which had fought on the side of the allies in the 1914–18 struggle, had recently signed the Molotov-Ribbentrop non-aggression pact with Germany.

There was obviously going to be opposition in Australia, as there had been a quarter of a century earlier, to sending Australian troops to serve compulsorily abroad. Labour leaders were naturally concerned at the possibility of Australia becoming entangled in European affairs that no longer directly concerned her as an independent state. They feared that total war would distract Labour from its real task of improving the lot of the Australian working man, and might even lead to a wage freeze or some other form of attack on the Australian standard of living. Labour argued that Australia could play her part in imperial defence by safeguarding her own shores and by providing the equipment which Australian factories were now well fitted to produce. Curtin himself had opposed conscription in the two referendums of 1916 and 1917 and could hardly reverse his views.

Nevertheless Menzies promised to provide a volunteer force of 20,000 men prepared to serve at home or abroad. He introduced compulsory training, for home defence, of enough men to provide a militia force of 75,000. He agreed to take part in the vast imperial scheme for training air pilots, gunners and navigators and he consented to Australia's only regular army division, the Sixth, being sent to Palestine to be trained for use in France.

And it soon became clear that Britain was going to need every ounce of help. Poland had fallen in a three-week campaign. Finland did not hold out much longer. Denmark and Norway were invaded and taken the spring of 1940. Holland and Belgium fell in five days. The British were flung across the Channel from the sand-dunes of Dunkirk. Italy formally declared war in June and France fell a few days later, with the result that the

Mediterranean life-line itself was threatened. Soon Italian forces, based on their African colonies, were moving towards the Suez Canal. French ports, not only on both shores of the Mediterranean but flanking the alternative routes round Africa, were now closed to the allies.

Against this background Australian troops took part in the Wavell's first offensive in the western desert against the Italians and helped to capture 45,000 Italian prisoners at Bardia, and another 26,000 at Tobruk before moving on to Derna and Benghazi. But British units had to be moved to Greece to stem or at least slow down the Italian invasion of that country and without any previous warning to Menzies, the British took the Australians with them. Once the British were involved in the mountainous territory south of the Jugoslav border, the Germans struck hard.

The Greek campaign became a rear guard action and the retreat had to be made without adequate air cover. Crete, to which the Anglo-Australian forces were withdrawn, was taken by the Germans in the war's first big paratroop offshore landing. The German invaders succeeded in securing the vital airfields for landing their air transport fleet, and administered another public defeat to the allies.

Meanwhile during the British absence in Greece the Germans counter-attacked in the western desert and drove the British forces back almost to their starting point. Only Tobruk, completely isolated on the landward side, was held. The Australians held on to it for eight months before it was relieved.

But meanwhile there were difficulties at home. The Australian General Election, held in October 1940, had left the two main parties with exactly the same number of seats in Parliament, and Government decisions depended on the views of the two remaining members who were Independents. Robert Menzies carried on under these unfavourable conditions, under heavy attacks for the misfortunes that had attended the Australians in Tobruk, Greece and Crete.

In August 1941 he gave way to Arthur William Fadden of the Country Party with whom he had made an alliance.

But there was a strong feeling that a firmer Government with a bigger majority was needed and in October the Independents

brought about the fall of the Fadden Government on the issue
of the Budget. The Governor-General called on John Curtin to
form a new Government and once more Australia was fighting
the war under Labour leadership.

The new Government soon had new shocks to bear, for in
December 1941 Japan, which had made a tripartite pact with
Italy and Germany, struck without warning at the U.S. naval
fleet in Pearl Harbour. The Japanese fleet had sailed secretly
from the Kurile Islands to the north of Japan and was able to
approach their target undetected through an area of mist and
fog in the north Pacific. The attack was launched on Sunday
morning, 7th December, from a distance of 275 miles. The
Japanese airfleet, 360 planes strong, found the U.S. fleet of
ninety-four ships including eight battleships completely unpre-
pared. The first Japanese bomb fell just before eight, the
torpedoes half an hour later. In two hours the fight was over
and the enemy had withdrawn. But in the meantime the
battleship *Arizona* had blown up, the *Oklahoma* had capsized,
the *West Virginia* and *California* had sunk at their moorings
and every other battleship except the *Pennsylvania*, which
was under repair, had suffered serious damage. More than
two thousand Americans were killed and as many more
wounded.

Japanese strikes were equally successful elsewhere. At dawn
on 8th December they struck the U.S. base at Cavite in the
Philippines and destroyed most of the aircraft on the ground.
The U.S. Asiatic fleet had to be withdrawn to Port Darwin
in Australia. Allied control had now been lost over every ocean
save the Atlantic. Australia and New Zealand were now open
to direct attack. On 10th December the two British battleships,
Prince of Wales and *Repulse*, which had just arrived in Singapore
in the hope of disorganizing the Japanese navy, sailed north to
attack Japanese forces which were already landing in Siam and
North Malaya.

The two battleships advanced beyond reach of fighter cover,
were detected and sunk. Hong Kong was attacked on 7th December and compelled to yield on Christmas Day. Borneo was
invaded on 16th December. Singapore, almost undefended on
the landward side, surrendered unconditionally at 8.30 p.m. on

15th February with the loss of some 20,000 captured Australian troops.

Thailand was overrun after a brief resistance. There were other landings on the North Gilbert Islands, lying midway between Hawaii and Australia; on Guam, to the East of the Philippines, and on Wake Island. Rangoon and Batavia fell. Manila was captured in January 1942. Lae, the capital of the Dutch portion of New Guinea, the large island 150 miles to the north of Australia, fell on 24th January and, soon after, the Japanese succeeded in marching across the Owen Stanley Mountains to within thirty-five miles of Port Moresby, the capital of the Australian sector. Already, in February, Darwin was bombed. Broome, once the centre of the Australian pearling industry, was attacked in March; likewise Wyndham. And Australia had no means of retaliating.

On 28th December, however, Mr. Curtin delivered a New Year's message which certainly altered the course of the war and, with it, Australia's future for many years to come. His speech was a direct appeal to the United States for help. The Prime Minister said, "Without any inhibitions of any kind, I make it quite clear that Australia looks to America, free from any pangs as to our traditional links of kinship with the United Kingdom. We know the problems the United Kingdom faces. We know the constant threat of invasion. We know the dangers of dispersal of strength. But we know too that Australia can go and Britain still hold on. We are therefore determined that Australia shall not go and we shall exert all our energies towards the shaping of a plan with the U.S. as its keystone which will give to our country some confidence of being able to hold out until the tide of battle swings against the enemy. The Australian Government's policy has been grounded on two facts. One is that the war with Japan is not a phase of the struggle with the Axis powers but is a new war. The second is that Australia must go on a war footing."

Curtin believed, probably rightly, that Japan would not invade Australia till Britain was occupied, in which case Britain would be unable to offer any help.

Three months later General Douglas MacArthur escaped in an open boat from Bataan, one of the last remaining footholds in the Philippines. He arrived in Australia on 18th March and was nominated by Mr. Curtin as Commander-in-Chief of all Allied Forces in the south-west Pacific. He set up his headquarters in Melbourne.

By the end of 1942 two-thirds of all Australian men aged between eighteen and forty had been called up, and men of up to sixty worked in the Civil Constructional Corps on "pioneer" road-making and building.

Within a little while the tide began to turn. In May 1942 a battle was fought with the two fleets out of sight of one another in the Coral Sea off Australia's east coast, the Americans being able to sink two Japanese aircraft carriers and eleven other craft for the loss of one aircraft carrier. The Japanese fleet had been on its way south to New Guinea. The following month the U.S. navy won another victory off Midway Island to the north-west of Hawaii, in which four Japanese aircraft carriers were sunk. Three midget submarines which tried to penetrate Sydney harbour were detected and sunk. At the end of 1942 the Australians and U.S. forces were back on the north coast of New Guinea. On 1st February 1943 the Japanese were compelled to withdraw from Guadalcanal, the large island in the Solomons. In April 1943 Admiral Yamamato, Commander-in-Chief of the Japanese Navy, was shot down on the way to Bougainville Island after Americans had broken the Japanese Code he was using and thus discovered his whereabouts. By September 1943 the Australians had forced their way up the Kokoda trail in New Guinea through tropical rain forest and, in a campaign in which no prisoners were taken (how could they have been guarded?), recaptured Lae in a paratroop operation. Some of their units had to be supplied entirely by air.

In January 1945 American troops returned as they had promised to the Philippines and during the summer of 1943 and for twelve months afterwards the Australian ground forces were able to relax slightly while the Americans continued to drive back the Japanese from their bases in and around New Guinea.

Towards the end of 1944 the Australians were in the fight again mopping up the Japanese in Bougainville Island, New Britain, and Wewak, which MacArthur had by-passed in his island-hopping progress towards the Philippines. Two hundred thousand Japanese had been cut off and trapped in little more than a year.

In June 1945 the Australians invaded Borneo in their final campaign of the war.

The end was now near. From November 1944 American Super Fortresses had been raiding Tokyo itself from a base in the Marianas, 1,500 miles away. Then they moved a thousand miles nearer setting themselves up on Iwo Jima, an island measuring three miles by five. Finally a bitter struggle began for Okinawa Island, midway between Formosa and Japan. The Japanese garrison of 100,000 resisted to the last. Japanese pilots, 90 per cent of whom died, made nineteen hundred "suicide attacks" on the U.S. forces. The U.S. Admiral Nimitz had to use the whole strength of his Central Pacific forces, including an army of 450,000 men, before the island fell.

Then, as the United States fleet moved in to bomb the Japanese coast, the first atom bomb fell on Hiroshima. Eighty thousand people died despite the many thousands of leaflets dropped in advance to warn them of the attack. Three days later a second atom bomb was dropped on Nagasaki. A Japanese surrender followed swiftly. The war was over.

Perhaps a history of Australia should end at this point, nearly twenty-five years away from today. Certainly it would be rash to pontificate about day-to-day events. But there have been some trends in Australia since the end of World War II that seem to have a permanent bearing on Australia's future history.

For example, in these last years of peace the ANZUS alliance between the United States, Australia and New Zealand, has been established (with Britain on the outside looking in). And, in some ways Australia, through the help that she has given to the U.S. forces in Vietnam, has assumed the special relationship that existed in Churchill's time between London and Washington. We must not forget, too, that ANZUS was the protection that Australia got when Japan was permitted to re-arm.

Then, inside Australia, there is the change which has taken place in the composition of the population of the sub-continent.

Since the war non-British immigrants have flocked to Australia. In 1951 the Australian Government made immigration agreements with the Dutch and Italian Governments. The following year it concluded one with West Germany, and in the seven years following 1947, when immigration began to rise from its war-time low, the percentage of British in Australia fell from 99·5 per cent of the total to 95·5 per cent. In Australia today there are sizable communities of Italians, Dutch, Poles, Germans, Yugoslavs, Greeks, Maltese, Ukrainians and Lithuanians. And the newcomers help to push the population towards the twelve million mark with an ever-growing natural increase that is independent of the flow of new immigrants.

This perhaps is one answer, though not a conclusive one, to the alarming population explosion now taking place in Asia, and a justification for the insistence still cherished today that Australia's sub-continent, as big as the United States, should be occupied by a population not much larger than Greater London's.

Australia's migration policy is also part of the effort which she is making to keep up with the progress being made in the rest of the world, an answer to the inevitable brain drain which she has had to live with now for nearly a century. But of course the argument may not seem so convincing to the Asians, particularly since Australia is far more dependent on the Asian market than she formerly was.

Since the war there have been vast discoveries of iron ore in Western Australia and there have been equally impressive efforts to make the most of Australia's scanty water supplies. Today, for instance, the man from the Snowy River is likely to have worked at one time or another on the £75 million Snowy Mountains Hydro Electric project, which involves eighty-five miles of tunnelling in the Australian Alps plus seven dams and sixteen power stations, in the process of which the water which would originally have flowed southwards through country that is already well watered runs west instead.

Australia is in touch with modern rocketry through the Woomera testing range in South Australia. Australians are well up too in outer space with their effective types of radio telescopes.

The airplane comes into its own in a country, like Australia, of big distances and ample space for vast airfields. Australia has been air-minded from the start. Australian pilots flew in World War I, and in 1920 the Commonwealth offered a prize of £10,000 to the first Australian to fly from England to Australia taking not more than thirty days. Q.U.A.N.T.A.S. (the Queensland and Northern Territory Aerial Service) started up in 1922. Planes are used by the game wardens who protect the buffalo, once imported as beast of burden, and now used as a target for big game tourists. Helicopters keep watch for sharks approaching bathing beaches.

Even the missionaries are now air-minded, for the Australian Inland Mission, originally set up by a Presbyterian Minister, the Reverend John Flynn, in order to provide medical attention as well as spiritual comfort for those living in isolated areas, has operated its flying doctor service since 1928. Prospective patients living in isolated areas call for help on radio transmitters powered by foot pedal.

Of course there is isolation still in a country where two-thirds of the population live near to the coast. Inland, the nearest neighbour can still be twenty, fifty or even a hundred miles away.

In some areas the postman comes only four or five times a year. There are still women living in the back of beyond under a tin roof with no running water, no coal, no electricity, no refrigerator and no indoor W.C. The creek beside the homestead may be dry perhaps for months in the year. It is still a man's world and the women are not welcome in the bush pub. Some people think little of chartering a plane for a 400-mile trip to a dance in the wool shed and a private race meeting on some big cattle station, with steak parties and rodeo on the side.

All this tends to make world problems seem remote and, after a day on the beach, hardly worth thinking about. It has been noticed that the original Russian air satellite Sputnik, launched in October 1957, was reported in only one Sydney newspaper and, even so, not as a lead story.

But who would like Australia to become one amalgam, with the differences between east, west, north and south ironed out

16

in one vast, air-conditioned, artificially watered, garden city?

The historian might well hope that this may never happen, for, if it did, the history of Australia would surely, for strangers at any rate, become too unreadable even to be written.

NOTES ON BOOKS

What follows is a small selective list of works, some scholarly, some popular, most of which can be regarded as stimulants in the search for a rapidly vanishing Australia. Among many general works, Arthur W. Jose's *History of Australia* (Angus and Robertson, 1929) is a compact introduction to the life story of the continent, but Marjorie Barnard's *A History of Australia* from the same publisher is far more comprehensive and takes the story up into the fifties.

Ancient Australia by Charles F. Laseron (1955) and *The Australian Aborigines* by A. P. Elkins (1954) (Angus and Robertson) set the stage for the whole performance, and *The 'Endeavour' Journal* of Joseph Banks (1768–1771), edited by J. C. Beaglehole, and published by the Trustees of the Public Library of New South Wales in association with Angus and Robertson, gives a good whiff of contemporary air to any inquirer. *The Historical Records of Australia* published by the Library Committee of the Commonwealth Parliament, and similar historical records of New South Wales, tell much of the story of the early struggles at a time when the Government really was the colony.

Barnard Eldershaw's *Phillip of Australia* (George Harrap and Co. Ltd., 1938) reanimates Australia's first Governor, and the various narratives of Captain Watkin Tench, published in 1789 and revised in 1793, are first rate diary material.

Two outstanding biographies by M. H. Ellis should on no account be missed. They are *John Macarthur* (Angus and Robertson 1955) and *Lachlan Macquarie* (same publisher 1952).

A number of travel books of no great literary merit describe various regions of Australia in the twenties, thirties and forties, as for example *Two Years in New South Wales* by P. Cunningham, Surgeon R.N. (Henry Colburn, London, 1827), *Excursions in New South Wales, Western Australia and van Diemans Land* by Lieutenant Breton, R.N.

(Richard Bentley, 1833), *Six Months in South Australia, with Advice to Emigrants* by T. Horton James (J. Cross, London, 1838) and of course *Old Melbourne Memories* by Rolf Boldrewood (Macmillan and Co. Ltd., 1896). *A Homestead History* by Alfred Joyce, written about 1850, was not published until 1942 (Melbourne University Press).

Then there are the various explorers' journals, also, I'm afraid, of little literary merit, by such people as Captain Charles Sturt, John McDouall Stuart, Dr. Ludwig Leichhardt, and others. The story of the Burke-Wills expedition has been readably revived in *Cooper's Creek* by Alan Moorehead (Hamish Hamilton, London, 1963).

Books providing dabs of local colour on various areas of Australia continue to appear regularly as, for instance:

> *Confessions of a Beachcomber* by E. J. Banfield (T. Fisher Unwin, 1908);
> *The Red Centre* by H. H. Finlayson (Angus and Robertson, Sydney, 1935);
> *Flying Fox and Drifting Sand* by Francis Ratcliffe (Chatto and Windus, 1938);
> *The Great Australian Loneliness* by Ernestine Hill (Robertson and Mullens, 1940);
> *Australia in Colour* by Dora Birtles (John Sandys, Sydney, 1946);
> *Return to Paradise* by James A. Michener (Secker and Warburg, 1951);
> *The Territory* by Ernestine Hill (Angus and Robertson, 1952);
> *With the Sun on My Back* by John K. Ewers (Angus and Robertson, 1953);
> *Spinifex Walkabout* by Coralie and Leslie Rees (Harrap, 1953);
> *The Pearl Seekers* by Norman Bartlett (Andrew Melrose, 1954);
> *Deep of the Sky* by Tom Ronan (Cassell, 1962), and so on.

The age of gold is described in *Victoria and the Australian Gold Mines* by William Westgarth (Smith Elder and Co., London, 1857), and *The Golden Colony* by George Henry Wathen (Longman, Brown, Green and Longmans, 1855).

Distinguished visitors who wrote about the Australia of the day included the historian James Anthony Froude, Mark Twain, Anthony Trollope, and, of course, in the twenties, D. H. Lawrence, who wrote his novel *Kangaroo* from a seaside suburb of Sydney.

Ned Kelly, the bushranger, is commemorated in *Australian Son* by Max Brown (Georgian House, Melbourne, 1956). *Australian Literature* is chronicled by Cecil H. Hadgraft (Heinemann, 1960), *The Story of Australian Art* by William Moore (Angus and Robertson, 1934) and both *National Portraits* by Vance Palmer (Melbourne University

Press, 1948) and *The Legend of the Nineties* by the same author (Melbourne University Press, 1954) are well worth seeking out.

William Morris Hughes, Welsh-born firecracker, dominated the Australian political scene for the first twenty years of the current century and stated his own case in autobiographical works of great readability and humour—among them *Crusts and Crusades* and *Policies and Potentates*, both published by Angus and Robertson.

War histories official and unofficial record the bravery of the Australian forces in the two World Wars, and the exploits of General MacArthur, with whom Australia co-operated to drive back the Japanese, have not remained unsung.

Finally, backing up the whole mass of documentation, is the invaluable *Australian Encyclopedia* published by Angus and Robertson in 1958. Though even this should probably be revised from year to year.

INDEX

A

Adavale, 211
Adelaide, 82, 89–95, 126, 134, 142, 178
Adelaide, River, 136
Albany, 126, 166
Albury, 210
Alexandra Station, 185
Alexander, 22
Alice Springs, 181, 186
Amalgamated Miner's Association of Victoria, 194
Anderson's Creek, 115
Anglo-Japanese Commercial Agreement 1894, 190
Anzac Corps, 219
Anzac Cove, 216, 217
ANZUS, 239
Ariadne, 19
Armstrong, Charles, 182
Arnhem Land, 130
Ashton, Julian, 199
Atkins, Richard, 51
Atlantic, 38
Attack Creek, 135
Austin, Thomas, 196
Australian Agricultural Company, 193
Australian Alps, 175
Australian Labour Federation, 194
Australian, The, 84
Australian Society of Compositors, 193

B

Backhouse, James, 97
Bakery Hill, 119
Ball, Captain, 31, 34, 36
Ballarat, 115, 119, 145
Ballarat Reform League, 119
Ballarat Times, 120
Balmain, 211
Bank of New South Wales, 60
Banks, Joseph, 10, 12–14, 16, 25
Barchester Towers, 147
Bardia, 235
Barkly Tablelands, 135, 185
Basilisk, 19
Bass Strait, 90, 198
Bataan, 237
Bathurst, Lord, 63, 66, 76, 77
Bathurst, 100, 113, 122
Batman, John, 95, 96
Baxter, 126
Baughan, John, 50, 51
Bayley, Arthur, 188
Beechwood, 176
Bellevue, 73
Bellona, 48
Benalla, 175, 176
Bendigo, 115, 116, 122
Bennilong's Point, 70
Bent, Jeffery, 63
Bentley, James, 119
Bigge, Thomas (commissioner), 75, 76, 103
Birdsville track, 186
Bismarck, 191

Blanchewater cattle station, 174
Blaxland, Gregory, 65
Bligh, Captain William, 52–5, 59, 63, 64
Bloodwood, 145
Blue Grass Swamp, 136
Blue Mountains, 40, 64, 66, 78, 82, 113, 114
Boldrewood, Rolfe, 110, 200
Bombala, 209, 210
Bombay, 60
Borneo, 239
Borrowdale, 22
Botany Bay, 10, 12, 14, 16, 18–20, 24–6, 33, 60, 72
Bougainville Island, 238
Boundary-riders, 157, 164, 175
Bounty, 52
Bourke, Governor, 96, 97, 103, 104
Bowen Downs Station, 175
Bower birds, 144
Brady, Matthew, 95, 173
Brahe, William, 139, 141
Brisbane, 78, 130, 133, 134, 177, 194, 211
Brisbane, Governor Thomas, 68, 75, 76
Britannia, 46, 49
British Australian Telegraph Company, 178
Broken Hill Mine, 189
Broome, 237
Bruce, Stanley Melbourne, 226
"Brumby", 201
Bullecourt, 221
Bulloo, 140
Bull-roarers, 30
Buninyong, 115
Bunny, Rupert, 199
Burke, 138, 141
Burns, Robert, 202
Bush ballads, 73, 200, 204
Bush rangers, 174
Butte de Warlecourt, 221
Buvelot, Abram Louis, 199

Byrne, Joe, 175

C

Caermarthen, 41
Caesar, John "Black", 173
Californian Gold Rush of 1849, 113
Cambridge, Ada, 200
Camel, 138
Clarence, River, 125
Comet, River, 130
Cook, Captain, 10–12, 14, 26
Coolgardie, 188, 189
Coonalpyn Downs, 197
Coopers Creek, 139–41
Coral sea, 238
Cosme, 196
Cotton, 144
Cox, William, 66
Crete, 235
Crick, William, 212
Cricket, 185
Crimean War, 177
Cross, Mrs., 200
Cunningham, Allan, 78
Cunningham, P., 69, 105
Curtin, John, 233, 234, 236, 238

D

Dalgety, 209, 210
Dalhousie Springs, 181
Daly Waters, 136
"Damper", 107
Dampier, William, 9
Dardanelles, 215, 217
Darling, Sir Ralph, 75, 82, 84, 85, 95, 102
Darling Downs, 78, 125, 130
Darling River, 78, 79, 139
Darwin, 179, 237
Darwin Charles, 103
Derwent, River, 198
Desert Pea Plant, 130
D'Ewes, John, 119
Dickens, Charles, 145, 202

Disarmament conference, 225
Dollfuss, Chancellor, 233
Domain, 71, 73, 211
Donahue, Jack, 173
Drover, 211
Droving, 186
"Dryblowing", 189
Duffy, Charles, 207
Duke of York Island (Mioko), 191
Dumaresq River, 125
Dundas, Right Hon. Henry, 42, 47
Dunkirk, 234
Dunn, J. G., 189
Durack family, 185

E

East India Company, 18, 22, 46, 198
Eleven Mile Creek, 175
Emden, 214
Emu Plains, 75
Encounter Bay, 90
Endeavour, 11, 12, 14
Eucalyptus, 21
Eugowra Rocks, 174
Eureka Hotel, 119
Euroa, 175
Europe, 19
Evans, George William, 66
Eyre, John, 126

F

Fadden, Arthur William, 235
Farrer, William, 198
Federation, 204, 206, 207
Ferguson, Lady Edith, 181
Fifty-seventh regiment, 85
Finlayson, W. F. 220
First Fleet, 23, 44, 196
Fish, River, 67, 113
Fishbourne, 22
Fisher, Andrew, 214, 218
Fitzroy, Governor, 101, 124
"Fly flat", 188

Flynn, Rev. John, 241
Forbes, Archibald, 145
Forbes, Sir Francis, 85
Forbes, William Anderson, 145
Ford, John, 188
Formosa, 190
Fowler Bay, 126
Frederick's Valley, 114
Fremantle, 82, 83
Fremantle, Captain, 82
Frew, James, 136
Frew's Ponds, 136
Friendship, 22
Froude, James Anthony, 187

G

Gallipoli, 214, 216, 217, 221
Game, Sir Philip, 231
Garden Island, 83
Gardiner, Frank, 174
Garibaldi, 126
Gawler, Governor, 126
Geelong, 196
German Southern Trading Company of Hamburg, 191
George Street, 71, 75
Gilbert and Ellice Islands, 191
Gilbert, Captain, 50
Gilbert, Marie Dolores Rosanna, 145
Gill, S. T., 199
Gipps, Governor, 103, 104, 113
Gippsland, 126
Gladstone, 206
Gold Commissioner, 115, 118, 119
Gold licence, 118
"Gold tent", 115
Golden Grove, 22
Gordon, Adam Lindsay, 145, 201
Goyder Line, 198
Grasmere, 111
Gray, 139
"Great North Road", 186
Greenway, Francis, 61

Gregory, Augustus Charles, 134, 135
Grenfell gold fields, 201
Grey, Earl, 206
Grey, Captain George, 94
Griffin, Walter Burley, 210
Grose, Major Francis, 45–9
Gruner, Elioth, 199
Guadalcanal, 238
Guardian, 38
"Gums" 21
Guyong, 114
Gympie, 211
Gympie Road, 149

H

Hall, Ben, 174
Halloran, Dr., 61
Hall's Creek, 186
Hamel, 222
Hargraves, Edward, 113
Harpur, Charles, 145, 200
Hart, Steve, 175
Hartley, 113
Hawaii, 237–8
Hawkesbury, 41, 69
Hawkesbury, River, 53, 62, 65
Hayes, Sir Henry Brown, 70
Henshall, T., 61
Henty, Edward, 96
Heyson, Hans, 199
Hill, Captain, 44
Hill 60, 221
Hitler, 233
Hobart, Lord, 52
Hobart, 96, 198, 207
Holdfast Bay, 90
Hoover, Herbert, 189
Hope, 47
Horrocks, John Ainsworth, 137
Horse-racing, 168
Horton, James, 109
Hotham, Sir Charles, 119
Hovell, William, 77
Howe, Lord, 15, 18, 19
Howitt, Geoffrey, 105

Howitt, Richard, 105
Hughes, William Morris, 210, 211, 212, 214, 218, 219, 220, 222, 224
Hume, Hamilton, 77, 95
Hunter, Captain John, 32, 33, 50, 51
Hunter River Valley, 200
Hunting, 170
Hyde Park, 60, 71, 185

I

Illawarra, 69
"Indians", 29–31
Irving, John, 42

J

Jackeroo, 185
Jail, 174
James, T. Horton, 88
Japanese, 190
Jerilderie, 176
Johnson, Rev. Richard, 38
Johnston, George, 55
Journeymen Tailors of Sydney, 193
Justinian, 38

K

Kalgoorlie, 189
Kangaroo, 21, 27, 35, 49, 151, 158, 159, 166, 167, 196
Kelly, Bowes, 189
Kelly, Dan, 175
Kelly, Ned, 173, 174, 175, 176
Kendall, Henry, 145, 200
Kennedy, Edward, 134
Kerr, Dr., 115
Kimberley, 188
King, John, 139, 142
King, Philip Parker, 51, 52, 82, 95, 198
King George's Sound, 82
King's Ponds, 136
Kingsley, Henry, 200
Knight Hill, 41

Koala, 21
Kokoda trail, 238
Kurile Islands, 236

L

Lady Juliana, 38
Lady Penrhyn, 22
Lae, 237, 238
Lake Eyre, 126, 134
Lake Woods, 181
Lalor, Peter, 119
Lambert George, 199
Lane, William, 195, 196
Lang, J. T., 228, 229, 230, 231
Larsen, Peter, 201
Lawson, Henry, 201–3, 228
Lawson, Lieutenant, 65
Lawyer vines, 144
League of Nations, 233
Leichhardt, Dr. Ludwig, 130, 133, 179
Lewis, Matthew, 45
Light, Colonel William, 88
Lilydale, 182
Lipson, Captain, 90
Lister, John, 114
Lithgow, 144
Liverpool, 73
Llansantffraid, 211
Londonderry Mine, 189
Lord Howe Island, 31
Lord, Simeon, 62
Ludendorff, 222
Ludwig I, King, 145
Lungfish, 144

M

MacArthur, General Douglas, 237, 238
Macarthur, John, 49–52, 54, 55
Macarthur, John Jnr., 76
McBrien, James, 113
McCrae, Hugh, 146
McCullock, George, 189
McGorrerey's Ponds, 136
McIlwraith, 191

McKinlay, John, 142
Macquarie, Lachlan, 55, 58, 59, 61–8, 76
Macquarie Tower, 70
Madras, 60
Maitland, Captain, 38
Mallina, 188
Manila, 237
"Man from the Snowy River", 204
Mannix, Dr., 219, 220, 221
Marchesi, Madame Mathilde, 183, 184
Marine Officers' Association, 194
Marsden, Rev. Samuel, 63
Marshall Islands, 191
Marsupials, 20, 21
Marx, Karl, 120, 122
"Mateship", 194
Matra, James Maria, 14, 15
Meehan, James, 62
Melba, Dame Nellie, 182, 184
Melbourne, 95, 97, 101, 105, 108, 112, 115–8, 145, 168, 176, 178, 185, 193, 209, 210, 238
Menindee, 139
Menzies, R. G., 229, 233, 235
Mesopotamia, 223
Messines Ridge, 221
Mioko (Duke of York Island) 191
Mitchell, Helen Porter, 182
Mitchell, 211
Monash, General, 222
Monitor, The, 84
Montez, Lola, 145
Moore, Joshua, 63
Moreton Bay, 101, 124
Morning Chronicle, 87
Mort, Thomas, 144
Mount Alexander, 115
Mount Gipps Station, 189
Mount Hopeless, 140, 141
Mount Lofty, 90, 92
Mount Morgan, 205
Mount Stuart, 135

Mount Twiss, 41
Mount Youle, 188
"Mrs. Macquarie's Round" 73
Mulga tree, 145
Mullenizer, 144
Muranji track, 186
Murchison, 188
Murdgee, 201
Murray, John, 95
Murray, River, 82, 138, 176
Murrumbidgee, River, 79, 80, 81
Mussolini, 233, 234
Myxomatosis, 197

N

National Labour Party, 220
Nepean, Captain Nicholas, 23, 50
Nettle trees, 144
New Caledonia, 190
Newcastle, 69
Newcastle waters, 135
New Guard, the, 231
New Guinea, 10, 12, 191, 205, 224, 238
New Holland, 11, 13, 17
New South Wales, 12, 14, 15, 17, 18, 52, 54, 64, 75, 76, 84, 94, 97, 101, 115, 123, 124, 142, 143, 144, 174, 190, 191, 193, 194, 196, 199, 201, 205, 206, 207, 209, 211-13, 230, 231
New South Wales Corps, 44-8, 49, 50, 51, 52, 54
Newspapers, 84, 87, 120
Nicholas, Isaac, 62
Nightingall, Miles, 59
Niemeyer, Sir Otto, 227, 228
Ninety Mile Desert, 197
Nore Mutiny, 62
Norfolk Island, 31, 34, 101
North Eastern Stock Protection Society, 175
Northern Territory, 190
North Gilbert Islands, 237

O

O'Hara, Robert, 138

Operative Stonemasons' Society, 193
Ophir Mine, 113
Orange, 211
Owen Stanley Mountains, 237
Oxley Plains, 175

P

Parkes, Sir Henry, 100, 207
Parramatta, 42, 49, 72-5, 95, 100
Parrot "Twenty-Eight", 144
Paterson, A. B. (Banjo) 204
Paterson, Colonel, 50, 55
Peel, Sir Robert, 82
Peel, Sir Thomas, 82, 83
Peninsular and Oriental Steamship Company, 121
Perth, 82, 83, 133
Pescadores, 190
Phillip, Arthur, 18-20, 22, 23, 25-7, 29, 32, 38-40, 42, 44, 46, 77, 49, 58
Pilbarra Creek, 188
Piper, Captain, 70
Pitcairn Island, 53
Platypus, 20
Poddy-dodgers, 174
Poetry school, 145
Polygon Wood, 221
Pony express, 180
Port Arthur Jail, 174
Port Augusta, 179-80
Port Dalrymple, 69
Port Darwin, 178-80
Port Essington, 130, 136
Port Jackson, 33, 40, 69, 70
Port Lincoln, 90, 98
Port Macquarie, 99
Port Moresby, 191, 237
Port Phillip, 82, 95, 96, 101
Portingales (Portuguese), 10
Portland, Duke of, 51
Pozieres, 221
Praed, Mrs. Campbell, 200
Prince of Wales, 22
Privy council, 52

Purdie's Ponds, 136

Q
Q.U.A.N.T.A.S., 241
Queen Victoria, 95, 102, 103, 206, 207,
Queensland, 79, 125, 143, 144, 145, 148, 154, 162, 163, 174, 177, 178, 190–92, 205, 207, 211, 220
Queen's Theatre, 117

R
Rabbits, 196, 197
Raffles, Sir Stamford, 178
Raiatea, 191
Railroad, 192
Rasp, Charles, 189
Redfern, William, 62
Redford, Harry, 174
Reid, William, 42
Regiment: 73rd, 59
Republic of Victoria, 120
Richardson, Ethel Florence, 200
Richardson, Henry Handel, 200
"Ringers", 186
Rivers, *see separate entries*
Roberts, Tom, 199
Robinson, Michael, 62
Rockhampton, 163
"Rocks" the, 49
Roebourne, 188
Roma, 174, 211
Rooster, fish, 144
Roper, River, 136, 179
Rosebery, Lord, 199
Rose Hill, 39, 41
Ross, Major, 34
Rouseabouts, 142
Royal Mail Hotel, 176
Royal Military College, Duntroon, 214
Royal Society, 11
"Rum Corps", 49
Ruse, James, 42
Rust, 197

Ryan, T. J., 221

S
St. Georges Sound, 82
Salt-bush, 145–97
Samoa, 191
Sand Hill, 93
"Scab", 194
Scarborough, 22
Schaffer, Phillip, 42
Scobie, James, 119
Seekamp, Henry, 120
Seringapatam, 60
Shearers, 150, 156, 164, 194, 202
Sheep farming, 108, 197
Sheep population, 192
Sheep station, 162
Singapore, 236
Sirius, 22, 32, 33, 34
Smyth, Father, 120
Snapper, Point, 91
Snowy, River, 210
Solomon Islands, 224
Somme, 221
Sorrell, 173
South Australia, 88, 91, 124, 177, 190, 194, 196, 205, 207, 220
Southern Cross, 188
Spence, William Guthrie, 194
Spiers and Pond, 145
Spinifex, 145
Splitters, 142
Squatters, 103, 104, 142, 143, 147, 150–53, 156, 158, 159, 164, 165, 174, 193
Squirrels, flying, 21
Staghounds, 169
Station-hands, 142
Steamships, 11, 12, 14, 19, 22, 38, 46–9, 82
Stirling, Captain, 82, 83
Stock-hands, 142
Stone-fish, 144
Streeton, Arthur, 199
Strikes, 193, 194, 212
Stringybark, 145

Strezelecki, Count Paul Edmond de, 113, 126
Stuart, James McDonall, 134, 141, 179
"Stump jump plough", 144
Stuart, Charles, 78, 88, 127, 134
Sudan Campaign, 191
Sudds, Joseph, 85
Suez Canal, 144, 177, 235
Sullivan, Sir Arthur, 183
Summer Hill Creek, 113, 114
Supply, 22, 35
Surprise, 44
Sulva Bay, 217
Swan, River, 82, 83
Sydney, Lord, 14, 15, 17, 26, 27, 42
Sydney, 12, 31, 41, 42, 60, 69–71, 73, 74, 78, 93, 99, 101, 102, 104, 108, 145, 155, 178, 201, 206, 209, 211, 238
Sydney Cove, 26, 32, 61, 62, 70, 74
Sydney Gazette and New South Wales Advertiser, 84
Syria, 223, 235

T

Tahiti, 11, 52, 53, 191
Tank Stream, 60
Tariffs, 205
Tasmania, 24, 55, 84, 101, 116, 119, 124, 168, 173, 198, 207
Theatres, 117
Theodore, E. G., 228
Thompson, Andrew, 62
Thompson, Patrick, 85
Timor, 53
Timor Sea, 134, 180
Tobruk, 235
Todd, Charles, 176, 177
Tom, James, 114
Tonga Islands, 53
Torrens, River, 90, 94
Towns, Captain, 144
Trade Unions, 193, 194, 212

Traveller, 63
Trollope, Anthony, 147, 154, 165, 173
Tudor, Frank, 219
Tumut, 209, 210
Turf club, 69, 85

U

University: Sydney, 122

V

Vale, Rev. Benjamin, 63
Vale, Elizabeth, 49
Van Dieman's Land, 95–7, 101
Victor Harbour, 89
Victoria, 97, 115, 121, 124, 143, 165, 175, 176, 190, 194, 196, 205–7
Victoria, Republic of, 190
Victoria, River, 135, 136, 186
Victoria River Downs Station, 185
Villers-Bretonneaux, 222

W

Wake Island, 237
Wakefield, Edward Gibbon, 87, 88
Walker, George Washington, 98
Wallaby, 21
"Waltzing Matilda", 204
Wambulalla, 211
Warlock Swamps, 181
Watson, John, 213
Webb, Robert, 42
Weddin Mountains, 174
Wellington, Duke of, 88
Wells Fargo, 121
Wentworth, William Charles, 65, 85, 123
Western Australia, 82–4, 101, 122, 126, 177, 178, 187
Western Port, 82, 190, 192, 196, 201, 205
"Wet" the, 178, 180
Whaling, 198

Wharf Labourers Union, 212
Whistling spider, 144
White Australia, 121, 190, 205
William's Town, 97
Wills, William, 138, 139, 141
Wilson, President, 224
Windsor, 74
Withnall, Jimmy, 188
Wright, Frank Lloyd, 210
Wyndham, 237

Y

Yamamato, General, 238
Yarra, River, 96, 199
Yass area, 210
Yilgarn, 188
York, Duke of, 202
York Peninsular, 134

Z

Zonnebecke, 221